# CULTURES, NATIONALISM AND POPULISM

This book examines the role of the cultural factor, and patterns of its interaction with social, economic and political developments, in fostering identity-based new populisms and various forms of political authoritarianism across the globe.

Comparing authoritarianism in the Asian and Western context, this book attempts to shed light on the different ways in which new political actors make use of cultural traditions or constructs in order to justify their claims to power and challenge the culture of modernity as understood in the Western world. Lastly, the book focuses on the consequence of these new challenges for multilateral cooperation at regional and global levels, asking the question: is the world moving towards fragmentation and anarchy or a pluralist and innovative form of multilateral cooperation?

This book will be of key interest to scholars and students of populism and authoritarianism studies, democracy, global governance and more broadly to international relations.

**Thomas Meyer** is Professor Emeritus of Political Science at the Technical University of Dortmund, Germany, and Editor-in-Chief of the monthly political magazine *Neue Gesellschaft/Frankfurter Hefte*.

**José Luís de Sales Marques** is President of the Institute of European Studies of Macau (IEEM), Macau.

**Mario Telò** is the Jean Monnet Chair of International Relations at the Université Libre de Bruxelles and Rome's LUISS, and a member of the Royal Academy of Sciences, Brussels.

# GLOBALISATION, EUROPE, MULTILATERALISM SERIES

Mario Teló, Institut d'Études Européennes at the Université Libre de Bruxelles, Belgium.
Series Managed by: Frederik Ponjaert, Université Libre de Bruxelles, Belgium.

This series delves into a given dynamic shaping either the global-regional nexus or the role of the EU therein. It offers original insights into globalisation and its associated governance challenges; the changing forms of multilateral cooperation and the role of transnational networks; the impact of new global powers and the corollary multipolar order; the lessons born from comparative regionalism and interregional partnerships; as well as the distinctive instruments the EU mobilises in its foreign policies and external relations.

**The European Union and Japan**
A New Chapter in Civilian Power Cooperation?
*Edited by Paul Bacon, Hartmut Mayer, Hidetoshi Nakamura*

**The Politics of Transatlantic Trade Negotiations**
TTIP in a Globalized World
*By Jean-Frédéric Morin, Tereza Novotná, Frederik Ponjaert, Mario Telò*

**Interregionalism and the European Union**
A Post-Revisionist Approach to Europe's Place in a Changing World
*By Mario Telò, Louise Fawcett, Frederik Ponjaert*

**Developing EU-Japan Relations in a Changing Regional Context**
A Focus on Security, Law and Policies
*Edited by Dimitri Vanoverbeke, Takao Suami, Takako Ueta, Nicholas Peeters and Frederik Ponjaert*

**Deepening the EU-China Partnership**
Bridging Institutional and Ideational Differences in an Unstable World
*Edited by Mario Telò, Ding Chun and Zhang Xiaotong*

**Multiple Modernities and Good Governance**
*Edited by Thomas Meyer and José Luís de Sales Marques*

**Cultures, Nationalism and Populism**
New Challenges to Multilateralism
*Edited by Thomas Meyer, José Luís de Sales Marques and Mario Telò*

# CULTURES, NATIONALISM AND POPULISM

New Challenges to Multilateralism

*Edited by Thomas Meyer, José Luís de Sales Marques and Mario Telò*

Routledge
Taylor & Francis Group

LONDON AND NEW YORK

First published 2020
by Routledge
2 Park Square, Milton Park, Abingdon, Oxon OX14 4RN

and by Routledge
52 Vanderbilt Avenue, New York, NY 10017

*Routledge is an imprint of the Taylor & Francis Group, an informa business*

© 2020 selection and editorial matter, Thomas Meyer, José Luís de Sales Marques and Mario Telò; individual chapters, the contributors

The right of Thomas Meyer, José Luís de Sales Marques and Mario Telò to be identified as the authors of the editorial material, and of the authors for their individual chapters, has been asserted in accordance with sections 77 and 78 of the Copyright, Designs and Patents Act 1988.



*British Library Cataloguing in Publication Data*
A catalogue record for this book is available from the British Library

*Library of Congress Cataloging-in-Publication Data*
Names: Meyer, Thomas, 1943– editor. | Sales Marques, Jose Luis de, editor. | Telò, Mario, editor.
Title: Cultures, nationalism and populism : new challenges to multilateralism / edited by Thomas Meyer, José Luís de Sales Marques and Mario Telò.
Description: Abingdon, Oxon ; New York, NY : Routledge, 2020. | Series: Globalisation, Europe, multilateralism series | Includes bibliographical references and index.
Identifiers: LCCN 2019018054 | ISBN 9780367202460 (hbk : alk. paper) | ISBN 9780367202477 (pbk : alk. paper) | ISBN 9780429260421 (ebk)
Subjects: LCSH: International organization. | Nationalism. | Internationalism. | Populism. | Authoritarianism. | Multilaterialism. | Globalization–Political aspects. | World politics–21st century.
Classification: LCC JZ1318 .C844 2020 | DDC 320.54–dc23
LC record available at https://lccn.loc.gov/2019018054

ISBN: 978-0-367-20246-0 (hbk)
ISBN: 978-0-367-20247-7 (pbk)
ISBN: 978-0-429-26042-1 (ebk)

Typeset in Bembo
by Taylor & Francis Books

# CONTENTS

**PART II**
**The EU and China: Diverse identities and political prospects** 85



**PART III**
**Challenges for a common agenda of a new multilateral convergence** 147

# TABLES

# CONTRIBUTORS

**Furio Cerutti** is Professor of Political Philosophy emeritus at the Università di Firenze and Adjunct Professor at the Scuola superiore S.Anna in Pisa. He has been a Visiting Scholar or Professor at Harvard, the Université de Paris 8, the Humboldt Universität of Berlin, the London School of Economics and Political Science, 外交学院 (China Foreign Affairs University) in Beijing, and Stanford University in Florence. Professor Cerutti is a member of the Harvard Law School Alumni Association and a Research Alumnus of the University of Heidelberg. From 2005 to 2010 he was a member of the GARNET Network of Excellence, under the auspices of the European Commission. In recent years, Professor Cerutti has published two books, *Global Challenges for Leviathan: A political philosophy of nuclear weapons and global warming* (2007) and *Conceptualizing Politics: An introduction to political philosophy* (2017), as well as several co-edited anthologies, including *The Search for a European Identity: Values, policies and legitimacy of the European Union*, with S. Lucarelli (2008); *Brauchen die Europäer eine Identität?* with E. Rudolph (2011); and 全球治理：挑战与趋势 (*Global Governance: Challenges and trends*), with Zhu Liqun and Lu Jing (2014).

**C. K. Martin Chung** holds a Ph.D. from the University of Hong Kong (2014) and a master's degree in European Studies from the University of Macau (2008). Previously, he was Research Assistant Professor of the European Union Academic Programme Hong Kong and a lecturer at the University of St. Joseph in Macau. His first book, *Repentance for the Holocaust: Lessons from Jewish thought for confronting the German past* (2017), explores the role of religious ideas in German *Vergangenheitsbewältigung* (coming to terms with the past). In *Reconciling with the Past: Resources and obstacles in a global perspective*, co-edited by Annika Frieberg (2017), he analyses the idea of apology in Chinese classics and the problem of its application in East Asian politics at present. At HKBU, he teaches the general education course on "The World of Contemporary Europe" and major elective courses, including "Contemporary Europe and Asia," "Government and politics of the United Kingdom," and "Political Philosophy: Chinese and European." Professor Chung is a recipient of the Asia-Europe Comparative Studies Research Project Grant 2014 from the Institute of European Studies of Macau for his project on Sino-European comparative cultures of remembrance, out of which a peer-reviewed article, "*Chinesische Vergangenheitsbewältigung: Hindernisse und Ressourcen in vergleichender Perspektive*" ("Chinese Coming-to-Terms with the Past: Obstacles and resources in comparative perspective"), was published in the *Jahrbuch für Politik und Geschichte* (2015). He has also participated in Model EU simulation exercises in Hong Kong, Macau and Tokyo.

**Renato G. Flôres, Jr.** is Director of the International Intelligence Unit at the FGV (Brazil), where he also serves as Professor at the Graduate School of Economics and Special Aide to the President. A member of the IISS, London, and of the Lisbon Academy of Sciences, he sits on the boards of several international relations research centers and think tanks, and on the Enlarged Board of one multinational bank. He also served as a Brazilian expert at the World Trade Organization. A specialist in global political economy, with a vast array of academic and less-specialized contributions, Professor Flôres has significantly contributed to international debates, particularly concerning the Asian dimension of FGV activities.

**Andrew Gamble** is Professor of Politics at the University of Sheffield and Emeritus Professor of Politics at the University of Cambridge. He is a Fellow of the British Academy and the Academy of Social Sciences, and a professorial Fellow at the Sheffield Political Economy Research Institute (SPERI). His most recent books are *Crisis without End? The unravelling of Western prosperity* (2014) and *Can the Welfare State Survive?* (2016). Professor Gamble, who served as a joint editor of the journals *Political Quarterly* and *New Political Economy* for over a decade, has published widely on political economy, British politics, and political theory. In 2005 he received the Isaiah Berlin Prize from the UK Political Studies Association for his lifetime contribution to that field.

**Lewis P. Hinchman** earned his A.B. in Politics from Princeton University in 1968. After three semesters as a Fulbright scholar in Frankfurt, Germany, he went on to do graduate work in the Government Department at Cornell University, from which he received his Ph.D. in 1979. He served on the faculty of the Humanities and Social Sciences Department of Clarkson University in Potsdam, New York, for almost 30 years before retiring in 2009. Since then, he has taught four times for the Semester at Sea program and acted as the English-language editor of the *International Quarterly: A journal of social democracy*. He also enjoyed teaching assignments at the University of Oldenburg and the University of Bonn, both in Germany. Professor Hinchman is the author or co-editor of three books in political theory, his area of expertise, and of numerous book chapters and articles on topics ranging from the rights of native peoples in the US and Australia to environmental political thought and battles over public lands in the American West, where he now resides.

**Yudi Latif** is a theorist of nationhood and statecraft. He recently headed the Indonesian Body for Enculturation of Pancasila (UKP-Pancasila, later known as the Badan Pembinaan Ideologi Pancasila). His numerous works on this subject form the basis for his contribution to the polity of Indonesia, including on the critical issue of local democracy, recognition in multicultural society, and Indonesian historiography. Professor Latif received his bachelor's degree in 1990 from Padjajaran State University and his Ph.D. in 2004 from Australian National University. He was admitted into life tenure of the Indonesian State Association of Science in 2016. He has served as senior advisor toward the founding of the Paramadina University in 1996, vice rector of the Paramadina University from 2004 to 2007, and the founder and senior advisor of NCMS (Nurcholish Madjid Society) since 2009. A former columnist for the Kompas daily, he contributes regularly to academic and state forums and pro-democratic civil society groups.

**Thomas Meyer** is Emeritus Professor Doctor of Political Science at the Technical University of Dortmund and Editor-in-Chief of the monthly political magazine, *Neue Gesellschaft/Frankfurter Hefte*. He has held visiting professor and guest lecturer positions at numerous universities, particularly in East and Southeast Asia, including Todai University, Tokyo; Beida University, Beijing; and the Indian Institute of Management, Bangalore. He directed projects for the prestigious German Research Foundation on such topics as political communication in the media (1995–2001) and the theory and practice of social democracy (2002–2006). From 2000 to 2007 he served as Academic Advisor to the European Commission for the Social Sciences and Humanities, and from 2004 to 2008 he was a member of the GARNET Network of Excellence, funded by the European Commission. Professor Meyer's research focuses on comparative social democracy, European studies, mass media and politics, religious and political fundamentalism, and the cultural foundations of politics. Among his many books are *The Theory of Social Democracy* (2007), *Identity Mania* (2001), and *Media Democracy* (2002).

**Qin Yaqing** is President and Professor of China Foreign Affairs University (CFAU), Chancellor of China Diplomatic Academy, Executive Vice President of China National Association for International Studies (CNAIS), and editor-in-chief of Foreign Affairs Review, the academic journal of CFAU and CNAIS. He served on the resource team for the UN High Panel for Challenges, Threats and Changes (2003–2004) and worked as Special Assistant to the Chinese Eminent Person, China-ASEAN Eminent Persons Group (2005). Professor Qin's main academic interest is international relations (IR) theory. Recently he has focused on the ways in which Chinese cultural and philosophical traditions can contribute to that field. He has also done research on global and regional governance and China's foreign policy. As a leading Chinese scholar and professor of IR, Professor Qin has published extensively on hegemonic systems and international conflicts; power, institutions and culture; and relations and processes. He received his Ph. D. and M.A. in Political Science at University of Missouri-Columbia.

**José Luís de Sales Marques** has been President of the Board of Directors of the Institute of European Studies, Macau (IEEM) since January of 2002. From 1993 to 2001, he served as Mayor of Macau. His research, teaching, and writing focus on Asian–European relations, EU–China dialogue, regional integration, and urban studies.

**Mario Telò** is the Jean Monnet Chair of International Relations at the Université Libre de Bruxelles, where he is the coordinator of the Global Europe Multilateralism (GEM) international doctoral program and the past president of the Institute for European Studies. He also teaches at the LUISS University and School of Government in Rome, and has been a visiting professor at numerous universities worldwide. Professor Telò has served as a consultant to the European Council, European Parliament, and European Commission. He is the author of 32 books and over 100 articles, published in seven languages. His recent works include *Europe: A civilian power?* (2006); *European Union and the New Regionalism* (2014); *International Relations: A European Perspective* (2016); and *Regionalism in Hard Times* (2016). He participates vigorously in public debates concerning international relations and the future of the European Union.

**Xinning Song** is the Jean Monnet Chair ad personam at Renmin University of China (RUC) in Beijing. He has served as Chairman of Academic Board of the Centre for European Studies at RUC and, since 2010, Director of the Institute of Comparative Regional Studies at Tsinghua University. Currently, he is China Director of both the Brussels Academy for China and European Studies and the Confucius Institute at Vrije Universiteit Brussel in Belgium. He is Vice President of the China Association of European Studies, Vice President of the China Association of British Studies, and a member of the Editorial/Advisory Board of a number of English-language academic journals in Europe. Additionally, he was the Vice Chairman of the International Politics Department and then the Associate Dean of the School of International Studies at RUC from 1988 to 2005; Director of Centre for European Studies at RUC from 1994 to 2007; and Senior Research Fellow at United Nations University Institute on Comparative Regional Integration Studies from 2007 to 2010. Professor Xinning's main research interests are in international relations theory, international political economy, European Studies and comparative regional integration, Chinese foreign policy, and EU–China relations. His recent publications include *The EU–China 40-Year Diplomatic Relationship: A new type of strategic partnership* (2017); *China–EU: Mutual benefit, strategic partnership and comprehensive cooperation* (2016); *An Introduction to International Political Economy*, 2nd edition (2015); *China and Europe in Post-Crisis Era: Opportunities and challenges* (2014); and *China and the European Union: The future direction* (2013).

# ACKNOWLEDGMENTS

This edited book, as well as the conference on Multiple Modernities that took place in December 2017 at Macau, organized by the Institute of European Studies of Macau (IEEM), would have not come to fruition without the generous support of the Macau Foundation, the leading funding mechanism for culture, science and education of the Macau SAR Government. The Conference was jointly chaired by the President of IEEM José Luís de Sales Marques; Thomas Meyer, visiting Professor at IEEM and former Chair of the Department of Political Science at the Technical University Dortmund; and Mario Telò, visiting Professor at IEEM, emeritus president of the Institut d Études Europeénnes of the Université Libre de Bruxelles and Member of the Royal Academies for Science and the Arts of Belgium.

We are grateful to the GEM program, the academic network coordinated by Professor Telò on behalf of the IEE-ULB, funded by Horizon 2020, EU Commission research DG, which supported research of several of the contributors to this volume and sponsors the book series of which it is a part. The editors are also indebted to a long list of individuals and institutions who have helped make this book possible in one way or another: Beatrice Lam for her excellent assistance throughout the whole process; the students and academicians of IEEM, the University of Macau; the conference participants, who enriched our discussions with their input; the anonymous referees of the book manuscript; and the staff of Routledge, who helped us to complete the project.

A special word of thanks goes to Professors Lew and Sandy Hinchman of the US, who provided professional assistance in all aspects of the editorial work.

# FOREWORD

The Institute of European Studies of Macau (IEEM) has organized a series of seminars on the topic of "multiple modernities," inspired by the pioneering work of Israeli sociologist Shmuel Eisenstadt and the subsequent academic discourse on it. We think that this discourse is of utmost importance both for understanding the dynamics of international politics today and laying the foundations for a genuine and sustainable multilateralism. The high quality of the academic dialogue generated during the 2016 inaugural session on "Multiple Modernities and Good Governance" encouraged us to continue promoting this series of debates. After submitting the manuscripts to an anonymous referee process, Routledge offered to publish the best papers of that first meeting in book form, albeit with significant revisions (*Multiple Modernities and Good Governance*, edited by Thomas Meyer and José Luís de Sales Marques), as well as the papers delivered at the second annual conference, which are collected in this edited volume. The 2017 meeting focused on a new segment of the challenges our world is facing today: notably those connected with the rise of many ominous "isms," including populism, nativism, authoritarianism and nationalism, among others. Readers will have an opportunity to sample views on the damaging aspects of this new political constellation as presented by scholars from around the globe. The latter hold very different perspectives, drawn both from the situation in their own countries and circumstances in neighboring or more distant states. The result is a comparative book of exceptional quality, one that is unmatched by most studies that draw on experiences in only one country. A third conference, held at the IEEM in November of 2018, focused more narrowly on the future of regional and multilateral relationships in an age of resurgent nationalism and identity politics.

We initiated the Macau seminars on multiple modernities not only because the world was changing fast, but because we wanted to understand (and help to influence) the direction that change would take. We were especially keen to assess the political consequences that the idea of multiple modernities might have, given that it led to questioning established notions of modernization, good governance, the good society, and the nature of people's individual and collective rights.

Recent events in the US, Latin America, and Europe have a tremendous impact on world politics, especially the Brexit decision made by the UK and the nationalist wave. Far-right and ultra-conservative forces went into several local and national elections energized both by Brexit and by Trump's victory. Although their electoral showings turned out to be less impressive than many had feared, the erosion of democratic societies continued, as stable democracies and mainstream political forces remained on the defensive. Due to the rise of populism, some governments took an openly nationalist or conservative turn in their social and economic policies. The exclusionary politics of ethnic identity has taken root, particularly in regard to migration and established immigrant communities, either as a direct consequence of the populist/nationalist electoral surge or in response to the potential strength of identity-based parties.

Global governance, multilateral cooperation, and interregional agreements such as the TTIP and the TTP have been jeopardized by the US's recent unilateral withdrawals. Meanwhile, new interregional projects such as China's Belt and Road Initiative are taking some time to be recognized as incipient forms of even and balanced cooperation. Global economic growth may be slowing, depending on how one reads the economic indicators; partly as a result, the world is drifting toward greater instability and mutual suspicion. Thus, collective efforts to find solutions to global problems such as climate change, sustainable development, and international peace and security face heightened challenges.

In this overall context, the research agenda of the second multiple modernities book reflected the state of affairs that the world already was facing by the end of 2017 and indeed continues to face even more starkly. The topics addressed by the various speakers suggest the ways in which the multiple modernities approach can shed light on a variety of concerns: de-civilization and/or clashing modernities; European identities; old and new cleavages; the new populism/nationalism; global multilateral governance; and multiple modernities within and between different cultures. We hope that this volume contributes to further academic debate on the issues covered in its pages and advances the quest to encourage dialogue and understanding among different cultures and modernities.

José Luís de Sales Marques
President, Institute of European Studies of Macau

# INTRODUCTION

*Thomas Meyer*

All around the world, various actors and cultural-political tendencies have been increasingly successful at challenging the Western model of modernization and its philosophical underpinnings. They maintain that the present crisis is the final proof of the inherent contradictions or even the bankruptcy of the Western way of life in every dimension, particularly for the establishment of just and inclusive government. They claim, further, that the shortcomings and crises of Western modernity show that the world needs fundamentally different models of development, culture, and politics.

Among the new actors that have challenged the culture of modernity as understood in the West and proposed far-reaching alternatives to it, three stand out. First, there are diverse forms of political authoritarianism that emphasize and draw strength from the particularity of national or regional cultural traditions. Next, there are several variants of religious and political fundamentalism that pursue the politics of identity and advocate certain forms of theocracy. Third and most recently, neo-populist political actors and parties have used ethnic and identity politics to win political power even in electoral democracies like the US and Hungary. Populist movements in both countries (and elsewhere) radically challenge the model of Western modernity.

In particular, during the present phase of global reorientation, the cultural factor, i.e. differing cultural world-views, identities, and their exploitation by political actors, plays a highly ambivalent—even contradictory—role in politics, ideological debate, and intellectual discourse. Both the trend to defy norms and values that always have been understood to be universalistic in the name of cultural regionalism and the trend toward aggressive religious fundamentalism in the form of identity politics that attacks the very foundations of human civilization have become more conspicuous and forceful. Some economically successful authoritarian models of development in East Asia have emerged as serious rivals to "Western modernity." Meanwhile, Islamic State activities in Syria, Iraq, and beyond continue to attract young people who are alienated from their own societies in Europe and parts of Asia and Africa. Finally, the Western model has been put on the defensive by populist and fundamentalist movements even within countries that had been bastions of Western modernity until quite recently.

The European Union sees itself as a culturally pluralist, democratic polity and a proactive agent working for peaceful cooperation, conflict resolution, and development in the world as a whole. Cultural diversity—in Europe and everywhere else—can be an asset that supports a society's creativity, helps to generate wealth, and enriches communal life. But it can also pose great risks when emergent political or socio-economic conflicts, especially in times of crisis, are interpreted in terms of cultural politics by identity entrepreneurs from various ethnic, political, and religious communities. The latter look to profit from instigating intercultural confrontation and hostility.

The present book is intended to help clarify the role of the cultural factor and the patterns of its interaction with social, economic, and political developments, especially when the latter create openings for new, identity-based versions of populism and/or forms of political authoritarianism around the world. Comparisons between authoritarianism in Asian and Western contexts help us understand the different ways in which political actors can exploit cultural traditions or constructs in order to justify their claims to power. Such comparisons tie into the "multiple modernities" discourse, pioneered by renowned sociologist S. N. Eisenstadt. The concept originally was designed to free the related ideas of modernization and modernity from implicit Western biases, yet without abandoning the principle that there is indeed a common core in all forms of modernity: namely, autonomous human agency. The Institute of European Studies of Macau, in connection with the University of Macau, a crossroad between East and West, aspires to become a place for the study of multiple modernities and their interplay with the forms and contents of multilateral global governance, a set of rules and conventions now under attack. To that end it held a first conference on the concept and its many applications in the autumn of 2016, dedicated to the broad topic of "Multiple Modernities and Good Governance." The present volume, based on a follow-up conference held a year later, deals with a more specific topic: the contradictions within modernization and their links to the recent global wave of political authoritarianism in its many guises.

To a great extent, political and academic debates about interactions between the crisis of modernity and politics have been carried on within the framework of two paradigms, Samuel Huntington's notion of a "clash of civilizations" and Francis Fukuyama's thesis regarding the "end of history." The first of these ideas rests on the claim that the world's major cultures are caught in a fundamental conflict over ultimately irreconcilable ethical-political values. The second postulates the final, historic triumph of Western political culture over its erstwhile rivals, the fate of which has been irremediably sealed by the collapse of the Soviet empire and its ideology of domination.

The multiple modernities approach explores the terrain between these two alternatives. It recognizes that almost every society, regardless of which civilization it belongs to, wishes to be modern—at least in some respects. But because the desire to modernize finds expression within quite different cultural contexts, it may turn out that modern societies will never converge on a single model. Instead, they will remain culturally distinct as far ahead as the eye can see. As Eisenstadt remarks in his by-now classic essay, "One of the most important implications of the term 'multiple modernities' is that modernity and Westernization are not identical" (Eisenstadt 2000: 2).

What makes Eisenstadt's viewpoint promising is that it does not stipulate anything close to Huntingtonian relativism. Instead, it presupposes a common core among all the different types of modernity. Eisenstadt's proposal for the definition of such a core has been the target of recent academic debates. He sees the key difference between modernism and traditionalism in "the conception of human agency, and of its place in the flow of time." Modernism embraces an idea of the future that is characterized by a number of alternatives realizable through autonomous human agency: the principle of subjectivism or reflexivity. The premises on which the social, ontological, and political order is based, and their legitimation, are no longer taken for granted as objective or given. Therefore, "Western patterns of modernity are not the only authentic modernities, though they enjoy historical precedence and continue to be a basic reference point for others" (Eisenstadt 2000: 2–3). In our previous anthology on this topic, we focused discussion on four new analytical concepts, which—much like the literature on multiple modernities—claim to represent a non-Western political perspective on modernization and seem well suited to define the common core of multiple modernities: good society, good governance, human security, and varieties of capitalism. One of the objects of the present work is to determine whether and to what degree such concepts enable us to discover commonalities and differences among the emerging multiple modernities in our time, particularly with regard to their political implications and consequences, and which cultural claims are nothing but outright negations of the narrative core of modernity as such.

This volume includes revised versions of the papers presented at the 2017 conference on populism and the new authoritarianism. They address a quite different—and very timely—set of issues: identifying the differences between populism and neo-authoritarianism; working out the political implications of the dialectic of modernization; and charting the consequences of multiple modernities for the future of multilateral relations.

There has been a tendency to treat the varieties of populism ascendant in Western-style democracies as somehow related to or even identical with the "new authoritarianism" that some regard as the most appropriate form of government for non-Western societies. There are indeed superficial similarities between the official ideologies and behavior of countries such as India, China, Malaysia, and Singapore, on the one hand, and Hungary, Poland, Turkey, the Philippines, and now Italy, the US, and Brazil, on the other. All speak the language of nationalism and sometimes even xenophobia; try to intimidate free media; occasionally brush aside the rule of law; and make life difficult for critics and oppositional figures. But most of the contributors to our proposed volume would distinguish the first group of countries from the second. The former, especially China and Singapore, are keen to join and work within global and regional associations to promote trade, financial stability, and effective climate change policies. They are ardent multilateralists who see global and regional cooperation as a "win–win" situation and at least verbally endorse the rule of law. Moreover, they justify their policies through a "discourse of human agency" that is in principle inclusive, meaning that the policies they endorse supposedly are designed to benefit most other countries and solve global problems. By contrast, the second set of countries, which represent the populist trend, are skeptical of and often hostile to transnational institutions and multilateralism as such. They have, at various times, expressed scorn for the European Union, the Eurozone, the G7 group, the North Atlantic Treaty Organization (NATO), the United Nations, the North American Free Trade Association (NAFTA), the Trans-Pacific Partnership, liberal immigration laws, and multiculturalism. Their leaders all have tried to subvert or discredit legal safeguards and/or to pack the justice system with their cronies and ideological soulmates.

To simplify, the first group of neo-authoritarian countries can and should be classified as having pursued alternative routes to modernization in which economic and technological development, anti-corruption policies, educational excellence, good governance, and social order overshadow human rights, democracy, press freedom and other desiderata of Western-style modernity, at least for the present. Thus, China, India, Singapore, and Malaysia display multiple forms of modernity. By contrast, Hungary under Orbán, the Trump administration in the United States, Poland under the PiS, Brazil under Bolsonaro, and the Philippines under Duterte display a certain degree of ambivalence toward (at least) the forms of modernity characteristic of the 21st century. Some of the extremist and/or funda-mentalist supporters of such governments have expressed hostility to democracy, implied that ethnic and religious minorities should not enjoy full political and legal rights, and construed membership in the political community as a matter of cultural identity (which they, the populist extremists, get to define). In short, some of the more radical elements in populist regimes would reject the potentially inclusive rhetoric, founded on the discourse of human agency, that we—following Eisen-stadt—have identified as core elements of the process of modernization. Let it be noted, however, that many of the scholars featured here acknowledge that even populist movements such as Brexit or the Trump voter-base in the US are by-products of modernity despite their opposition to some of its constitutive values. Populists are by no means unreflective proponents of "traditional ways," regardless of what they claim. What follows is a brief comparison of neo-authoritarian and populist regime types as depicted by the authors of this volume.

First, as noted, for Eisenstadt the characteristic feature of modern life is the princi-ple of reflexivity, which states that the social order and its future evolution should be subject to the decisions made by autonomous human agents. In neo-authoritarian countries such as China or Singapore, this remains the case in theory, even though in practice the circle of those who make such decisions, and the range of options they must choose from, is relatively limited. As one of our authors (Chung) argues, in China an "external" understanding of freedom (freedom vis-à-vis the outside world) has tended to smother the internal, morally-oriented variety. By contrast, in populist regimes—especially those of a fundamentalist tinge—the idea that citizens should choose their own social order and future has come under suspicion. Instead, some populist leaders seek an objective standard of value that expresses the (supposedly monolithic) will of the people in their respective countries, such as religion, ethnicity, language, or culture. They then seek to anchor that essentialist idea of the nation and the popular will in laws, institutions, schools, the media, etc., while censoring alternative visions.

Second, multilateralism, regional and global cooperation, and a rules-based international system of trade and monetary stabilization have emerged since World War II as linchpins of modernity and bulwarks against the impoverishment caused by extreme protectionism and competitive devaluations during the Great Depression. If populist regimes had their way, they would destroy many if not all of those liberal-internationalist networks of cooperation as well as the norms that underpin them, returning instead to a "Westphalian" system of nation-state competition and balance-of-power politics, or perhaps even to a Huntington-style clash of civilizations. Some of the essays collected in this volume (e.g., those by Telò and Qin) reflect on the dangers posed by these assaults on the global order and the increasing weakness of some regional schemes of cooperation such as the EU and NAFTA.

The authors of the papers collected here do not overlook the failures and blind spots of the "globalist" international order and its efforts to aid and abet the modernization process, given that it has been so thoroughly intertwined with the Washington Consensus and neo-liberal policies imposed on developing countries and often harmful to their long-term interests. Some authors (e.g., Flôres) worry that the "standard model" of modernization, especially when accompanied by the rising tide of information technology, undermines crucial representative institutions of (Western) modernity and alienates the broader populace from modernity altogether. And they see that modernization in the economic sense frequently has deepened inequality, especially in Latin America. But they also note that the shortcomings of Western-style modernity might encourage countries in the Global South,. such as Brazil, to carry out "revolutionary multiple modernities experiments." Ironically, efforts by the Western powers to impose a single standard of modernity may ultimately generate a plethora of competing and multiple modernities.

Finally, a few of our contributors have chosen to speculate on the next phase of modernization or even on the post-modern era and the new brand of politics that will be needed to grapple with unprecedented problems such as climate change (cf. Cerutti). Some scholars (e.g., Telò) even speculate that Western modernity, once seen as relatively uniform, is on the verge of splitting into two camps: a United States hostile to international cooperation, bent on bullying weaker nations, and committed to pursuing a mercantilist trade policy, versus a European Union hard-pressed by populism but still inclined to value regional ties, rules-based international relations, a more generous welfare state, and exhaustively negotiated peace deals such as that with Iran. Moreover, the respective roles of religion in the United States, where it remains a powerful force, and in the EU, where the secularizing process is quite complex, should become a major topic of discussion (Katzenstein 2006). A growing rift between the US and the EU would intensify the trend toward multiple modernities even within the countries that, in a sense, "invented" modernity in the first place. As the United States withdraws from its former role as a champion of a rules-based international order, it may be that Europe could or should assume that responsibility (cf. Gamble), even though it too has been assailed by populist/nationalist challenges.

The Fukuyama–Huntington controversy has found echoes in wide-ranging philosophical debates over multiculturalism and the degree to which other cultures (whether within Western societies or elsewhere) should be treated as monolithic and thereby "essentialized," or whether they should be understood as being engaged in dialectical processes of renewal and reinterpretation of their traditions: i. e., as open to innovation and the adoption of patterns, ideas, and practices from other cultures and the interactions among them. Our anthology sheds light on these questions as well. It may turn out that different forms of modernity converge on certain aspects of honest, effective government via distinct political and cultural traditions. Singapore, for example, is renowned for its efficient and highly trained civil service. While the West, too, evolved an efficient and responsive model of bureaucracy, Confucian traditions likewise provide strong support for an elite civil service capable of acting in the public interest even against the wishes of authoritarian political leaders. As Amartya Sen has pointed out (Sen 2000: 231–234), so-called "Asian values" of authoritarianism are in fact challenged from within their own traditional context. After all, it is clear that allegedly Western values such as toleration and dissent have long lineages in Asian thought as well.

Therefore, it is obvious that the dialogue between the West and the representatives of various version of Asian cultural traditions must focus on the ways by which the shared notions of good and inclusive governance, rule of law and basic rights can be institutionalized most reliably. Western countries should avoid "weaponizing" human rights and honest government, turning them into polemical tools in political power struggles. Furthermore, they should carry on a dialogue in a self-critical spirit about what concepts like human rights or good governance might mean in the cultural traditions of non-Western countries (cf. Chung).

## Part I: Competing modernities and models of modernization

**Thomas Meyer** (Chapter 1) offers an introduction to this section and indeed the entire book by clarifying many of the concepts and arguments associated with the multiple modernities approach. He points out that, in a globalized world, there are no more "homogeneous cultures." All cultures constantly are being contested and reinterpreted. Moreover, the basic units of sub-cultural structure are social milieus, not entire cultures. So we should not suppose, as Huntington does, that the main fault lines run between cultures; rather, those rifts cut across them, dividing some socio-cultural milieus from others (e.g., cosmopolitans from communitarians). Applying those insights to the study of modern-day populism, we realize that the sources of populist support flow from a certain milieu: those who have suffered socio-economic decline coupled with cultural destabilization. Identity entrepreneurs have tried to explain their discontent as the result of elite policies that favor immigrants and foreign trade interests. As the antidote to those ills they offer isolationism, protectionism, and closure, both symbolic and practical. The proper remedy, argues Meyer, is an inclusive form of government that combines both "input" and "output" legitimacy.

In the US, nationalism and religious fundamentalism have been a witches' brew nourishing the populist wave led by Donald Trump, while secularization and cultural diversity have been the antidote. In Indonesia, as **Yudi Latif** explains in Chapter 2, the overriding political task has been more complicated: building a nation (cementing the country's 500+ nationalities, religious communities, and language groups together) while pushing economic development and maintaining a tolerant, civil polity. He argues that Islamic intellectuals have played a crucial role in all these endeavors. They helped shape the founding five principles of Indonesia's constitution (Pancasila), infusing them with a broadly religious yet democratic and tolerant spirit. As Latif remarks, "There is no doubt that Islamic thinking contributed greatly to the ideals of the nation." This is especially the case because Islam was engaged in a long struggle against authoritarian and even totalitarian tendencies in the country. The key to Islam's moderating role, he asserts, lay in the resolve of Islamic intellectuals to weave their religious ethics into the country's political life without forming an overtly Islamic party that would be perceived by non-Muslims as a threat to their own beliefs and institutions. He insists that Muslim intellectuals have always supported "openness." It remains to be seen whether that openness will endure in the face of the rising tide of religiously-tinged populism (as in the Ahok affair) in Indonesia that even Latif, for all his optimism, recognizes as a threat.

According to **Renato Flôres** (Chapter 3), technological developments in past decades, especially the growing dominance of the information and social media behemoths, have caused a deep rift in the socio-economic fabric of communities and societies. Traditional channels of collective action (e.g. via representative democracy) are yielding to a virtual democratic world community. As a result, authoritarian and populist reactions look increasingly appealing to some as ways to change the unfair status quo and empower neglected social groups. The concept of multiple modernities can help us to shed light on the existing *confusión de confusiones*, especially (as Flôres shows) in South America. A glance at Brazil, in particular, introduces another dimension that we also find in some other cases under study: the intrinsically static structures prevailing in certain developing countries that give rise to the phenomenon that the author calls the *éternel retour*, one that in the context of multiple modernities may lead to an implosive outcome. As Flôres concludes, "Persistent forces, ones anchored in structures that often may be traced back to the Empire, have stifled and frustrated… innovative impulses." In short, the developing world may not be the ideal venue for multiple modernities to flourish, yet this chapter suggests the possibility that some developing countries after all might become a crucible for revolutionary experiments in multiple modernities.

We often think of multiple modernities theory as a response to the claim that modernization is simply Westernization by another name. Advocates of multiple modernities see different roads to modernization being tried around the globe. In Chapter 4, **Lewis Hinchman** calls this the "horizontal" or geographic idea of multiple modernities. To it, he contrasts a different idea: that modernity is not a threshold that countries cross, never to go back. Instead, in his vertical or temporal theory, modernity itself must be subdivided into waves or phases, of which we allegedly are now entering the fourth. Modernity is thus a moving target that is never complete and is always undoing or revising the work done in previous phases. Moreover, it is like an archipelago in which the most modern regions and cities have more in common with each other than with their own hinterlands. Hinchman calls populism the "voice of modernities past" rather than a revolt against modernity as such. Voters for Trump, Brexit, Le Pen, and other right-wing populist leaders and movements do not seek to rescind modernity; rather, they want to cling to the phase of modernity in which they felt at home and could prosper (such as the heavy industrial era, or the preceding period of small towns and small farms). Hinchman shows that populism, if successful, would likely block or retard the next wave of modernization, leaving a country stagnant and floundering, as was the fate of Argentina after Perón.

## Part II: The EU and China: Diverse identities and political prospects

The contribution of **Xinning Song** (Chapter 5) highlights the complex interplay between modernization and modernity, while focusing on "authoritarianism with Chinese characteristics." After both Western (Sun Yat-sen) and Soviet (Mao) modernization models had failed, only the Deng Xiaoping approach, revolving around the "four modernizations" launched in 1978, really worked in accelerating development, stimulating high growth rates, and waging a successful fight against poverty. Yet, all the Chinese models he mentions rested on varieties of authoritarian governance. Xi Jinping, in search of more thoroughgoing reforms, wants to spur the domestic market while also enhancing the power of the Communist Party. While Deng Xiaoping implemented political authoritarianism for the sake of economic development, Xi Jinping's authoritarianism is intended to cope with more complicated domestic challenges. It harbors the ambition of turning China into a world power.

According to **Furio Cerutti** (Chapter 6), the plurality of approaches to modernity goes hand in hand with the failures of the Washington Consensus, which imposed upon the world a single understanding of what it means to be modern. In his view, modernization creates the conditions for citizens to enjoy better lives, but in itself it does not generate that favorable outcome: Everything depends upon the distribution of the social product and the political, legal, and cultural circumstances under which modernization happens. Although technical and industrial development accompanied Europe's progress towards modernity, the latter esteems civilizational, ethical, and political values and aims, which modernization does not. Cerutti then turns his attention to the political identity of Europeans, which also relates to modernity, since—among other things—this identity is essential to the legitimacy of the EU. The latter is a fledgling post-national polity (not a state) threatened in its very existence by the resurgence of nationalism and protectionism and the rise of populism. Finally, he argues that the modern structure of politics (labeled "Politics 1") is in a dangerous crisis, since it has failed to generate a scheme of governance suited to a globalized planet, especially given the unprecedented threats from nuclear proliferation and climate change. To meet that challenge, Europe will have to generate a legitimate form of "Politics 2."

Chapter 7, by **Mario Telò**, includes both analytical and normative sections focusing on several features of a new multilateral agenda. The analytical part features three main conclusions drawn from research on global governance. First, even if challenged by populism and its allies, the new grass-roots, democratic regionalism is a structural rather than a merely transitional phenomenon. Second, both regional entities and major powers are entering into multidimensional interregional relationships of various kinds. Third, after the collapse of the bipolar world, it remains unclear what kind of multipolarity is likely to follow. Telò is alert to the prospect that a new form of multilateralism might emerge to remedy the deficiencies of the current Bretton Woods legacy. At this point, the normative section follows from the analytic conclusions: A new, more institutionalized, pluralistic system of multilateral cooperation is already foreshadowed by certain incipient trends in practical politics. A rules-based global governance scheme for the 21st century will serve the purposes of containing power politics and countering the fragmentation inherent in populism/nationalism. To accomplish all that it will have to be post-hegemonic, multilayered, obligatory, legitimated more fully through the participation of civil society, and deeply committed to reciprocity.

Offering a fresh analysis of the causes and consequences of populism, **Andrew Gamble** (Chapter 8) illuminates some crucial sources of the populist revolt. The social impacts of the financial crash of 2008, global uncertainties affecting the post-Cold War international environment, unregulated globalization, slow recovery, wage stagnation, and rising inequality have been just a few of the factors adduced to explain the rise of new anti-system, anti-globalization movements within Western democracies. Neo-liberalism, Gamble says, launched what amounted to still another utopian project, of a kind familiar from Western political history: a scheme of government that could rely primarily on markets rather than politics to achieve order and prosperity. But as globalization proceeded and generated novel problems such as mass migration and nuclear proliferation, there was an ever-greater need for different actors (e.g., NGOs, international organizations) and enhanced cooperation at the international level. And that, in part, is what created the populist backlash against globalization, especially in the United Kingdom and United States, but even in the European Union, now beset by disintegrative tendencies.

## Part III: Challenges to a common agenda for a new multilateral convergence

How might multilateral cooperation for the common good overcome populist and nationalist challenges? **Qin Yaqing** (Chapter 9) renovates Chinese internationalist theory by developing an original synthesis of classical Chinese thought, the new institutionalism (Ikenberry), neo-realism (Mearsheimer), and constructivism. His approach highlights the quest to establish a post-hegemonic world order based on "new multilateral institutionalism." Toward those ends, Qin seeks an intercultural consensus on several basic principles, including an upgraded and non-instrumental notion of multilateralism and a strong conception of institutions able to cope with global power imbalances, inequalities, and deficits. But he recognizes the dangers posed by an alternative scenario for the evolution of world politics. To describe it, he coins the term "populist realism": the anti-globalization movement linked to revived power politics, state-centrism, and the resurgence of extreme nationalism.

In Chapter 10, **Martin Chung** addresses a crucial theoretical challenge, the relationship between internal and external freedom, in which the internal dimension relates to the nation state while the external aspect points to international constraining forces. Sun Yat-sen, like other prominent anti-colonialists, argued that too much individual liberty weakens the nation-state while simultaneously undermining its bid for international independence from imperialist pressures and potential domination. This line of reasoning, while understandable, risks justifying hard nationalism. By contrast, European thought (as exemplified here in the work of Thomas Mann) distinguishes between liberal freedom vis-à-vis the state and republican freedom with the state and within the state. The difference between European traditions and the views expressed by Sun is visible not only in Mann's emphasis on internal freedom but also in Kant's and Rousseau's simultaneous defenses of both internal liberty and international independence.

In short, the concept of multiple modernities describes a Janus-faced political reality. Multiple cultures, whether in a geographical or temporal sense, can be divisive. Populist identity entrepreneurs do their best to intensify those divisions, driving wedges between ethnic and religious groups and between countries or even civilizations and stoking nostalgia for past versions of modernity. Modernity, by contrast, can potentially unite what has been put asunder. Modernization and eventually modernity tend to confront countries with similar sets of problems: securing honest, uncorrupt governance; cleaning up the environment; carrying on mutually beneficial trade; promoting cooperation in science, education, anti-terrorism efforts; and much else. And, perhaps most crucially, modernity disposes countries and their leaders to take a "reflexive" approach to those problems—i.e., to think that human ingenuity, solid, fact-based research, and multilateral cooperation can help us to solve them. The multiple modernities approach is all about striking a balance between these imperatives: preserving cultural differences while deepening cooperation and consultation among modern and even semi-modern countries.

## References

Eisenstadt, S. (2000). "Multiple Modernities." *Daedalus* 129(1): 1–29.
Katzenstein, P. (2006). "Multiple Modernities as Limits to Secular Europeanization?" In T. Byrnes & P. Katzenstein (eds.), *Religion in an Expanding Europe*. Cambridge: Cambridge University Press, pp. 1–33.
Sen, A. (2000). *Development as Freedom*. New York: Anchor Books.

# PART I

# Competing modernities and models of modernization

# 1

# MULTIPLE MODERNITIES AND ANTI-MODERNISM TODAY

*Thomas Meyer*

## Introduction

Donald Trump, Marine Le Pen, Victor Orbán, Recep Tayyip Erdoğan, Narendra Modi—to drop just the most familiar names from different spots on the globe. This list suggests that we are living in a time characterized by tremendous and permanent changes, shifting backdrops, and disruptions, some of which are driven by the growing power of populist movements and authoritarian leaders. They threaten not only democracy and the rule of law but the very foundation of modern political culture. Some of them undermine the foundations of peaceful regional cooperation (such as the United Kingdom, Poland, and Hungary) or global governance (the US). Consequently, when the late Tony Judt a few years ago called the present age an "epoch of insecurity" (Judt 2011: 11), he was referring to both the domestic situation in Western-style democracies and the international order.

The unprecedented Trump phenomenon in the US, both a result and a catalyst of the decay of civic culture, the soft power of reason, and democratic rule of law—and all this in a country that used to be a global beacon of freedom and a guarantor of a liberal world order—has become an unpredictable factor sowing confusion, destabilization, and increased insecurity.

The European Union, aiming to become a peaceful world power and a haven against the onslaught of "negative globalization," is caught in a multi-dimensional crisis. It is beset by the populism-driven Brexit decision of the UK as well as by ascendant right-wing populism in all member states and especially in parts of Eastern Europe. All too many of the citizens of Europe seem to have fallen in love with ethnic identity politics and a new kind of authoritarianism.

India, the world's largest democracy for over seven decades now, seems caught in the grip of a populist movement/party that exhibits features of both cultural fundamentalism and intolerant nationalism.

China is reversing the direction of its reform agenda in almost every sphere of society, but only in its domestic politics; it is maintaining course in international relations. Increasingly, it seems determined to establish the legitimacy of its social order and governmental power by harking back to pre-modern traditions.

Turkey, once the pioneer of secular and democratic modernization in a Muslim society, now finds itself regressing toward re-Islamization and increasingly authoritarian rule.

And these are just a few of the flash points. What is happening in today's world? We see two things going on. First, there are more countries in which the elites claim the right to choose a non-Western, alternative path to modernization. Multiple modernities seem to proliferate (Russia, Turkey, China, Iran). Second, we are witnessing a spectacular process of rebalancing the relative cultural and political weight of modern vs. anti-modern socio-political orders in most Western democratic countries (the US, Europe).

People from countries all over the globe once greeted modernity—together with the culture of cosmopolitanism with which it is associated—as a great hope for permanent progress and peace. But now prospects have grown less sanguine due to a series of severe economic and cultural crises that have arisen in the arch-modernizing West. The list is long and includes the over-exploitation of nature (with its well-known attendant risks); the destructiveness of an untamed market economy, which threatens social cohesion and security; increasing socio-economic inequality and alienation; and the rise of a new wave of often racist identity politics. It frequently appears as though big corporations dominate politics and social life at the price of social disintegration. The global credibility of the West is at stake, along with the moral universalism with which it is often associated.

Around the world, various actors and cultural-political tendencies have been more and more successful in challenging the Western model of modernization and its cultural underpinnings from both within and without. They maintain that the present crisis is the final proof of the inherent contradictions or even the bankruptcy of the Western way of life in all its dimensions, particularly in regard to the establishment of just and inclusive government. They claim, further, that the shortcomings and crises of Western modernity show that the world needs fundamentally different models of development, culture, and government.

In particular, during the present phase of global reorientation cultural factors play a highly ambivalent, even contradictory role in politics, ideological debates, and intellectual discourse. By "cultural factors" we mean the growing impact that distinct world-views and identities are having, as well as the uses political actors make of them. Both the trend to defy universalistic norms and values in the name of cultural regionalism or particularism and the trend towards aggressive political-religious fundamentalism in the form of an identity politics that attacks the very foundations of human civilization have become more conspicuous and forceful. In their wake, a new wave of authoritarian neo-populism is sweeping across many parts of the world.

We need new, clearer concepts to help us analyze and understand these unprecedented developments and their role in the contemporary world. In debates about globalization, modernization, and multiple modernities, too little attention is usually paid to some basic facts that can make the complex situation more comprehensible. What is modernization? What is the common core of multiple modernities, if any? What is anti-modernism? What is the role of cultural and political agency here? What basic socio-cultural units play the key role in the political arenas, both domestically and globally? And what are the root causes, forms, and consequences of the authoritarian neo-populism that has infected liberal democracies?

## Modernity, culture, and styles of civilization

The discussion surrounding multiple modernities suffers from a lack of clarity concerning the basic cultural units of reference. The questions are: whose modernity and whose anti-modernity? When we talk about multiple modernities, are we referring to entire cultures, to sub-cultural or regional units, to societies, to nations, or to something else? In order to find an appropriate answer to these questions, it would seem helpful to start with the observation that two distinct ideas—modernization and civilization—have much in common. Civilization as an historical process has been understood as nearly equivalent to modernization ever since the path-breaking work of Norbert Elias (1979) on the topic. I suggest that we should adopt Elias's definition, since it combines two related dimensions: the process and consequences of the *internalization* of cultural norms and precepts into the individuals' motivational structure and the rapid *differentiation* of societal and political institutions within societies (division of labor). In every culture, processes of civilization as understood here are evolving. They are not isolated elements; instead, they continually interact, particularly in the modern age of intensified globalization. Cultures—the specific pattern of narratives, of meaning, values, myths, general explanations, and rituals that help us make sense out of life—are the original content or context in which these processes of internalization and differentiation take place.

Understood in this way, culture and its norms embed all other social structures (politics, economy, group solidarity) while remaining in permanent flux and interaction with them (Parsons 1951). More specifically, modernization can be understood as the process in which tradition is transformed according to the logic of subjectivity, secularization, rationality, and universalism with degrees of rapidity, comprehensiveness, and depth that vary from one society to another. Or, as Richard Münch describes this process, the ongoing *logic* of modernization in diverse contexts of cultural tradition creates the *dynamics* of modernization, i.e., different cultural constellations that preserve to varying degrees the specific character of each culture even under conditions of modernization (Münch 2001). To this extent, at least, modernity is necessarily multiple.

Cultures have proved to be fluid social discourse-formations or dynamic and contradictory discursive spaces. They are reproduced in daily life under the impact of social and political power structures, occurring in a social space with conflicting collective actors (Bourdieu 1987). Hence, a shared cultural tradition will have a variety of meanings in everyday life for the diverse socio-cultural *milieus* in which these collective actors are embedded. All these meanings are influenced by current experiences and competing interpretations, by social positions in society and related habits, by power structures and their dynamics, and via interactions with the outside world. In this sense modernization can be seen as a global system. Inevitably, cultures are constantly interpreted and re-interpreted. Therefore, internal differentiation and arguments about what traditions mean is an ineluctable feature of cultures. The belief that there are still homogenous cultures in a globalized world is a fiction. Thus, Hinduism, Buddhism, Islam, the "West," and Judaism, for instance, all are internally highly differentiated and dynamic "cultures" that display different faces from one place or milieu to another.

Today the most basic alternative ways of understanding and practicing a given cultural heritage within the broad frame of each given culture are traditionalism, modernism, and fundamentalism (Meyer 2001; Marty & Appleby 1995). They epitomize conflicting ways of understanding the content of a given culture and putting the relevant tradition into contemporary practice. Therefore, they may be termed "styles of civilization" in much the same sense as the economic styles identified by Werner Sombart (2001). They differ in dealing with a cultural heritage by highlighting certain aspects of it, forgetting others, stressing differences, and reinterpreting traditions in the light of new experiences and particular milieu interests. Styles of civilization belong to the most crucial factors that create varying social-cultural milieus in each society. Similar milieus in different cultures may have more in common than different milieus in the same culture (like fundamentalist or modern milieus across cultures against each of them toward other milieus in their own culture). In this sense modernity/modernization is understood as one of the three principal styles of civilization that are active in all cultural contexts. It is a way of re-interpreting a cultural tradition through the lens of reflexivity: a principle that has been identified by paradigm-building authors, notably Max Weber and Shmuel Eisenstadt, as the essence of modernization. Traditionalism as a style of civilization is selectively reflexive, in that it defends as much of a tradition as it can without resisting modernization across the board. By contrast, fundamentalism pretends to retrieve the original essence of a given culture/religion in its totality without any re-interpretation or hermeneutics—i.e., without reflexivity.

As extended research on religious/political fundamentalism in all cultures of the world has demonstrated, modernization everywhere takes place as project that is always contested among differing socio-cultural milieus (cf. Marty & Appleby 1995; Kepel 1991; Meyer 2001).

The basic dimensions in which modernization takes place include the following:

- Discursive spaces are marked by differences and contradictions.
- Rival actors (or milieus) and coalitions of actors, drawing on their cognitive, social, and political resources, attempt to "capture" whichever interpretation of tradition is the dominant one at any given place or time.

- The continuing dominance of certain interpretations, as well as political stability, requires a sufficient degree of correspondence or connectivity between popular cultural traditions and elite culture.

Similarly, the process of modernization reshapes cultural identity-formation at the following five levels.

- Belief culture: metaphysical world views.
- Everyday life and work culture: ways of life.
- Social culture: national solidarity.
- Civic culture: behavior in the life-world and civil society (e.g., human respect and equality; "feminism" vs. "machismo").
- Political culture: ways of living together as citizens.

In modern milieus, the levels of cultural identity become relatively independent of one another. For example, one might share a certain religious belief with other persons, but not their lifestyle or political culture. Alternatively, one might share the political culture without holding the same belief or way of life. Contrary to modernity, anti-modern milieus (fundamentalism, *intégrisme*) claim the invariant holistic unity of all identity levels. We cannot share a political culture with people with whom they do not share what I have termed belief and everyday life cultures. Thus, liberal democracy and the rule of law require a sufficient level of cultural modernization. They are built on an idea of citizenship that involves common norms of political behavior while allowing for the free individual choice of belief and lifestyles. This fact helps explain why fundamentalism transcends the character of a religion to function as a political ideology in which the representatives of certain confessional or ethnic groups claim the right to define the content of all the different levels of cultural identity and to exercise total cultural hegemony and power.

## Socio-cultural milieus: The basic units of culture

The confluence of competing styles of civilization, the logic of cultural modernization, and the diverse interests of differing social groupings gives rise to a wide array of internal differences in value orientations within contemporary societies. Pierre Bourdieu (1987) has shown that the basic units of social structure and socio-cultural belonging (identity) in all contemporary societies cannot be cultures, religions, or nations as a whole, but instead the smaller units of socio-cultural milieus. More specifically, the rise of anti-modern milieus in the midst of modernization in the West has proven to be an inseparable part of this process. As we observe today in so many parts of the world, these milieus react to the often painful, disorienting, and threatening contradictions of modernization—including social deprivation, the devaluation of socio-cultural self-esteem, and general insecurity in their life-worlds and workplaces—by rejecting the entire project of modernization, both its norms and most of its means. These milieus, known in the West today respectively as radical nationalist authoritarian populism, right-wing extremism, and religious/political fundamentalism, actually extend well into the socio-cultural upper middle strata of their societies and embrace a broad palette of attitudes either skeptical about or downright hostile to modernity and its proxy, globalization. Usually they take refuge in ethnic or religious identity politics in tandem with aggressive scapegoating. They dismiss democratic pluralism and embrace political authoritarianism, nationalism, and xenophobia. In general, they hope to overcome the problems of an open society and cosmopolitan openness for which modernization stands by closing their identity groups and their countries against the onslaught of (under-regulated) globalization.

The anti-modern milieus that have arisen both in the global South and in the West are always hybrids combining modernity and anti-modernity in varying ways. They are modern in the formal sense that they have issued from the contradictions and fractures of modernization itself and make use of modern forms of organization, communication, recruitment, and weapons technology. Yet the content and strategic approaches of their activities are anti-modern; at bottom, they seek to replace the principle of autonomous subjectivity and its social-political implications by the principle of a homogeneous collective (Marty & Appleby 1995). As the Indian historian Pankaj Mishra most recently documented, from the very outset, even in the heartlands of Western modernization, an intrinsic process of counter-modernization has been at work (Mishra 2017). It found expression on both the cultural-ideological and the political planes as a persistent undercurrent. That undercurrent varies in intensity as a function of existing circumstances, sometimes showing up as a cultural-ideological force and at other times as a claimant (occasionally successful) for political power in the state.

The milder cultural-ideological variant of anti-modernism began relatively gently in the early 19th century in the form of European romanticism in art, philosophy, and politics, in various shapes and forms of staunch conservatism or as a counter-revolution. A reaction to the French Revolution, it has been an alternative voice in civil society, political discourse, and politics up to this very day. A more aggressive version was the violence-prone anarchism or anarcho-syndicalism in parts of southern Europe and within the American workers' movement in the late 19th and early 20th centuries. The historic zenith of this form of conservative-revolutionary politics was exemplified in fascism and National Socialism, both extreme forms of "modern anti-modernism" in Europe between the Twenties and Forties. They still persist in the form of mentalities in smaller milieus and of parties posing a challenge to the dominant political institutions and structures of Western modernity. Together with the bulk of Western modernity, these mentalities have been exported to many societies of the global South, where they have appeared in various locally-influenced guises.

However, in the context of our discussion it is crucial to investigate the difference between two highly divergent forms of response to the often-forceful export of Western modernization and its intrinsic contradictions to places that lie outside the heartlands of the West: autochthonous modernities and fundamentalist anti-modernism. In principle, the two usually clash. The ways in which the dynamics and the crises of modernization generate the ups and downs of repeatedly updated (or "modernized") versions of anti-modern revolts seem to follow a cyclical logic. The more severe and far-reaching these crises of modernization, which are typically accompanied by decreasing output legitimacy, the greater the risk of anti-modern revolts.

## Multiple modernities and anti-modernism

What exactly are those elementary criteria or values that indicate the demarcation line between different varieties of modernization and the outlook of their anti-modern adversaries? Is there some kind of consensus among all those who represent the different varieties of modernity that might distinguish them from those who practice plain anti-modernism? As mentioned above, it was Eisenstadt (2000) who identified the principle of subjectivity (reflexivity; legitimate difference) as the required minimum consensus. It stakes out a demarcation line within the styles of civilization. *Traditionalism* is selective in its relation to the process of modernization and tries to defend inherited social norms and institutions in social life, family relations, and gender issues without dismissing modernization altogether. *Modernity* promotes subjectivity and reflexivity across the board, such that everything needs justification in order to be acknowledged. By contrast, *fundamentalism* attacks sub-jectivism and reflexivity in all their forms and pretends to embody the pure truth of the original cultural identity.

Consequently, from a Western vantage point, the political cultures and institu-tional settings of the systems of governance that emerge in and through diverse processes of modernization worldwide must comply with these principles, albeit in their own ways. Politically speaking, genuine modernization requires a form of governance that sufficiently includes the political will of all subjects (persons) in both the input and output dimensions of political decision-making. Only then are individuals the ultimate source of legitimacy and the final addressees of governance. The concept of "good governance" has been put forward as a means of establishing an innovative framework for meeting those requirements without connecting them with the usual set of Western political institutions (World Bank 1996). Good governance does not presuppose any specific institutional setting; instead, it postu-lates that both the input and output sides of the political process need to be sufficiently (or increasingly) inclusive, paying equal respect to all subjects in terms of opportunities for participation and to social resources.

The good governance approach also allows for non-Western criteria when it comes to placing political systems on the spectrum between full inclusion in inputs and full inclusion in outputs. This approach corresponds to the interrelated con-cepts of liberal rights and social rights as articulated in the 1966 United Nations Covenant on Basic Rights: the legal and the social resources needed to have a self-determined life (i.e., the principle of subjectivity). The Covenant was transcultural in both its drafting and its legal confirmation. As such, it is an appropriate expression of the fundamental conditions of human agency and reflexivity as well as of the core principle of modernity.

If a given regime achieves inclusion at both poles of the political process, it deserves to be considered a good government. If only one of those poles is sufficiently inclusive, the verdict must be mixed: neither altogether good nor altogether bad governance. If both poles are predominantly exclusive, then the assessment is unambiguous: bad governance (see Table 1.1).

It is always desirable that both input and output legitimacy should be high and in balance. Obviously, the merely technical institutionalization of a Western-style political system does not guarantee outputs that will meet the standard of good governance—not even the criterion of real, effective political participation. By contrast, a high degree of social inclusion that entails a fair amount of output legitimacy is in itself an important ingredient of good governance, especially when it improves those social goods that concern the basics of human development (health, education, income). This generalization applies in particular to countries with very low standards of living and social security. Such an assessment, to be sure, follows directly from a non-Western reading of the Covenant on Basic Rights.

Nevertheless, the extremes of bad governance remain clear enough: One extreme is characterized by complete exclusion in both input and output, as exemplified, by the dictatorial regimes of North Korea and certain African countries. Inclusive authoritarian regimes differ substantially from "extractive/non-inclusive" systems, since they continue to stake a popular claim to traditional cultural legitimacy and rule of law while remaining largely inclusive in their output. Singapore is the classic example of such "hybrid" regimes (cf. *The Economist*'s democracy index). There is yet a third case, which usually has been neglected in Western-style political analysis such as that provided by Freedom House. It consists of countries that are formally input-inclusive (albeit with defects in reality) but highly output-exclusive (like the US). Even in the West, few countries are equally inclusive in terms of both input and output. The Scandinavian countries probably approximate most closely to that standard. From the viewpoint of the multiple modernities approach, the challenge is to develop and apply appropriate criteria for a fair and genuinely informative yet non-Western assessment of political regimes along the matrix of input and output inclusion. An enhanced democracy index for the input

**TABLE 1.1** Varieties of political regimes

| **Democratic regimes** | | |
| --- | --- | --- |
| *Input-inclusive* | *(a) Output-inclusive* → | Good governance |
| | *(b) Output-exclusive* → | Mixed governance |
| **Authoritarian regimes** | | |
| *Input-exclusive* | *(a) Output-exclusive* → | Bad governance |
| | *(b) Output-inclusive* → | Mixed governance |

side in combination with an enriched human development index, representing the output side, might make a good starting point. In most of the countries in which popular political culture (as opposed to repression masquerading as political culture) supports authoritarian rule to a certain degree, political power is usually justified by some combination of two "resources": a partially modernized traditionalism and strong output legitimacy. The ruling elite, even when it enjoys mass support, continues to be challenged in various ways by milieus that represent competing ideas of governance or even modernization. The process of modernization always remains contested and open.

Modernity, with its core norms of subjectivity in the sense of the equal value of all subjects and good governance with its crucial yardstick of input- and output-legitimacy is thus based on a holistic idea of inclusion. The concept of inclusion comprises the legal, political, social, economic, and cultural dimensions of human life, all of which deserve equal weight. We must keep in mind that this political philosophy was part of the answer of the United Nations to the catastrophic collapse of European civilization after National Socialism and fascism had seized power in the wake of the Great Depression, which brought unprecedented mass unemployment and misery for millions of people.

Applied to our own time, these "lessons of history" demonstrate that the systematic and permanent exclusion of large strata of a society (today increasingly the global society) from the social, political, or cultural resources on which their lives depend increases the risk of radical revolt. The risk intensifies when social and cultural exclusions accumulate. At present broad sectors of many Western societies, indeed more or less the entire bottom half of some of them, have suffered from stagnating or decreasing incomes and increasing social and cultural insecurity for nearly three decades now. This development has been caused by economic megatrends like the digital revolution and the advance of globalization in connection with serious cuts in social safety nets. The sector of precarious work has substantially increased everywhere, just as standards of social protection have been lowered and the prospects for improvement have grown bleak. In this situation yet another powerful factor has influenced the way many people in Western societies understand themselves and their lives: sudden, irregular mass immigration into Europe and the increased political focus on the large numbers of undocumented immigrants from Central America already living in, or newly moving to, the US. Populist agitators attribute these trends to liberal globalization and liberal government. Growing numbers of people increasingly see the latter as the principal sources of their social or cultural deprivation and insecurity. They (or the agitators to whom they listen) tend to identify open borders and globalization in all its forms as the main causes of their tribulations. They claim that social inclusion, cultural recognition, and security cannot be revived except through a new politics of nationalism, social closure, and authoritarian government. This is the hour of neo-populism and political fundamentalism in its diverse manifestations everywhere in the world.

As mentioned above, in all cultures of the world, religious-political fundamentalism thus far has been the most striking form of anti-modernism. Its many variants emerged in structures that, to a great extent, resemble one another across cultures while standing in opposition to all other milieus within each culture. Comparative studies spanning all cultures show that, under certain conditions, each of them generates currents of fundamentalism alongside the modernizing and the traditionalist aspects (Marty & Appleby 1995). Thus, the global fault lines run not between cultures but within them. In essence, this is a battle between those who seek political supremacy for their own understanding of cultural tradition and those who demand a political-legal framework for the coexistence of different socio-cultural milieus. The present crisis of economic modernization and globalization has given rise to a broad variety of old and new forms of political revolt that dovetail with, reinforce, and "legitimize" each other in today's open global arena. The key axis of political conflict in the West and partly also in the global arena is shifting, and the consequences of this for the global order are still obscure—as demonstrated by the politics of the US under Trump.

## New political cleavages

Electoral behavior in recent years has nudged academic democratic theory to redefine the crucial cleavage lines of political conflict in contemporary liberal democracies (Merkel 2017). A new core divide that has come onto center stage substantially shapes political culture, party competition, and partisan affiliations: the conflict between cosmopolitans and communitarians. More generally, this new cleavage in Western liberal democracies has also been described as a conflict between "modernizers" vs. "anti-modernizers" (Bertelsmann 2017). It downgrades or supersedes the classic left-right divide and cuts across social classes beneath the upper middle strata. Cosmopolitans or modernizers favor liberalization, globalization, multiculturalism and migration; they are or feel themselves to be among the winners of liberalism and globalization. Communitarians or anti-modernizers, who oppose those developments, are or feel themselves to be the losers of globalization and the liberal order. In particular, they are against open markets on the basis of either their socio-economic degradation or their perceived threat to cultural identity, or both of these factors in tandem. They champion nationalism and closed communities as well as closed economies.

This is the historic moment for authoritarian populist entrepreneurs and their scapegoat narrative that blames painful socio-economic degradation and cultural discontents on immigrants, minorities, and unfair international trade. Both problems, they say, can be overcome solely through strategies of general closure. The core of such closure, in turn, is identity politics: the degradation or exclusion of cultural minorities. As the economist Joseph Stiglitz put it recently, the new wave of nationalist and populist authoritarianism in the Western world is a "revolt of the modernization losers" against liberal democracy and liberal globalization.

However, we should emphasize that political (as distinct from philosophical) communitarianism today comes in two versions: one that is liberal and another that is identity-centered. The liberal variant aims at a communal consensus on the level of civic culture but allows for ethnic and religious divergence. In contrast, identity-communitarianism stipulates the ethnic and/or religious homogeneity of the entire community. The latter is always conducive to political fundamentalism (e.g., Germany's NPD), whereas the former can express itself either as national conservatism (e.g., the mainstream of the Alternative für Deutschland) or as authoritarian right-wing populism (e.g., the Front National in France, the Tea Party in the US, or the supporters of Viktor Orbán in Hungary) in electoral democracies.

It is characteristic of nearly all the societies of Western modernity that, throughout their entire histories, three variants of socio-cultural and political anti-modernity have been at work alongside the gradually broadening and more nuanced spectrum of modern and traditionalist milieus. There are religious fundamentalist milieus that influence society and the political process everywhere, although their significance varies considerably from one country to another. Such milieus are fairly unimportant in the Scandinavian countries, but enormously important in the United States. Likewise, political romanticism is quite common, although its range of variations is broad. It is found not so much in tight-knit milieus, but more typically in the form of tendencies or currents. In many places two secular milieus of anti-modernity can be found whose representatives turn up as actors in the political process: the strict ethno-fundamentalists and the radical populists. These milieus can overlap regarding party membership, although they need to be distinguished in respect to their cultures (in France this cultural divide runs between the Front National of Jean-Marie Le Pen and its new iteration, led by his daughter).

Let us now examine more closely the three main types of anti-modern politics current in the West, some of which can be found in the Global South as well, albeit in different forms.

*Political romanticism* champions "community" against "society." For long stretches of the 19th and 20th centuries, anti-modern romanticism has inspired not only numerous offshoots of the political right but also some of the left as well. A powerful current in the European radical left presented a counter-plan for a utopian socialist community that was thoroughly fundamentalist in character. It was to be the crowning achievement of the historical critique of an individualistic society that, in presumed contradiction to its own claims, long had denied the majority of its members the freedom and equality they should have enjoyed. Instead, so it was argued, societal individualism had ushered in nothing but alienation and repression. The vision of a liberated community, in which all individuals would be at one with others as well as with themselves, was offered as a counterweight to the forces of alienation that ultimately rupture healthy relations. The alienated society was supposed to be supplanted by an integrated, socially harmonious community. When this message experienced its first major flowering, Ferdinand Tönnies contrasted the two key concepts (or rather ideal types) in a manner that has become famous:

> The theory of society depicts a circle of people who live and reside peacefully side by side as in a community, but are not closely associated, rather, largely

> separated from each other … In line with this definition the theory of community assumes the complete unity of the human will as an original and natural state which is preserved despite, and all through, empirical separation …
>
> *(Tönnies 1987: 8, 39)*

In the case of the communists, such an integral community was to arise mysteriously from their party dictatorship. In the case of the left wing of democratic socialists of the 19th and early 20th century, on the other hand, it was to emerge from the sum of numerous reforms as a qualitative leap within the frame of democracy. Today, under the impact of increasing social and economic individualization, the factors that once gave birth to this dream in history again are on the rise. The principle of community remains alive and vibrant as a counterweight against globalization, if only in small isolated groups, both on the left and the right.

*Authoritarian populism* has two dominant versions. The first type, which emerges from the activism of "radical" or grass-roots democracy, fights for more democracy through extra-parliamentary methods. This version is legitimate, or even desirable, from the standpoint of modernity and democracy. The second type comes in many forms, all of which must be distinguished clearly from the first. This version of populism dismisses political pluralism and basic universal rights by appealing to an understanding of "democracy" that presupposes a homogeneous populace: i.e., a "community" possessing a unitary political will. In fact, populists often brand as "traitors to the people" the very representatives who sit in parliaments and governments, despite the fact that they were chosen through a pluralistic process of political competition and free choice. The mental world inhabited by this type of populism implies a negation of both of the crucial principles of modern culture from which the latter's social and political ideas emerged: subjectivity and legitimate difference. Because it denies the legitimacy of pluralism, populism of this second kind is always bound to be political authoritarianism on the basis of a presumed homogeneity of the people. Where the respective "people" is already highly diverse, they defend the status quo against ethnic or religious newcomers. They restrict themselves to limited infringements on the rule of law and democracy and favor the idea of a merely electoral, sometimes plebiscitary authoritarian "democracy." This is in different forms the approach taken by Trump, Le Pen, and Orbán.

*Ethno-fundamentalism or outright right-wing extremism* is an ideology that has spread throughout Europe, sparking a resurrection of the precept of racial purity, now understood as the purity of ethnically defined cultures. This is the core purpose of what is termed the "identitarian movement" (*movement identitaire; identitäre Bewegung*). The "intermingling" of cultures, it is argued, is the cause of their present decline and a violation of the right of every individual culture to define its own identity. Each culture that wishes to preserve its integrity is bound to the geographical environment of its origins. This principle holds true not only for European countries, which—so the ethno-fundamentalists argue—mistakenly take in immigrants from the countries of the South, but also for the original cultures of the immigrants themselves. The kinship between the theory of the clash of civilizations and the chauvinistic concept of "ethno-pluralism" (de Benoist 2017) has become the European New Right's favorite discourse with increasing influence in intellectual life, right wing parties, and even sectors of the establishes conservative parties. The "ethnic cleansing" practiced in the 1990s in Bosnia laid bare the mechanisms by which identity politics of this type accumulates and exercises power. Ethno-fundamentalism is both an intellectual discourse and a growing trend in cultural and political life whose protagonists are active in diverse political parties trying to influence their identity and politics.

## Conclusion

In sum, it is a dialectical interaction between socio-economic factors (degradation, insecurity) and cultural factors (threatened identity, disparagement) that in most cases works as the driving force behind the global wave of authoritarian neo-populism, the "revolt of the losers" of modernization. In its soft form its objective is a substantial correction of the present course of globalized modernization that brings about broader social and political inclusion and control. In its extreme forms it demands a reversal of modernization and globalization and a reversion to fundamentalist forms of identity politics, nationalism, and exclusion. The driving forces here, either individually or in combination, are as follows:

- Cultural-social crises of identity and recognition (identity insecurity).
- Status insecurity or downward mobility without prospects of improvement.
- General uncertainty of cultural and/ or political orientation.
- Economic crises in the absence of social insurance to cushion the shocks and with no hope in sight.
- Glaring shortcomings of political representation in connection with failures to deliver the elementary requisites of human life (output breakdown) as well as the corruption or failure of political elites.

It is becoming more and more probable that the fundamentalist and anti-modern rejectionist tide will rise in those socio-cultural environments that are hit by several or all of these contradictions. Although the forms taken by this revolt against modernization will be context-specific the world over, their overall content will be similar. It always will involve a coalition between social and cultural losers, although of course the two groups inevitably will overlap in many cases. To a great extent, this is what is happening currently in the US and in Europe, as well as in many other parts of the world.

The British-American historian and staunch social democrat Tony Judt (2011) called the beginning of the 20th century the "age of insecurity." The French economist Thomas Piketty (2013) discerns in this epoch the structures of increasingly provocative inequality. The Chinese intellectual Wang Hui sees a global crisis of representative politics (Wang 2012), an estrangement between politics and societies. Samuel Huntington's thesis of a "clash of civilizations" (Huntington 1996) may not be empirically tenable but, to the extent that it is an ideology to which people subscribe, it generates a global mood in which cultural identities are felt to be under strong mutual threat. There is much evidence to support the idea that major socio-cultural milieus both in the West and in parts of the Global South have begun to sense the growing convergence of all these tendencies. As noted above, it is stoking feelings of what Pankaj Mishra (2017) has called the "age of anger."

We must emphasize again that there is a substantial difference between the various autochthonous "alternative modernities" that have been developed or discussed in the Global South since the late 19th century and the out-and-out anti-modernism that is rising in both the Global South and the West. The great traditions of alternative modernities in the South that to date have continued to have such a powerful cultural and political impact mostly emerged from an early assessment of both the experiences and the expected destructive and marginalizing consequences of Western modernization. Some of these movements or intellectual currents developed indigenous roads to modernization that are, or aim to be, socially and culturally inclusive and are capable of gaining the support of the popular mainstream. Frequently they are ready to play an active and rational role in the global arena as well.

In opposition to them are the various types of unvarnished anti-modernism apparent both in the West and in the South, mainly in the guise of religious or ethnic fundamentalism. Beyond all their marked differences in form and content they share one outstanding trait: They are all based on identity politics, scapegoating, and systematic exclusion or closure, both in terms of domestic and international politics. They contribute to the destabilization of the global political arena and make multilateral global governance less likely. In essence, anti-modernization issues ever-more-urgent calls for a rethinking of modernization and globalization.

The liberal global order of past decades has given way to a multiplex globalized reality and to oligopolistic open markets that no longer offer anything stable and secure and are always open to new and dangerous conflicts. Given this state of affairs, it should surprise no one that the hardest-hit groups—and not only in the theaters of acute crises—should seek refuge among the protagonists of anti-modernity. After all, the latter pretend to offer security and justice through authoritarianism and homogeneity. In this way, they try to reduce the current irritating complexity to a few simple and familiar patterns for which the groups in question yearn. Crises and the multiplex challenges of Western modernity seem to have become the sign of our times. Their ultimate source, of course, is modernization itself with its hybrid face and often dubious outcomes.

The dialectic of modernity has gone global with all its ambiguities and self-destructive risks. It seems that negative globalization and the under-regulated openness associated with it have been overextended in recent years. A spirit of localism and closure is spreading, but the real challenges of today's world demand an inclusive cosmopolitan spirit and fair political cooperation, regionally and globally. What is required is a renewed awareness of the current global risks of modernization and a new strategy to insure both fair social and political inclusion and mutual cultural/religious respect. It is vital to reduce the fear and insecurity that are the breeding ground for neo-populism and the new authoritarianism. What we need, in short, is a different type of globalization. Here again, a dialectic is at work: better global governance—i.e., much fairer globalization—appears to be the key factor for weakening the political forces that oppose multilateral cooperation.

## References


Bertelsmann. 2017. *Populäre Wahlen*. Gütersloh: Bertelsmann Verlag.

Bourdieu, P. 1984. *Distinction: A social critique of the judgment of taste*. New York: Routledge.

De Benoist, A. 2017. *View from the Right*. London: Arktos Media.

Eisenstadt, S. 2000. "Multiple Modernities." *Daedalus* 129(1): 1–29.

Elias, N. 1979. *The Civilizing Process*. Malden, MA: Blackwell Publishers.

Huntington, S. 1996. *The Clash of Civilizations and the Remaking of World Order*. New York: Simon & Schuster.

Judt, T. 2011. *Ill Fares the Land*. London: Penguin Books.

Kepel, G. 1991. *La Revanche de Dieu: Chretiens, juifs et musulman à la reconquete du Monde*. Paris: Éditions du Seuil.

Marty, M. & S. Appleby. 1995. *The Glory and the Power: The fundamentalist challenge to the modern world*. Boston, MA: Beacon Press.

Merkel, W. 2017. *Kosmopolitismus versus Kommunitarismus: Ein neuer Konflikt in der Demokratie*. Berlin: WZB.

Meyer, T. 2001. *Identity Mania: The politicization of cultural difference*. London: Mosaic Books.

Meyer, T. 2013. "Cultural Conflict, Global Governance, and International Institutions." In M. Telò (ed.), *Globalisation, Multilateralism, Europe*. Farnham: Ashgate, pp. 287–300.

Meyer, T. 2014. "Cultural Difference, Regionalization and Globalization." In M. Telò (ed.), *European Union and New Regionalism*. Farnham: Ashgate, pp. 55–74.

Meyer, T. 2018. "Multiple Modernities and Good Governance." In J. de Sales Marques & T. Meyer (eds.), *Multiple Modernities and Good Governance*. London: Routledge, pp. 15–28.

Mishra, P. 2017. *The Age of Anger: A history of the present*. London: Allan Lane.

Münch, R. 2001. *The Ethics of Modernization*. Lantham, MD: Rowman & Littlefield.

Parsons, T. 1951. *The Social System*. Glencoe, IL: The Free Press.

Piketty, T. 2013. *Capital in the 21st Century*. Cambridge, MA: Harvard University Press.

Sombart, W. 2001. *Economic Life in the Modern Age*. New Brunswick, NJ: Transaction.

Tönnies, F. 2001. *Community and Society*. Cambridge: Cambridge University Press.

Wang, Hui. 2012. "Rethinking Equality: The decline of representation." In J. Nida-Rümelin & W. Thierse (eds.), *Die Gleichheit neu denken: Der Verlust des Repräsentativen*. Essen: Klartext Verlag, pp. 15–76.

World Bank. 1996. *Governance and Development*. Washington, DC: The World Bank.

# 2

# NATION-BUILDING IN THE ERA OF POPULISM AND THE MUSLIM INTELLIGENTSIA

## The Indonesian experience

*Yudi Latif*

## Introduction

As the presidency of Joko Widodo (or Jokowi, as he is familiarly known) began, the incoming government espoused the idea of a "revolusi mental," a mental revolution.[1] Indeed, this psychological shift was a key campaign theme advocated by Joko Widodo prior to the presidential election of 2014. Once in office, the new president issued a regulation on this very topic, known as "Instruksi President" (Presidential Instruction) number 12, in 2016. It was anticipated that this move would draw criticism for being "jargonistic," which turned out to be the case, as the Instruction generated considerable controversy. For several weeks, the new edict remained a hot topic in the country's newspapers. Some of the attacks in the media revived an issue that had lain dormant for a while: what it could or should mean to be Indonesian in the post-authoritarian era.

Some critics recalled that Jokowi's move paralleled what the country's first president, Sukarno, did during the formative years of Indonesia that lasted from 1945 up to the epoch of "guided democracy." Sukarno once employed the phrase "character-building, nation-building" as an ideological framework for public policy intended to mobilize the newly independent (post-colonial) polity. Criticism of Sukarno's initiative has now become associated with the current phenomenon of populism. References to the term "nation-building" were quite frequent in Sukarno's speeches beginning in the mid-1950s and continuing into the mid-1960s, including his state speech of August 17, 1957 and another delivered at the Asian Games of 1962. Historians later would provide inconsistent accounts of what Sukarno actually did within this conceptual framework. Some observers acknowledged the importance of integrating the diverse citizenry of the new nation, while others strongly condemned the populist and authoritarian tone of Sukarno's speeches. Especially when we remember that the Cold War formed the backdrop to Sukarno's presidency, evaluating his ideas becomes a more complex and challenging task.

In what follows, I intend to link the current *revolusi mental* with the memory of Sukarno-style nation-building as a way to illuminate the problems of a country like Indonesia. To begin with, the term nation-building is enshrined in the formal content of Inpres 12/2016 issued during the presidency of Jokowi. The problem of integration in Indonesia is acute, since the country—a sprawling archipelago—contains as many as 500 ethnic groups[2] as well as a variety of distinct religious communities, all swept up in a wave of drastic change. Nor should we overlook the fact that Indonesia has millions of increasingly affluent consumers assailed daily by barrages of often-conflicting information. All of these factors influence the functioning of Indonesia's government. Leading figures in and out of the government therefore are trying to channel this new-found prosperity into a positive process of nation-building.

The question then becomes, how to revisit the meaning of nation-building while taking into account the diversity of contemporary society. To frame the problem more generally, we might also inquire whether populism is likely to push Indonesia into an era of uncertainty and whether at this point nation-building has lost its meaning.[3]

With these issues in mind, the present essay is intended to determine how Indonesian Muslim intellectuals shape the discourse of nation-building, and how their role displays both continuity and change.

## Formulation of nation-building in Indonesia

As all of us are well aware, the post-World War II period brought with it some very fundamental changes. The broad interests of humanity found expression in a variety of new moral and political movements, including anti-slavery, anti-colonialism, and anti-imperialism. Furthermore, the postwar era introduced reforms in multilateralism and envisioned a different set of obligations, with distinctive roles attached to them, that governments were now expected to fulfill. It was in this context that Indonesia achieved international recognition as an independent nation. What we might learn from the post-war period is that legitimate government is obliged to respect human dignity. That principle manifested itself in certain core institutions of the modern nation-state and international bodies, especially their charters and constitutions. Denmark approved its constitution in 1953, (West) Germany approved the Basic Law in 1949, and the transition from the Fourth to Fifth Republics in France took place in the 1950s. In addition, the UN Charter was adopted in 1945, the same year in which the process of independence for Indonesia was launched. And the birth of Indonesia as a nation also coincided with the formulation and acceptance of the Indonesian constitution, often abbreviated as UUD 1945. The set of principles known as Pancasila was enshrined in the preamble of UUD 1945, and it therefore serves as the underlying premise of the entire constitution.[4]

Pancasila was proclaimed by Sukarno on June 1, 1945. Because it is incorporated into the constitution, it has been the foundation of Indonesia's polity. Pancasila consists of five principles: *Ketuhanan yang Maha Esa* (belief in God the Almighty); *Kemanusiaan yang Adil dan Beradab* (just and civilized humanity); *Persatuan Indonesia* (union of Indonesia); *Kerakyatan yang Dipimpin oleh Hikmat Kebijaksanaan, dalam Permusyawaratan Perwakilan* (democracy guided by the inner wisdom of the deliberation of representatives); and *Keadilan Sosial bagi Seluruh Rakyat Indonesia* (social justice for all Indonesians).

Sukarno offered an alternative version of those values in a speech given on June 6, 1945, although he continued to refer to just five *sila* (principles), or Pancasila in the Indonesian language. He called Pancasila the founding self or *"dasar falsafah"* (*philosofische grondslag*), and the *"pandangan dunia"* (*Weltanschauung*) of the nation and state of Indonesia. The principles, thus redefined, are as follows: (1) *Ketuhanan yang berkebudayaan* (theism with civilization); (2) *Internasionalisme (kemanusiaan universal) yang adil dan beradab* (internationalism; universal humanism with just and civil virtues); (3) *Persatuan dari keragaman Indonesia* (unity from the diversity of Indonesia); (4) *Demokrasi permusyawaratan* (democracy of deliberation); and (5) *Keadilan sosial* (social justice).

In Sukarno's view, those five *sila* could be further reduced to three: (1) *Kebangsaan dan internationalisme* (*sosio-nasionalisme*, or nationhood and internationalism/socio-nationalism); (2) *Demokrasi-politik dan demokrasi/keadilan-ekonomi* (*sosio-demokrasi*, or democracy of politics and democracy/justice of the economy/socio-democracy); and (3) *Ketuhanan yang berkebudayaan* (theism with culture). Further, he said, "If I am to reach the very heart of those principles: five to three, three to one, then I will arrive at one original Indonesian word: *gotong royong*.[5] The state of Indonesia should be founded as a state of *gotong royong*."

To express this point in a slightly different way, the foundation of all the principles of Pancasila is *gotong royong*. This notion has numerous applications across many fields. First, it implies that theism must be of *gotong royong* in its core (i.e., it should be a theism that is broadly cultural and tolerant, not one that is aggressive and pits each person against every other). The principle of internationalism should be of *gotong royong* (humanistic and just); it should not be an internationalism that is colonialistic and exploitative. The principle of nationhood should be of *gotong royong*: capable of developing unity out of diversity, *bhinneka tunggal ika*,[6] rather than eliminating differences and diversity, or refusing unity. The principle of democracy should be of *gotong royong* (deliberative); democracy should not be confused with majoritarianism (majorocracy), nor should it allow rule by a narrow elite of powerful, resource-rich groups (minorocracy). In economics, the principle should be of *gotong royong*: that is, the economy should encourage wider participation and emancipation, yet the market should be modified by the spirit of family. In sum, a Pancasila-based economy would not involve a vision of welfare drawn from individualistic capitalism. Yet neither would it allow the state to sharply restrict individual economic liberty or oppress individuals in the way that old-fashioned statism permitted (Latif 2011).

With the spirit of all five principles, Pancasila is a guiding vision and a durable worldview for the nation-state of Indonesia. The principles enable us to anticipate and reconcile competing elements. The one-dimensional statecraft of secularism is avoided, as is religious radicalism. Pancasila also arbitrates between homogeneous nationalism and atavistic tribalism, between inward-looking chauvinist nationalism and triumphalistic globalism, between autocratic governance and individualistic democracy, and between an étatist economy and predatory capitalism.

## Nation-building in a country with a Muslim-majority population

For most Indonesia specialists, the relationship between Islam and the Indonesian polity has been a matter of intense interest. In this context I would like to focus more on aspects of nation-building in which Muslim intellectuals played a key role and envisioned a modern ethical polity.

Prior to independence in 1945, the nascent Indonesian leadership and the most effective political organizations of that era gained energy and inspiration from the civilization of Islam. Agus Salim[7] and Haji Oemar Said Tjokroaminoto,[8] two leading Muslim intellectuals in the 1920s, not only commanded strong retinues of followers but also learned how to establish a democratic nation. Both Sukarno himself, whose views were more deeply rooted in the "domestic" political movement, and Moehammad Hatta,[9] who came out of the pan-anti-colonialism movement in Europe, derived their political theories and movements from Islamic values. Considering everything that those men did and the enormous impact they had on modern Indonesia, there is no doubt that Islamic thinking contributed greatly to the ideals of the nation. The generation of Muslim intellectuals who worked towards Indonesia's independence (the "founders") contributed to the idea of emancipation as the key message of independent Indonesia (*Indonesia Merdeka*), according to which all human beings are equal before God, and therefore serfdom and exploitation (by way of colonialization and imperialism) of human by human are totally unjustified.[10] This belief system is often characterized as religiously based emancipation.[11] Nation-building in Indonesia has been powerfully shaped by this understanding. It gives inclusive space for individuals and groups with varying ethnic, religious, and linguistic backgrounds, while providing an early understanding of otherness within one family or nation.

The diversity within Islam, which includes everything from its jurisprudence and traditions to its socio-political environment, has been the ultimate factor in moderating conflicts. In Indonesia, this has been especially true given the country's extraordinary geographical and cultural diversity. Its islands reach from Aceh in the west all the way to Papua in the east. Each region of the country has its own heritage, written works, and emphasis on particular values. In the early 1970s, a great deal of energy was devoted to developing a synthesis of Islam and modern Indonesian life, an effort in which Nurcholish Madjid was one of leading figures. What was happening during that decade actually was a reflection of efforts made to address the mess of the 1950s and 1960s.[12] In this effort, renewal was not primarily associated with "post-colonialism" (as was the case during the first 15 years of the nation's history), but rather with "post-ideology." Abdurrahman Wahid (Gus Dur, later to become Indonesia's president in the post-authoritarian era), Nurholish Madjid and to certain extent Soedjatmoko warned the new regime and the larger society about the growing over-emphasis on "technocratism" and "depoliticization," which they attributed to the post-ideological polity. These men, it turned out, bequeathed an enduring legacy to the very ideas of "modernity" and "development." What remains significant, for the purposes of this essay, is their shared conviction that religion never ceased to play a role in the nation's life, and that development is a process of joint learning. In this respect, it is worth considering the value of Islam and the important role it has played in the development of Indonesian democracy. In the context of the development of democratic institutions in the post-reform (or post-1998) era, we should recall that democracy is partly about preventing tyranny and totalitarianism. One notable support for that observation is provided by Mohammat Natsir, a leading Indonesian national and international figure of the 1940s through the 1960s, who argued that Islam is "*democratic* in the sense of being *anti-istibad* (anti-mob or anti-anarchy), *anti-absolutist, anti-authoritarian,* and *anti-totalitarian*" (quoted in Latif 2003: 452).

More specifically, I would like to cite the late Nurcholish Madjid, a prominent Muslim scholar. He maintained that the only eternal entity is God; everything else is ephemeral and contingent. Knowledge of their own contingency should enable human beings humbly to approach the "Truth" and understand that well-being is best attained through uprightness (*hanif*), submission, humility, mutual recognition (*ta'aruf*), and deliberation in an open, just, civil, and social environment. Coming from this Islamic perspective, he reiterated that the humanistic Islamic message asks Muslims to empower themselves to make Islam a living grace for all, or *rahmatan lil-alamin* (Latif 2003).

Madjid viewed nation-building in the context of the "nation-state"; that is, he regarded it as a state for all the communities within the nation, one that is founded on consensual social terms and that produces an open "contractual and transactional" relationship between the parties to the agreement. He further described the foundation of the nation-state as being designed to attain the general welfare (in the Salafic conception, this would be expressed as *al-maslahat al-ammah* or *al-maslahat al-mursalah*, the foundation of the concept of the general welfare), and to disseminate a concept of goodness of and for all without discrimination and exceptions. The problems and difficulties faced by Muslims are not something that they alone must try to solve. In the search for common ground, the universal message of Islam calls for a process of dialogue about local situations and dynamics, and instructs Muslims to face persisting and emerging challenges. Muslims are asked to empower themselves to live without barriers between being Islamic and being Indonesian citizens (Madjid 1992). More fundamentally, Indonesian Muslims are optimistic in welcoming all future challenges in the spirit of both Islam and Pancasila. Islam involves, in fact, a significant participatory element, a pillar and source of Indonesian values. Having said that, it is natural to expect Islam to keep playing an important role in the development of Indonesian values in the Pancasila.

## Populism as a challenge to nation-building

At times, populism has posed a challenge to the legitimacy currently enjoyed by the Indonesian polity, in part because it has emerged as a "post-truth" movement. It is not hard to imagine that some forms of populism could lead to the phenomenon often labeled "state failure." Here, the polity can no longer sustain its own legitimacy or perform the usual functions of governing, much less wield power wisely and bring about progress. Of course, there is much debate about how populism should be assessed or framed. That debate has special relevance for multicultural Indonesians and their nation-building project, since it raises questions about whether the populist wave, whether motivated by religion or ethnicity, might undermine the country's longstanding multicultural life. Could the great experiment that is Indonesia perhaps outlive the post-colonial legitimacy it acquired earlier in its history? Can the Indonesian nation still be considered legitimate in a world shaped by populism?

Indonesia is a hybrid country whose many constituent cultures have endured and cross-fertilized over many decades and even centuries. It can be analogized to an ecosystem in which different ethnic and racial groupings cohere, following shared ideals and maintaining unity. Indonesia is also an excellent place for dialogues between different civilizations. Those civilizations enrich each other in the long term, albeit with many ups and downs. Such enrichment is still going on, in a process that shapes not only governance, but also relations among ethnic and religious groups.

The ups and downs relate to the capability of Indonesians to understand the sources of conflict, which cultural gaps and differences in beliefs potentially could foster. But conflicts arise for many reasons, not only due to differences in culture and beliefs. Other factors that should be recognized as important in provoking discord include social inequality and unequal access to or participation in power. Those factors have been present in many of the conflicts that have occurred in Indonesia, although it is not always easy to pin down their precise role.

The first factor behind social tensions does indeed involve cultural gaps and differing beliefs, or what are often called cultural issues. That should come as no surprise, given the country's extreme diversity and the need to manage it wisely. One Indonesian social scientist, Supardi Suparlan, has suggested that we should pay attention to the balance of power relations between ethnic communities and national systems. That balance is a prerequisite for social stability. If the national system is too strong or dominant, then the values espoused by ethnic communities will be depressed and weakened. This condition could lead to expressions of disappointment in satire or farce. When addressing diversity policies in Indonesia, Suparlan argues, one should emphasize the diversity of cultures. In this case he distinguishes between the ethnic diversity of perspective and cultural diversity. We must take a community perspective, since we are a multicultural society, not a plural one. He understands multiculturalism as a way of life that celebrates the cultural differences or a belief that recognizes and promotes cultural pluralism. Multiculturalism protects cultural diversity, including the cultures of the minorities. "In multiculturalism," he says, "all cultures are in a position of equality. Not only that, but cultural enrichment has a unique dynamics in that each culture adopts elements of the others—a cross enrichment" (PSIK-Indonesia 2017: 7–8).

In practice, the degree of social equality that prevails might end up playing a major role in determining whether multicultural life can function smoothly. The current level of equality could be assessed by looking at many different variables, such as changes in socio-economic life. Particularly important here is the state of rural life today and the ability of farmers to earn a decent income. Related issues include the flight from the countryside ("de-agrarianization") and marginalization (on both topics, see van Klinken 2007). I would argue that the factor of equality/inequality should be assessed not merely in economic but rather in socio-cultural terms.

## A closer look at religion and the state in the polity of Indonesia

If we wish to understand how religious communities and other associations within the Indonesian polity live and interact, we must first grasp the distinction between "the state that protects religion" and "the state that represents religion." Religion and politics are not necessarily separate as long as the state acts as a neutral referee and is committed to protecting the liberty of each and every faith to express its convictions and conduct its affairs as it sees fit. However, what must be avoided is the identification of the state with the creed or practices of any one religion. This is especially true of Indonesia since, as we have seen so often, it is a nation-state that contains a multicultural society.

The politicization of religion, or rather the manipulation of religion for sectarian political gain, should be prevented. When religion becomes politicized, certain groups will claim that God is always on their side, an assertion that leads to triumphalism, attitudes such as "I own the truth," and the danger of theocracy. Religion can contribute most to public life by emphasizing that the views of all groups must be taken seriously and understood. Fortunately, this scenario is quite plausible, given that all religions have as their core message the virtues of peace and understanding. It is also important that political parties and the nation should allow the true prophetic voice of religion to be heard and felt. Belief in God should encourage the faithful to feel free to challenge the ideological dichotomy of "left" and "right" and to subsume those ideologies under a broader moral canopy. This is the deepest meaning of the credo of Nurcholish Madjid, as expressed in his saying: "Islam, yes; *Partai* Islam, no" (quoted in Latif 2003: 575). On this reading of Madjid, society and politics should interact in such a way that all citizens will be guaranteed the right to live together. It is on such a foundation that the constitutional rights of religious freedom in Indonesia have been built.

In the aftermath of the overthrow of Suharto in 1998, Indonesia carried out a reform of its constitution by adding four crucial amendments. The second of those concerns the constitutional sanctity of human rights, a clause that firmly protects the human rights of all citizens. This amendment expands the grant of rights to Indonesia's citizens that had been incorporated into the original text of the constitution.[13] Essentially, the constitution also provides the legal basis for citizens to defend their lives, and to achieve and manage their welfare in a timely manner through political means and organizations, law, and public reasoning, all without being stamped as subversives or enemies of the state. This conception also implies citizens' right to access information that is vital to their personal security. Citizens thus develop, practice, and enjoy their constitutional rights through various means and by leading active lives, including by consulting the media.

However, Indonesians have raised legitimate questions about whether religious freedom has been protected and upheld sufficiently. Many wonder whether such constitutionally-guaranteed freedoms are being used or abused, and even whether the constitution has outlived its usefulness where religion is concerned. There is no perfect constitution under the sun. Nevertheless, when it comes to the nation's ethical principles and the objective of safeguarding diversity, the constitution (of which Pancasila is the very foundation) is unambiguous. As matters stand, Indonesia continues to face crises and conflicts relating to religious freedom. Yet it has also achieved significant progress, something that cannot go unrecorded in the history of the world.

Today, nation-building in Indonesia undoubtedly is moving toward greater democratization and the progressive realization of human rights. However, opposition and antagonism to this move also have emerged. Our world today is significantly influenced by the tidal wave of identity politics pushing people toward ways of life centered around ethnicity, language, and religion. Every search for identity calls for a form of self-realization. That, in turn, may create a gap between one kind of identity and another. Indonesians should be alert to learn more about how to understand the unavoidable dialectic of self-realization and to refuse an atavistic simplification in which persons may think that the only way for their own identities to survive is for difference and otherness to perish.

The present and future of nation-building lies in its capacity to promote and enhance the ongoing integration of a society that increasingly must cope with divisive forces. Thus, its champions must try to develop a politics of recognition designed to guarantee individual rights, especially those of diverse cultural groupings and social strata, so they can peacefully co-exist and to be actively engaged in the life of the republic.

Ethics and religiously-based systems of morality play important roles as the foundation and catalyst for efforts to unify the nation-state and ensure its survival. It is important that religious communities should understand more fully the need to separate scrupulously "the public affairs of religion" from "the private affairs of religion": i.e., to know when they should be integrated and when they should be kept distinct and separate. Still, all religions should have a shared concern about public affairs that touch on matters of justice, welfare, humanity, and civility.

The Pancasila value-system on which Indonesian nation-building is based includes the legitimate expectation that the nation will protect and support the development of religious life as the vehicle for introducing ethical values into public life. Yet Pancasila never aspires to the creation of a theocratic state that would exclusively represent the goals of one single religion or faith community. Its very existence does a great deal to deter the rise of a religiously-based tyranny that would leave no room for plurality in the life of the nation, and that would create a two-tier system of citizenship whereby the lower tier would be reserved for "different" religions or religious communities.

## The role of the Muslim intelligentsia in Indonesian nation-building

The Indonesian Muslim intelligentsia played a fundamental role both in developing a nationalist movement leading to independence and in clarifying the challenges that would have to be faced both then and in the future. This conjunction of nation-building and Islamic thought has been arguably the most pivotal development in the history of multicultural Indonesia. In the formative years following the country's independence, the intelligentsia dared to reflect upon the very essence of a nation called Indonesia. They also were able to inspire future debates about how Indonesia should be envisioned.

In most cases, those debates echo many of the experiences of the Indonesian intellectuals themselves. Their constant concern was, and is, to transform post-colonial Indonesia into a living, dynamic, multicultural nation. Of course, matters concerning the balance of power, the shape of institutions, socio-economic policy, and limits of government authority always have been controversial. Nevertheless, Muslim intellectuals repeatedly urge their audience to understand and value the very existence of multicultural Indonesia.

Soedjatmoko, in his concept of "the intellectual in developing nations," explained the matter as follows:

What changed in the light of the post-independence experience was the intellectual's awareness of power, its function, its limits, and its character. Among intellectuals there is now a greater awareness of the need for a strong central government capable of pursuing the goals of nation-building and economic development in the face of intractable obstacles posed by tradition, ignorance, and backwardness. There is also a greater awareness of the need to establish and develop countervailing forces within the society that can limit abuses of power and ensure voluntary popular participation, initiative, and organization. The intellectuals of developing nations have aligned themselves on both sides of this dividing line … [T]he difficulties of setting economic development in motion, especially in some of the larger developing nations, have made many intellectuals realize that power is not an indifferent commodity that can be applied to all problems and all tasks …

*(Soedjatmoko 1994: 22–23)*

On another front, Cak Nur (Nurcholish Madjid) held leadership in high esteem:

> The founding fathers of the state held a preliminary but crucial idea of the
> state and the nation of Indonesia. But … the idea has not yet come to full
> fruition. Parts of the idea that already have matured, especially the state form
> of the Republic of Indonesia, furnish us with an important foundation. They
> are the legacy of the nationalist-patriot element of the founding fathers. Other
> parts, the ones that have yet to emerge fully, include the issue of national
> development for the common good based on justice and honesty. This is the
> source of everything that has gone wrong with our national life. Reflecting
> the youth of the founding fathers, which was partly responsible for the
> immaturity of the new nation, the excellent idea (of the founding fathers), in
> the manifestation of the nation's life, faced what Bung Hatta called a
> dwarf-soul of our leader …
>
> *(Madjid 2004: 68)*

Both thinkers are among the many proponents of the role of the intelligentsia in
shaping the nation-building process. Soedjatmoko won fame as a United Nations
diplomat during the independence movement (Lake Success, New York, 1947),
then later as the rector of United Nations University. Cak Nur himself was a
Muslim intellectual and, at present, the role of the Muslim intellectual is alive and
well. The intelligentsia has developed numerous initiatives to address the challenge
of populism as it appears in the midst of the transformation from post-colonial to
multicultural life. Its members also played a considerable role in governance, especially those who eventually served in one way or another as public officials. This
great contribution has been a hallmark of the Muslim intelligentsia from its
beginnings in the 1900s up to the present day.

Reflecting on such contributions, one sees that the Muslim intelligentsia in
Indonesia always has supported openness and recognition both in public life
(especially in governance) and in inter-communal relations. Their contributions
have been notable in several fields, including education, discourse, and even
advocacy in behalf of minorities. At the same time, space for recognition also
means being able to live with many contributions from other groups.

The role of the Muslim intelligentsia gives greater legitimacy to Pancasila, in a
historical sense. The promulgation of Pancasila at the dawn of the nation has continued to influence Indonesia ever since, not least through the acknowledgement
that Indonesia is a highly diverse nation. Several conflicts with religious overtones
remind Muslim intellectuals of their continuing role. Repeatedly, they have made
an effort to respond to the "contest of legitimacy." This too provides a deeper
understanding of Pancasila even in several uniform parts of the nation.[14]

The arrival of "electoral life" in 1999 and its continuing role, and of decen-
tralization from 2004 onwards, confronted the Muslim intelligentsia with both
problems and opportunities. The values of "emancipation" and "renewal" still
were framed by the Muslim intelligentsia as a process of nation-building (see Latif

2003; Madjid 1984; Madjid 1992; Feillard 1997). The likes of Syafii Maarif, Azyumardi Azra, Syafii Anwar, and (later) Budhy Munawar-Rachman and Yenni Wahid played prominent roles in responding to the new wave of democracy with openness. They saw an opportunity to influence the contemporary understanding of emancipation, such that distinct forms of otherness can coexist. They also saw that democracy helps to prevent the rise of a "strong person" and "autocratic rule," and that it affords greater scope for broad participation in the nation. At the same time, this kind of democracy requires them to be active in promoting the discourse of emancipation and renewal. This consciousness by Muslim intellectuals of their own responsibilities has broadened the space of recognition for othernesses.

As early as the period from 1999 to 2010, the active role of the Muslim intelligentsia in developing the space of recognition was challenged by a series of sectarian conflicts and episodes of ethno-nationalism. Furthermore, the contest of transnational persuasions in an intra-faith context posed another problem. The social and human costs of those conflicts have brought about a rather different situation than the one that prevailed during previous decades. Those challenges have induced Muslim intellectuals to revisit the ideals of Indonesia. They have often collaborated with intelligentsia from various other communities to examine the meaning of multicultural life of Indonesia and underscore its importance to the country.

Part of this collaboration has involved the question of representation. The electoral dynamics of Indonesia raise the question of whether representation should or does take place exclusively through electoral processes (i.e., government by elective officeholders, political parties, and rules and regulations). How much should political life be changed by elections? The collaboration among intellectuals from different faiths and world-views resulted in the advocacy of inter-communal relations that would be shaped by one of two factors: electoral processes or local practices and traditions. The exchange of visits between religious leaders happened more often in this period. Especially influenced by the Ambon and Poso conflicts,[15] cooperating religious leaders dedicated considerable time and energy to nurturing a new generation of leadership that would continue to reflect on and reform the matter of representation. Pancasila has been interpreted in novel ways that amplify this type of leadership.

Members of the Muslim intelligentsia also have had to face the new wave of populism in which the wisdom of emancipation and renewal are disputed. The advocates of this kind of populism exploited both electoral processes (as in the context of the Jakarta election of 2017 and the Ahok case[16]) and socio-cultural life (as in the context of Hizbut Tahrir) in order to advance their ideas and political agenda. This form of populism argues for unilateral and uniform ways of life, thus offering a challenge to the usual notion of representation. The challenges posed by populism are not easy to deal with, since its advocates have called into question all of the assumptions behind emancipation and renewal, thereby undermining the foundations of Indonesia's constitution and political institutions.

The concepts of emancipation and renewal offered not only an understanding of the era of colonialism (explaining why independence was a must), but also emphasized the equality of all human beings in a nation called Indonesia. The idea of religiously-based emancipation is an integral part of the active role played by the Muslim intelligentsia in framing nation-building. That role, in which they supported both the broader narrative and the specific measures of the central government,[17] further revealed that nation-building is justified and should be progressive. In socio-cultural life, they have been stimulating discourse on Pancasila and the socio-historical roots of the Muslim intelligentsia and working with Islamic boarding schools (*pondok pesantren*). Their varied and changing roles have proved important in shaping the Indonesian polity.

When they see Western-based modernization in many parts of the world, Muslim intellectuals may respond by placing a high value on an aspect of their own traditions: the principle that the "face value" of truth should be questioned. The generation of Muslim intellectuals that rose to prominence during Indonesia's struggle for independence played a major part in fostering this atmosphere of free inquiry. They questioned the worth of colonialism and paternalism, rejecting the conceit that somebody else ought to think for them rather than letting them do their own thinking. Furthermore, they transformed the tradition of learning up to the present day, even including the practices of faith-based (Islamic) educational institutions. The Muslim intelligentsia sees free inquiry and questioning as one part of modernity that they want to foster. They also emphasize that the message of earlier generations of Muslim intellectuals should continue to shape public life. Religion, they believe, should play a prophetic role in civic affairs rather than withdrawing from them. However, they still think that Pancasila should be the common ground and agree that nation-building should continue to be based on Pancasila.

Perhaps, when looking into the challenges raised by present day modernity, Indonesia has much to ponder. When it comes to models of governance, the use of persuasion in public life, inequality, contemporary conflicts, and many other things, Indonesia must collaborate with other countries in developing and refining the discourse of nation-building. The Indonesian polity has engaged in nation-building, but that process is still very much ongoing. The transformation of the post-colonial polity is supported by intellectuals from various communities, with the Muslim intelligentsia playing a very strong role. In that context, Indonesia combines a tradition of learning from Western-based modernity with the process of encouraging the many communities of Indonesia to share their lives and experiences. Also remaining vital is the question of representation: i.e., whether and in what ways various communities are and should be legitimate members of the public sphere. Of course, persistent and emerging challenges always should be faced by the Muslim intelligentsia. By keeping the standard of learning high, and high enough, the Muslim intelligentsia provide a large pool of wisdom in the context of nation-building, not least by re-examining the rich civilization of Islam in Indonesia.

The intellectuals' role continues to supply the energy for renewal, and never has failed to revive the capability and willingness of Indonesians to absorb and manage contradictory forces throughout critical phases of their country's history. Those are the aspects of continuity that I have come to see in efforts by the Muslim intelligentsia to advance nation-building, both in their own setting and with others in public space.

## Notes

1 Unless otherwise noted, all translations are by the author.
2 The United Nations even has pioneered a special kind of analysis tailored to "small island" and/or "archipelagic nations" in its report on sustainable development. This could be considered an indication of increasing recognition that the ecosystems of such nations need an additional and quite different approach than most other types.
3 Papers and serious journals keep reminding both government officials and the intelligentsia establishment, often in gloomy words, that they should examine more seriously the type of populism that thrives in today's Indonesia.
4 Today's literature provides an extensive list of readings on what constitutes a charter, and how a charter would serve as the legal basis for a nation-state's judiciary system.
5 Loosely translated or paraphrased, "jointly shouldering, sharing, tying up the loose ends." This word arose from certain practices of rural populations: providing (public) services, arranging work according to a roster/schedule, eating from one or two big plates in times of prayer or festivals, moving homes, and creating terraces and providing irrigation.
6 This saying is the only verbal symbol (the other symbols are based on numbers, animals, or things) in the national insignia or coat of arms: Garuda Pancasila. It comes from the book of *Sutasoma*, written by Mpu Tantular during the height of Majapahit (the reign of Rajasanagara). A more complete version of the saying is, *bhinneka tunggal ika, tan hana dharma mangrwa*, or "diversity, but consistent with oneness"; truth is not equivocal or scattered, but always one and integral. The phrase is from Old Javanese, the early Javanese language that was mixed with Sanskrit. For a more thorough observation, see Poerbatjaraka (1952), Zoetmolder (1974), and Gonda (1952).
7 Salim was a Muslim intellectual and early educator who joined Sarekat Islam in 1915. He was a member of BPUPK (preparatory committee for the independence of Indonesia), and later part of a diplomatic negotiating team at the United Nations working out the terms of independence for Indonesia (Lake Success, New York, 1947). Eventually, he became a minister in the newly independent Indonesia.
8 Tjokroaminoto was the leader of *Sarekat Islam* "Union of Islam," which was founded in 1905 as *Sarekat Dagang Islam* and renamed *Sarekat Islam* in 1912. The organization was a union from which many Indonesian leaders—including Sukarno himself—and national movements arose.
9 Hatta was the founder of the nationalist movement, *Perhimpunan Indonesia* (Association of Indonesia), established in 1922; he later became the first vice-president of Indonesia and prime minister during the formative years of the newly independent country.
10 This point is quite similar to the Islamic understanding that human beings are tasked by the Almighty with tending to life on Earth, to make Earth worth living for all (for example, in Surah al-Baqarah verse 30).
11 This emancipation is based on the understanding that humanity is contingent, the creature, while God is absolute, the creator. Emancipation thus conceived is to be found in most religions, including even the smallest streams of beliefs. This type of emancipation is powerful, since it offers an understanding of the genesis of life, and the ultimate destiny of the life of humanity. This gives strong justification (Latif 2011).

12  The 1950s and 1960s witnessed a sharp swing in the Indonesian polity. During the 1950s, governments in the country's parliamentary democracy rose and fell quite rapidly, averaging between eight months and about three years. The sharp contrast between ideologies of party politics compromised the effectiveness of any sitting government. This period also saw religiously motivated armed struggles and, separately, armed struggles waged due to the neglect of economic development outside Java by the central government. At the same time, this period also included the Asia-Africa Conference, the first free election in the nation with universal suffrage, and discussions about the proposed constitution (Konstituante). Many important Indonesian thinkers rose to prominence during this era. Muslim thinkers were important in shaping the debate on how to integrate the core value of "emancipation" in Islam as a crucial integrative factor for the nation.

The 1960s began the era of "guided democracy", during which the institutions of democracy were overshadowed and "reorganized" by Sukarno and his dominating personality. This was also an epoch of inflation-prone economic life. Moreover, it saw the comeback of Indonesia's original constitution, UUD 1945, which again was invoked as the chief means to frame the polity of Indonesia. During that decade, too, Indonesians had to live through the tragic violence and killings of 1965 and then the coming of a New Order. In this particular time, Muslim thinkers and creators of solidarity still tried hard to frame the discussion so as to highlight the unity of Indonesia based on emancipation, even in a decade of huge existential problems. They obviously tried hard to prevent a further breakdown in the political cohesion of Indonesia, seeing the novelty of the proclamation of Indonesia in 1945. In effect, the incoming New Order regime in 1966 sought legitimacy from Muslim thinkers and solidarity makers when they claimed that they were adopting new forms of governance.

The extremes during this period constituted the intellectual background for a new generation of Muslim thinkers, the likes of Nurcholish Madjid, Abdurrahman Wahid (Gus Dur), and Munawir Sjadzali. This new generation took the extremes seriously during the Fifties and Sixties while espousing a polity based on the "emancipation" value of Islam, which they saw as integral to the proclamation of Indonesia as a nation-state. Undoubtedly, they framed a new generation of discourse that combines Islamic thinking with the socio-history of Indonesian thinking without relying on one or more particular ideologies of party politics. For further general historical reference, see, for example, Ricklefs (2001).

13  The original (pre-amendment) text of the Indonesian constitution (UUD 1945) enumerates the rights and immunities of citizens in articles 29 to 34. These articles essentially already enshrined the rights of the citizen in the polity. However, during New Order, with its autocratic tendency, discourses and legal procedures based on this set of articles were profoundly neglected. This neglect spurred Reformasi-era lawmakers to make human rights protections more obvious, stipulative, and readable by the average citizen.

14  In several regents (*Kabupaten*), administrative levels below the Province, there are situations in which ethnicity and/or the local spoken language and/or religion is much closer to uniformity.

15  Although inherently complicated, the Ambon and Poso conflicts (circa 1999–2001) were highly influenced by religious persuasions. Especially in those areas, religious affiliations are often confined to one particular ethnic group (*"cuius regio, eius religio"*). This makes it much harder to respond to such conflicts. In any event, the local leaders themselves "woke up" and dealt with the matters by themselves with the understanding that their futures would be shaped exclusively their own decisions.

16  History will assess further the context of the Jakarta election of 2017. What many agreed concerning that particular cycle is that the use of social media with strong negative language, especially those that stirred up popular passions against Ahok, the Chinese-decent candidate for governorship, played a role in his fall.

17  Including the 2017 administrative ban against Hizbut Tahrir.

# References

Feillard, A. 1997. "Traditionalist Islam and State in Indonesia: The road to legitimacy and renewal." In R. W. Hefner & P. Horvatich (eds.), *Islam in an Era of Nation-States: Politics and religious renewals in Muslim Southeast Asia*. Honolulu, HI: University of Hawaii Press.

Gonda, J. 1952. *Sanskrit in Indonesia*. Nagpur: International Academy of Indian Culture.

Latif, Y. 2003. *Inteligensia Muslim dan Kuasa: Genealogi inteligensia Muslim Indonesia abad ke-20*. Jakarta: Mizan Pustaka.

Latif, Y. 2011. *Negara Paripurna*. Jakarta: Gramedia Pustaka Utama.

Madjid, N. 1984. *Islam, Kemodernan and Keindonesiaan*. Bandung: Mizan.

Madjid, N. 1992. *Islam Doktrin dan Peradaban*. Jakarta: Yayasan Wakaf Paramadina.

Madjid, N. 2004. *Indonesia Kita*. Jakarta: Gramedia Pustaka Utama, Universitas Paramadina, Perkumpulan Membangun Kembali Indonesia.

Poerbatjaraka, R. M. N. 1952. *Kepustakaan Java* [*Writings of Java*]. Jakarta: Djambatan.

PSIK-Indonesia. 2017. *Indonesia, Chain of Tolerance*. Jakarta: PSIK-Indonesia (Indonesian Center for Islam and Studies) & FES (Friedrich Ebert Foundation Indonesia).

Ricklefs, M. 2001. *A History of Modern Indonesia Since c.1200*, 3rd edition. Basingstoke: Palgrave.

Soedjatmoko. 1994. *Transforming Humanity: The Visionary Writings of Soedjatmoko* (ed. K. Newland & K. C. Soedjatmoko). West Hartford, CT: Kumarian Press.

van Klinken, G. 2007. *Communal Violence and Democratization in Indonesia: Small town wars*. New York: Routledge.

Zoetmolder, P. J. 1974. *Kalangwan: A survey of Old Javanese literature*. Jakarta: Djambatan.

# 3

# CAN WE EXPLAIN MULTIPLE MODERNITIES?

## Suggested insights and their test in a South American context

*Renato G. Flôres, Jr.*

### Introduction: Betrayal and revenge

Socio-economic evolution during the past century was strongly conditioned, particularly in its second half, by rapid and far-reaching scientific and technological development. However, beginning in the final decades of the twentieth century, a subtle turn can be identified. A notable shift of emphasis and redirection of research efforts toward the information sciences gradually developed.[1] The advances achieved in that branch—intertwined with telecommunications technology, miniaturization techniques, extremely sophisticated software, and artificial intelligence algorithms—have brought about a thorough overhaul in most industrial and product realms, leading to more concentrated ownership of productive capital, even though in a physical sense the latter has been disseminated more broadly around the world. At the same time, these changes have tended to enhance the already-existing hermetic side of modern science, thus considerably increasing the gap between the creators of science, on one hand, and the designers of technology and laymen, on the other. No wonder that Beck (1986), in a pioneering insight, denounced the "new societal risk" that ensued, in which millions of people were at the mercy of opaque but seemingly irresistible procedures, products, and systems fashioned by single-minded technicians, however well-intentioned those technicians might be.

To some extent, such outcomes can be considered an ironic betrayal of the original promises and expectations that accompanied scientific progress, through which strife and hard, relatively unproductive labor eventually would be banished in favor of more human, freer, and more efficient societies, in which further progress would come under collective control. As in any global trend, the big picture is neither black nor white; positive shades of improvement may be ranged alongside dismal outcomes. Inevitably, technological and scientific progress stimulated new forms of social interaction.

The purpose of this introductory section is not to evaluate whether the overall result has been beneficial on balance, despite the dozen or so ticklish problems it has spawned. Nor is the point to decide whether a predominantly bad outcome is broadly acceptable; this is a matter for (many) other papers. Rather, what counts here is that the subtle inflection mentioned, "betraying" a more social view of scientific development, increased the degree of alienation, concentration, and control in modern societies. Citizens, victims of an overwhelming flow of information, were treated as (often passive and involuntary) experimental subjects beset by all kinds of innovations, systems, or "apps." Especially when combined with encompassing data-analytic techniques operating in real time, the flood of information—which is largely unchecked, and nowadays even generated by robots—continually disrupts established social and economic patterns.

People as well as institutions generally acquired a multiplicity of identities that generated two opposing movements. On the one hand, individuals are tempted to take advantage of such multiplicity, which in principle (and many times in an illusory way) gives them the ability to act in several contexts under different guises. Hackers offer an extreme example of this Protean identity-switching. On the other hand, control mechanisms—aided by the same techniques—have increased enormously, as they try to capture the same, unique person no matter how or where he or she acts in the web galaxy. From citizen-based issues to those involving external security, this tension unleashes a host of domestic and trans-border problems (not least those related to the protection of individual privacy), the solutions of which remain out of reach.

These highly technical and knowledge-intensive developments have increased inequality among countries, while concurrently generating deep fractures within national and local societies. Those able to pioneer new software developments, innovative algorithms, and applications increasingly separate themselves from the rest, who remain doomed to dependency on those very systems, obliged to purchase and use them but with an unavoidable time lag. On a country basis (cf., among others, Valladão 2014 and Collins 2013), the purchasers of algorithms and robots are likely to become producers of traditional goods, with ever decreasing value-added, while the "Masters of Algorithms and Robots" extract world rents from their unrivalled technical prowess. At the individual level, the latter are also responsible for creating and providing powerful escapes from reality. The electronic-era amusements industry is, after all, essential to keeping masses of people appeased and unquestioning.

The shift to information science and technology ultimately has reinforced the widespread expansion of capitalism's far-reaching control capabilities—ones that jeopardize our humanity—as well as their silent, pervasive domination. Norms, standards, protocols, and (in a broader, more dangerous way) regulations, all constrain and determine individual action. Relying on arguments of complexity and high technological imperatives, they create an environment that the ordinary citizen is obliged to accept without communication, without dialogue and, even worse, without access to the caste of rule-makers. Beck's gloomy vision (notwithstanding its 1999 update) has been overshadowed by an even gloomier reality.

Meanwhile, though giants like the information and social media companies present themselves as producers of public goods, freely available to all citizens of the global community, they are extremely profitable mechanisms of social control, generously paid, among others, by most international (and domestic) providers of goods and services. This massive, rapid, pervasive development has triggered wrenching changes in the socio-economic fabric of communities and societies. Traditional channels for collective action in domestic democratic constituencies are evolving progressively into an impersonal, virtual democratic world community, insulated as far as possible from economic processes and ultimately controlled by the very same high technology producers (cf., among others—with different nuances—Crouch 2004 and Willke 2014). Representation, especially in its traditional democratic form, is becoming an elusive concept. Authoritarian and populist reactions are starting to look like efficient ways to try to change the unfair status quo and give voice to the huge number of outsiders.

It is in this world characterized by permanent, often unexpected changes and strongly conditioned by the phenomena described above, that the concept of multiple modernities can help shed light on the existing *confusión de confusiones*. In addition to or alongside intellectual movements challenging the Western model of modernization and its philosophical underpinnings, we interpret populism as a kind of backlash or revenge against the gently suffocating and predatory world that mainstream modernity has been imposing on the planet.

Building on this core argument, the following sections outline a thesis that justifies the title of the paper. The "revenge" dimension is elaborated in Section II. Then, after an intermezzo (Section III), and remembering that it is always dangerous to advocate universal theories in political and social contexts, in Section IV we examine some South American cases in search of support for this line of reasoning. Caution in making generalizations is warranted, since situations in Africa, Asia (including the especially complex cases of India and China), and even the US may require revisions to our thesis that go beyond mere amendments and corrections.

Section V, on Brazil, adds a further pinch of salt to the debate by introducing another dimension that is valid in many instances: namely, the intrinsically static structure prevailing in certain developing countries' societies (which yields a phenomenon we have labelled the *éternel retour*) that may lead to an implosive outcome within a multiple modernities context. Brazil is the chosen case study for this possibility, although studies done of that country may apply to others on the same continent.

The concluding section highlights the fact that the multiple modernities construct may open a helpful window of observation, and in many cases also of analysis, on the baffling transformations that the world has been experiencing. Nevertheless, two points must not be forgotten: the surprising capacity for response and absorption displayed by mainstream globalization and the specificities of development contexts, which draw renewed attention to old, unsolved riddles like fairness, and the shape and effectiveness of democracy.

## Reaction

Trying to extract a uniform pattern of reaction from modernity movements ranging from those in the European Union to those in South Africa, while bypassing the Americas and ignoring the enormous diversity in Asia and the Middle East, does not seem like a defensible procedure. Moreover, the social sciences generally take a dim view of the attempt to import concepts from a hard science like physics. Yet we are speaking precisely of a dynamic comparable to that in the famous law in the Newtonian model, in which the new modernity arises as a countervailing response (i.e., a reaction) to the impact caused by the standard modernity, a main feature of the latter having been outlined in the previous section of this chapter.

The concepts of alienation, concentration, and higher control are indispensable if we wish to construct a persuasive theoretical formulation of that insight.

*Alienation* implies that, hemmed in and constrained by the techno-regulatory apparatus, various segments of the populace feel completely left out of the political decision-making process. The *concentration of power* exacerbates those sentiments, since the exercise of real, efficacious power becomes ever more conspicuously the privilege of a few: those individuals most deeply enmeshed in the capital-technological core. The debate on the legitimacy and, ultimately, the meaning of belonging to the European Union, now evident in so many countries, has roots in this feeling of alienation from a true polis, alienation from the fact of being governed by clearly defined cliques of bureaucrats, big corporations, flamboyant global politicians, and a few romantic idealists.

Examples of alienation and concentration are numerous. Consider the case of the former Commissioner Durão Barroso, who behaved in a highly questionable manner during the Ukrainian crisis, openly advocating the dissolution of a democratically elected government. Just two years after resigning his elite European Commission post, he changed course swiftly—again in a highly controversial way—by assuming the presidency of the Goldman Sachs International financial conglomerate. Consider also the Visegrád countries (the Czech Republic, Hungary, Poland, and Slovakia). Feeling excluded and searching for their own identity, they have begun to experiment with modes of governance far outside the ambit of Western European norms. So far, though, they have not sought to leave the European Union. Furthermore, it is worthwhile to study the case of Marine Le Pen and her followers, still a force in French politics who see their nemesis in the *parvenue* "modernity" of Emmanuel Macron, a politician barely known until his breakthrough victory in 2017. Nor should we overlook the nationalist upsurge implicit in Brexit and the ticking time bomb of regional independence movements, of which the push for a state in Catalonia is but a first laboratory trial. As beauty is in the eyes of the beholder, many people—optimists surely included—perceive in most of the previous cases solid proof of the flexibility of the system, the power of liberal democracy, or just a series of stumbling blocks the dimensions of which should not be exaggerated and which will prove unable to stop the positive march towards full union.

The optimistic camp does not include the present author. The multiplicity invoked by populism, which is hard to square with positive qualities of the system, signals a search for a new modernity that decisively breaks with the prevailing one. Even if, at first glance, the populists may appear unmodern, if not as throwbacks to the past—viz., the rhetoric of some of Le Pen followers' rhetoric or the nostalgia to return to the old United Kingdom, free from interference by Brussels—they are essentially modern in the sense that *they have been generated by the very modernity they oppose*; without it, they would have been inconceivable. "How far do they contest the Western path of globalized development?" is a question not easy to answer, since many—like most of the Visegrád countries, or nearly all regional independence movements—are searching for another route *within* the broadly modern reality that they are rejecting in part.

*Control* enters the picture in a different mode. Border controls, increasingly automated and aided by sophisticated surveillance systems, block the flow of people who (for a variety of reasons, such as flight from war or catastrophe) seek a different place in which to pursue their livelihoods and opportunities for self-expression. Domestic controls, thanks to the technological advances already mentioned, demand ever more from citizens, in real and in personal time, in states that often do not deliver public goods comparable to the expected level of quality and reliability. This mismatch is more acute in developing and underdeveloped countries than in advanced ones.

Aided by powerful computing capabilities, control spreads to multiple aspects of civil life, in the form of rankings and evaluations strictly based on quantitative indicators in which matters of quality recede behind sheer output volume. These range from academic ratings, blindly reliant on the number of publications in previously ranked journals (a poor proxy for true scientific and social impact), to economic, social, and even artistic performances, where sheer numbers are the usual and sole measure of success and achievement. All these are powerful sources of dissatisfaction, further social alienation, and "civic anxiety."

Some modernities may focus primarily on the latter issues, such as movements for a less GDP-focused society, zero-growth initiatives, or campaigns to include quality in several instances where control has simply ruled it out. Often, modernities outside of or contesting the alienation/concentration trend form alliances as a way of recovering a voice in the public debate and avoid being overwhelmed by the tyranny of the quantitative. Nevertheless, one common thread linking this multiplicity of modernities is the will to use the very tools that initially provoked their negative reactions. In Section I of this essay, the word *revenge* was employed because nearly all modernities, engendered by the disruptive and disconnecting technologies, have recourse to those tools as essential instruments for disseminating their ideas and consolidating their organizations.

Beginning with the rough attempts at change such as the Arab Spring, passing through the various huge Brazilian street protests from April to July of 2013—another frustrated call for an alternative modernity in politics and public administration that failed to bear fruit—to the anti-EU nationalist governments in Poland and Hungary and the ever more popular Alternative für Deutschland, in each case there is a single root cause of the dissatisfaction they express.[2]

Pure scientists, in their comfortable Olympus of scientific truth, would say that such populist protest movements are to be expected, since science and technology are not responsible for the uses mankind makes of their discoveries and gadgets. After all, the latter can serve opposing groups as well as more pro-modern forces. However true it may be its abstract formulation, the presumed response of scientific elites lacks insight into the real nature of present-day problems. The dilemma consists in the difficulty of distinguishing the mainstream version of modernity that is at stake here from the plethora of its techno-scientific causes and components. Does this difficulty undermine the novelty or freshness of the multiple modernities concept? In some cases, yes it does; in others, not. To obtain a deeper view of the symbiosis of pro-and anti-modern forces and to grasp how similar or dissimilar the proposals and movements in question really are—i.e., to justify fully the idea of multiple modernities—we need to take a closer look at some specific examples. But first we must elaborate a bit further on the very essence of this multiplicity of modernities.

## Intermezzo: The system fights back

The concept of multiple modernities assumes the existence of a kind of modernity against which all the others are contrasted as alternatives. Such core modernity is the one to be found in the Western globalized ("advanced") world, best represented by the societies of the United States and the European Union. However, it may be misleading to lump together those two regions of full-fledged modernity. Given the existence of significant differences between the two, we will take the case of the US as the paradigm. Even so, one runs the risk of entering into a kind of fractal definition, where dualisms and even multiplicity pop up at each lower level to which one moves in the elusive pursuit of precision. Thus, for example, it might be said that under a Republican presidency the model differs from that under a Democratic one, but differences persist when one gets inside the different party factions, and so on—down to a point where further analysis becomes pointless. To avoid this Byzantine trap, we postulate that the standard modernity is the one observed at the level of US society broadly understood, as seen at the country level and in the form that has been exported to the rest of the planet since the end of World War II.

The identification of a "standard modernity" is important because it helps us specify what the concept of multiple modernities really connotes. Does it suggest that the standard modernity co-exists with other forms, but under a perspective that it still is predominant? Or does it imply that such co-existence is dynamic, such that multiple modernities are successfully pushing back where co-existence already almost had become the norm? For instance, is Evo Morales's Bolivia a fully robust alternative modernity, or will it disappear if Bolivia rejoins the standard model in a future election, or even after an unfortunate *coup d'état*? Are Marine Le Pen's followers just a vogue fueled by several clear points of dissent (anti-EU sentiment, hostility to sharing space with large communities of immigrants, etc.), or the embryo of a sustainable alternative?

This essay argues that the reality is situated somewhere between these two poles. Of course, that makes for a complex picture in which the standard form still counts as predominant, but a plethora of modernities lead more or less stable lives, sending clear signs of a state of flux in both the global scene and also internally in many regions. In such a predicament, the standard model fights for its continuation and, consequently, strikes back in all possible ways against its rivals, whether subtly or in more violent outbursts. In the latter case the standard version of modernity will make full use of capitalism's extraordinary capacity to absorb rivals and re-invent itself.

If the tremendous developments in information technology and data analysis have been almost universally adopted by the alternatives to mainstream modernity, then the latter must come up with new concepts, regulations, and techniques to limit, control, or if possible forbid certain uses of those advances. Cybersecurity thus became a buzzword for a whole set of procedures that can duly protect sensitive files and crucial systems and installations and simultaneously can mar or impair important features useful to the alternative modernities. A whole narrative—and related algo-rithms—on robots, invaders, and fake news automata has been developed to curb or discredit devices that once sabotaged the system but by now have been turned against the very alternative modernities that pioneered their dissident uses.

Another narrative, that of catastrophes and situations involving high risk and damage, has been enhanced and refined for various reasons, but especially to call attention to the inability of the alternatives to cope with them. This is a point grasped by Klein (2007), among others. The financial system, a redoubtable power in itself and one that remains allied to the standard model, mutates into several products that, like an oasis in a desert, foster the illusion that they are working to alleviate key problems raised by other modernities. Green finance is a conceptually rich but certainly controversial example.

Labelling different outcomes of specific historical contexts, shaped by distinct cultures, as "authoritarian" or "populist" sometimes may function to undercut their likely legitimacy and suppress their content, lumping them together in a third-class set of protests against the system. It is senseless to discuss multiple modernities in themselves without considering the existential challenge that they pose to the dominant order, and the way that order responds to it. When we study concrete examples, we always must be cognizant of the possibility that an orchestrated effort by the dominant order will threaten to change or destroy rival modernities. The study of concrete examples always must bear this point in mind.

## Multiple modernities in South America? The case of former Spanish colonies

Because it is less vast and diverse than either Africa or Asia and shares with the developed world the imprint of Western culture, South America seems to offer a manageable yet quite extensive testing ground for evaluating the concept of multiple modernities. Furthermore, in the context of this paper, field studies are doubly important because they add concrete social and historical dimensions to the reasoning outlined in the previous sections, thus sharpening the country studies that the multiple modernities approach favors.

As a continent featuring subsidiary and in some cases peripheral economies, none of which is a center of scientific or technological innovation, South America absorbed or adopted the discontents and reactions described above. Despite their shared history of being on the receiving end of waves of modernity, South American countries—or at least some of the social groups within them—have responded to it in their own unique ways. That insight suggests that, as societies on the global periphery, the responses of South American countries to modernity have been shaped more strongly by social forces and historic dysfunctions (among other causes) than is the case in more developed societies.

From the societal viewpoint, inequality turns out to be one of the crucial causes (if not the most important one) of discontent with the standard model. Time and again it reveals different faces, generating ever new forms of unfairness. Here, we will not elaborate on these different manifestations of inequality, or their measurement and distribution. We wish only to point out that (a) the South American continent may well harbor the most egregious examples of inequality on the planet, and for that reason (b) it provides a complex and varied menu of responses to modernity—responses often labelled as populist, but that in fact display a far more subtle character than any such broad generalization might convey. Nuances, as usual, are better revealed and understood with the help of history.

We start with a trio of countries usually and wrongly lumped together as having found similar answers to the challenges of modernization and modernity: Bolivia, Ecuador, and Venezuela.

To understand the first of these cases, it is necessary to go back to the era of independence in the early 19th century. In 1825, this huge country—named after its first president, Simón Bolívar, who was arguably the most famous liberator in the history of Spanish America—faced the problem of how to establish a European-inspired nation-state with a majority-indigenous population. Europeans and *criollos*, though a minority, would seek to retain power by drafting a constitution that included an article stating: "All Bolivians are equal and share the same rights." Yet the framers of that constitution qualified the grant of rights in a detail buried in an attached explanatory addendum, which stated that the "the rights of the native Indians will be detailed later." With this single line they transformed half of the country into non-citizens.

It would oversimplify things to call Evo Morales a populist, because that expression would obscure and underplay the stark drama of a country still in the making, where indigenous Bolivians (the original ones) found in him the leader they needed to help them integrate fully into their own country.[3] This does not absolve Morales from his mistakes or excuse his recent urge to try to cling to power, but it does introduce a new and fundamental variable for analyzing his socio-political model: a variable that sets his policies apart from most other modernities. Morales's way of conducting economic policy is mostly conservative, and the economy has not been faring badly. Of course, as pointed out above, the ever-present threat of a backlash from those who wish to defend the standard model of modernity forces him to operate within an often adverse if not downright hostile environment.[4] Has Morales managed to create an alternative form of modernity? Yes and no. Those who favor and work toward social progress inevitably must take into account his large constituency. In this respect, what he has done indeed suggests that a new version of modernity is underway. Yet his style of socio-economic management is not really new at all.

Ecuador, a country where indigenous nations are also a sizeable fraction of the population—though less so than in Bolivia—adds another dimension to the debate, since it is well-endowed with natural resources and riches. To some extent, that endowment is due to the diversity of the ecosystems it contains.

Rafael Correa, the well-educated son of a middle-class family, eventually gained the support of many indigenous people, especially those affiliated with the Pachakutik Party, in the course of his first campaign for the presidency. Rather than focusing on the Indians, his political platform pledged to create a fairer society and a more efficient system of public goods and services. Infrastructure investment was given priority, and during his ten-year rule as president he undeniably altered the face of the country in this respect, providing modern transportation complexes of roads, ports, and airports, together with improved telecommunications. Correa fought for an independent trade and foreign investment stance (not necessarily a protectionist one) and, in spite of two major crises, had a broadly successful performance. Although criticisms of his allegedly authoritarian posture are quite commonly voiced, he generally did respect democratic institutions and stepped down peacefully in 2017, after passing the presidency on to a former collaborator who won in a fair and free election.

The same question applies to Ecuador as to Bolivia: Was an alternative form of modernity created there? Again, the answer is nuanced, comprising a yes and a no. Recently, a public referendum in Ecuador eliminated the possibility of indefinite re-election to the office of president. In this way, an amendment that Correa had introduced before leaving power, probably to assure his own re-election, was overturned. It is not clear how far his former ally, the current president Lenin Moreno (in principle now Correa's adversary), will pursue policies akin to his own. However, it is most likely that Moreno will hew more closely to the standard model of modernity.

Of the three countries canvassed here, the most extreme example of possible alternative modernities is Venezuela, where the strong, unique personality of the late Hugo Chávez, as well as his early death, ended up derailing his experiments and leading to unfortunate outcomes.

Background realities matter, as usual, and the Venezuelan elite before Chávez could be considered perhaps the least enlightened on the continent. Thanks to the immense oil and gas reserves of the country, that elite had set up a socially monopolistic model of exploitation in which their sons would attend universities in the United States, usually choosing to study engineering and management sciences. Eventually, they would fill the technical and executive posts of the national oil company, PDVSA, the main provider of both white collar and blue collar employment in the country. Oil exports supplied enough revenues to import everything the nation needed—quite a lot, it turned out, since harmonious, diversified domestic economic development (which gas and oil revenues could have supported) was not encouraged. As early as 1974, one perceptive development thinker, Celso Furtado, already had identified Venezuela as a unique case of underdevelopment despite its abundance of financial means (Furtado 2008). The country had, and continues to have, few industries; moreover, the gap between the elite and the rest—already extremely wide by the 1990s—has been worsened by absent or poor-quality public services.

Hugo Chávez can be understood as the leader of one of several protest movements. He launched a failed *coup d'état* in 1992 and spent years in prison for the attempt. But eventually he succeeded in gaining power through democratic elections. Sooner or later such an upheaval was inevitable, given that the PDVSA elite-driven model clearly had been exhausted and discredited.

Like the two presidents of our previous examples, Chávez concentrated his efforts on reducing inequality and creating a network of public services and social assistance, notably in the health sector, to alleviate the burdens weighing on the poor. It is not easy to evaluate the dynamics of his several years in power, but what differentiated his case from the former two was his much more active international role and ambitions. Indeed, buoyed by oil exports revenues, he wanted to create a new model that could be adopted by (at least) most of South America. Though his model of development remained vague and heavily dependent on revenues from a highly volatile international commodity, Chávez fought for an alternative modernity that featured rhetoric that was heavily equalitarian and anti-US (the unavoidable hegemon and oftentimes patron of the Americas).

The multiple tasks demanded by the situation on both the domestic (still unresolved at his death) and international fronts progressively led Chávez to ever more dictatorial behavior, at least until he ended up a victim of cancer. His death added confusion to an experiment that already showed severe cracks and fissures. Relying on considerable skill and savvy political and leadership instincts, he had managed to keep a lid on the problems. But his demise plunged the country into relative chaos that only deepens as the months and years go by.

Two other examples complement the views articulated in this section. The first is that of Chile, a modernity project that, since the dramatic overthrow of Salvador Allende's socialist experiment in 1973, has made a 180-degree turn. Chile now figures in all the glossy pictures of model countries treading the virtuous path toward standard modernity, mostly on account of its capitalist and pro-globalization strategies. Why then should it be included in a treatise on multiple modernities? Because fatigue with that model, exacerbated by patterns of increasing inequality and spatial exclusion, has started to creep into Chilean society. The country, long since under democratic rule, vacillates between a more leftist, less globalized path and a fully globalized, liberal one. In this way, it somehow managed to lose its character as a model and drifted closer to standard mainstream economies in crisis.

The tension between those two paths acquires nearly tragic overtones in Argentina, where sharp oscillations have occurred within a political ecosystem that is difficult to grasp from the outside. Different groups and parties in that country claim for themselves the "Peronista" label or heritage. A liberal spell, plagued by a worsening external debt situation and macroeconomic mismanagement, was followed by a populist period under the Kirchner regime that was both more socially oriented and internationally closed. Deteriorating economic conditions led to the victory of a new liberal who, since taking power in early December, 2015, has been striving to realign the country with the standard model of modernity. After two years, the result—particularly in view of Argentina's political fragmentation—remains uncertain.

These five examples, beyond calling attention to the nuances that economies of the periphery bring to the concept of multiple modernities, show that innovation and true alternatives, which would give a clearer meaning to the adjective "multiple," are as hard to find in the South as in the North. Moreover, South America's lack of linkage (and self-identification) with the long history of European industrial revolutions and their related social class conflicts changes the object of protest and the purpose of change. This is particularly the case in countries like those we have highlighted here. Less than 200 years ago, they were colonies and, after a brief taste of liberty, soon became essentially exporters of commodities and raw materials with deeply stratified societies.

Nevertheless, as in more advanced economies, multiple alternatives are triggered by core inequalities, public services dysfunctions, and harsh failures in both the public sector and the democratic process more generally. All of these problems display a far darker side than they do in the North. If we attempt to draw lessons from the examples discussed here, they seem to reveal out-and-out class struggle in more or less democratic (albeit fragile?) environments rather than alternative forms of modernity. Aren't all of these cases really examples of works in progress in terms of nation-building, rather than instances of multiple modernities?

## Multiple modernities in South America? The case of Brazil

The biggest and most highly diversified country on the continent offers an intriguing case study. To begin with, Brazil has had a unique past. It is the only ex-colony in history to achieve independence through a practically bloodless transfer of power from a father to a son, who then became emperor of the new state, with the expectation that later the two kingdoms would probably reunite under his crown. For 67 years Brazil—to the great envy of Simon Bolívar—was a vast and solid empire. It finally became a republic due to certain shocks: notably, the economic consequences of a major war against Paraguay and the somewhat unexpected end of slavery.

It is not my purpose here to relate the long history of the Brazilian republic in its 120 years of existence. After a period of rapid development in the years from 1956 to 1960, during the Juscelino Kubitschek presidency, the country was swept up in the United States' anti-communist Cold War strategy from 1964 to 1985, as a military coup toppled the left-leaning president Goulart and led to a dictatorship. The supposed point of the US strategy orchestrated on the South American continent was to prevent the Cuban example from influencing other countries there.

The 21 years of military rule brought development at very high growth rates but significantly increased inequality, urban concentration, and social problems, while creating a huge state apparatus. Of the four directly elected presidents since the end of that period,[5] two have been impeached and one has been convicted of corruption and is now in jail. There is a notable lack of new names and proposals on the political scene, showing that one of the worst legacies of the dictatorship has been the fragmentation of the political class that existed before 1964 and the absence of a younger generation of politicians. Thus, the long authoritarian interlude had a chilling effect on all political activity.

From 1995 until 2010, the country experienced a fairly virtuous cycle with two presidential mandates going to Fernando Henrique Cardoso (8 years), followed by two more for Luís Inácio (Lula) da Silva. President Cardoso conducted a liberal, globalization-friendly policy, though in a more moderate tempo than Collor de Mello, the first president to be impeached in the recent history of the republic, who governed from March of 1990 to early October of 1992. He also profited from a more stable economy that he had been bequeathed by Itamar Franco, under whom he had served as Finance Minister.

Lula da Silva, without destroying his predecessor's accomplishments, pursued a much more socially oriented policy, one that successfully reduced inequality and rescued millions from poverty. He also sought, with some success and thanks in large measure to his brilliant Foreign Minister, Celso Amorim, an alternative modernity on the international scene, casting Brazil as an important independent voice within the capitalist framework.

By 2011, Brazil was preparing to amalgamate reforms that had been pursued by the two previous presidents and largely had complemented one another. The idea was to advance along a path of development that might actually lead to an original modernity, *in which the system would have been changed from the inside*, in full accordance with the democratic playbook. The popularity that Lula da Silva enjoyed at the end of his second term in office allowed him to name one of his closest aides, Dilma Rousseff, as his successor. It is outside the scope of this paper to speculate about why Rousseff was chosen, or to pass judgment on her level of competence. What matters is that she proved herself to be completely unable to carry out the momentous and crucial task that had fallen to her lot. As a result, a generalized deterioration on all fronts took place, ending in her impeachment in 2016, the second year of her hard-won second mandate.

As this book goes to print, the country has just held new elections, won by the populist, pro-military candidate, Jair Bolsonaro. The first round of the presidential balloting revealed a deep divide between established political forces (including even Lula's Workers' Party) and the populist forces. Although Lula continues to claim that he represents the poor and the marginalized, it is Bolsonaro who mobilized the winning majority, which included plenty of the very people Lula wanted to champion.

The liberal measures taken under Enrique Cardoso included privatizations and the installation of several regulatory systems (some of them hastily designed), as well as certain industrial arrangements and structures. In retrospect, the latter set of reforms, which suffered from alternating waves of protectionism and spells of more free-trade oriented policies, seem to have generated about a mixed outcome. The pervasive oligopolistic structures of the Brazilian economy remain nearly untouched. The gains achieved in reducing inequality appeared to be sustainable only if development-oriented and ancillary policies were pursued while stable conditions for securing the livelihoods of middle and low-middle class Brazilians were maintained. Since this has not been the case, those gains risk being lost as time goes on. Although the post-Dilma government under Michel Temer desperately tried to implement reforms intended to improve (and boost) the traditional model, Brazil remains mired in a deep economic contraction, with growth only now resuming.

From this brief overview it is not easy to perceive a continuous upward trend in Brazil's economic policies that might portend positive developments for the country's future. This is a point that has been elaborated more fully elsewhere (Flôres 2014). Instead, Brazil seems to follow a pattern similar to the "eternal return," a metaphor put forward by Friedrich Nietzsche and inspired by ancient Greek philosophy.[6] Brazil's structural problems never disappear; they change and seem to improve, only to return later in a more or less different setting but in an equally dramatic way. Even with the help of information technology—as in any active modernity nowadays—the country hasn't left behind its old ways or its structural dysfunctions. It is bewildering to identify, in a superficially dynamic society, the same constraints and lack of any autonomous capacity to overcome the conditions the country endured long ago when the standard model of modernity gained prominence.

Did Brazil's history offer alternatives? Intermittently, over shorter or more prolonged periods of time, original solutions and confirmations may have been discovered and tried. Yet persistent forces, ones anchored in structures that often may be traced back to the empire, have stifled and frustrated those innovative impulses. They insure that any original solutions found for Brazil's problems lack continuity, endurance, and minimal stability. Hence, they really do not qualify as alternatives at all.

A roughly similar pattern may be observed in other big and complex developing countries, such as India. Nevertheless, Brazil inevitably stands as a unique example of a country in which mainstream and alternative modernities coexist in a nearly anarchic way. They are often locked in a recurrent conflict that makes it hard to determine which kind of reality one is dealing with.

## Conclusion: Limits to the multiplicity of multiple modernities

The multiple modernities concept provides a lens through which to analyze and interpret the present variety of protests and claims for alternative social, political, cultural, and economic approaches to organizing political life. This essay has attempted to locate a common thread to all these manifestations of dissatisfaction without overlooking other possible causes of them. That common element is related to a kind of betrayal that occurred in techno-scientific development. As a result of that betrayal, the masses became estranged from the whole process of modernization. In addition, the deeply capitalist motivation behind the chosen course of development made it clear that the standard model of modernity was a construct imposed on an alienated, easily controlled society entirely dependent upon—but also mystified by—the encompassing power of the IT environment.

This trend has introduced some drastic shifts in political praxis. It has destroyed capabilities for collective organization and weakened efforts to formulate and attain well-defined, effective goals to be implemented by real groups and parties. This disintegration of political processes has been the object of many studies (see the essays in Streeck 2016, for instance). For a time, it seemed as though the very factors responsible for the transformation could be re-purposed to stimulate change and provoke reactions to the standard model. Nevertheless, the forces behind the rise of technological modernity have proven to be highly adaptable and flexible. In fact, they have shown an ability to embrace and absorb the very multiple modernities intended to counteract the standard model. As a result, it is often the case that newly emergent multiplicity is short-lived, and that yesterday's modernities can be labelled as (at best) populism or authoritarianism. In this way, they are made to appear to be unhealthy deviations from the standard model, in need of a cure.

This paper has sidestepped one essential issue at the core of the problem: whether or not the omnibus idea of democracy—invoked so many times in a hypocritical way—continues to be useful and modern.

We have attempted to test the concept of multiple modernities in the context of developing countries, notably in the not truly backward yet still peripheral region of South America. The outcome of our investigation has raised further doubts about the concept's utility. It is difficult to frame the supposedly modern realities as essentially efforts to create multiple modernities. In fact, the weight of historical determinants and path dependency unveils a pattern of societies still in the making; thus, their relative incompleteness vitiates the multiple modernities aspects of experiments undertaken in the countries we reviewed. In the biggest country at stake, Brazil, a somewhat ironic fact can be invoked: a nearly doomed eternal return *Gestalt*, in which the same problems cyclically recur, while their context and rhetoric are transformed by forces of modernity that are, despite all efforts, *unable to change the basic social structure and forms of stratification, particularly the strongly defining patterns of inequality*, many of which were inherited from late colonial times.

Summing up, the examples cast doubt on the possibility of a more autonomous flourishing of multiple modernities in the developing world, or rather, considered in a broader context, whether this group of countries might become an effective cradle for the emergence of radically new instantiations of modernity. That, at any rate, was something expected at the beginning of the BRICS (Brazil, Russia, India, China, South Africa) experiment. The concept of multiple modernities, assuming that they do exist, appears more likely to make sense in the developed regions. Even so, they do not point to a harmonious transition of systems or models. Conflict, concentration, reaction, and counter-reaction will continue to set the rules of the game in a world where genuine, true multiplicity tries hard to gain more ground.

## Notes

1  This shift does not mean that developments everywhere else ceased; biological sciences together with biochemistry and biotechnology flourished.
2  Though naturally triggered by specific dissatisfactions, many but not all of which are related to the information society.
3  Voting rights for Indians were first granted during the 1950s under the presidency of Paz Estenssoro, more than 100 years after the original constitution was ratified.
4  A striking example of some developed countries' lack of goodwill toward President Morales is the often-forgotten incident that took place in July of 2013, when he was returning from meetings in Russia. In open violation of international rules, and as an offensive gesture toward a democratically elected head of state, the presidential aircraft allegedly was denied routes over southern EU countries (notably Spain and Portugal), under vague accusations that he was protecting Edward Snowden, then confined to a Moscow airport.
5  If one includes the two vice presidents who ruled after each impeachment (Itamar Franco and Michel Temer) and the one (José Sarney) replacing the first civilian ruler, Tancred Neves, who was indirectly elected by Congress and died soon thereafter, Brazil has had seven acting presidents.
6  The "eternal return" allows manifold and slightly different interpretations (see, for example, Eliade 1989 and Deleuze 1965). Roughly, as utilized below, the concept refers to a situation in which a given structure repeatedly comes back, even while changes in conditions and in ancillary features may occur.

## References

Beck, U. 1986. *Risikogesellschaft: Auf dem Weg nach einer anderen Modernität*. Frankfurt am Main: Suhrkamp Verlag.
Beck, U. 1999. *World Risk Society*. Cambridge: Polity Press.
Collins, R. 2013. "The End of Middle-Class Work: No more escapes." In I. Wallerstein, R. Collins, M. Mann, G. Derluguian, & C. Calhoun (eds.), *Does Capitalism Have a Future?* Oxford: Oxford University Press, pp. 37–70.
Crouch, C. 2004. *Post-Democracy*. Cambridge: Polity Press.
Deleuze, G. 1965. *Nietzsche*. Paris: Presses Universitaires de France.
Eliade, M. 1989. *Le Mythe de l'Éternel Retour*. Paris: Gallimard.
Flôres, R. G., Jr. 2014. "Brazil." In B. Currie-Alder, R. Kanbur, D. M. Malone & R. Medhora (eds.), *International Development: Ideas, experience and prospects*. Oxford: Oxford University Press.
Furtado, C. 2008. *Ensaios sobre a Venezuela: Subdesenvolvimento com Abundância de Divisas*. Rio de Janeiro: Contraponto.
Klein, N. 2007. *The Shock Doctrine: The Rise of Disaster Capitalism*. Toronto: Random House.

Streeck, W. 2016. *How will Capitalism End?* London: Verso.
Valladão, A. 2014. "Masters of the Algorithms: The geopolitics of the new digital economy from Ford to Google." Discussion paper. Brussels: German Marshall Fund.
Willke, H. 2014. *Demokratie in Zeiten der Konfusion*. Berlin: Suhrkamp Verlag.

# 4

# TIME, MODERNITY, AND THE RESURGENCE OF RIGHT-WING POPULISM

*Lewis P. Hinchman*

Most scholars attracted to the "multiple modernities" approach to comparative politics agree that they are trying to navigate between two rather extreme positions, identified respectively with Francis Fukuyama (1992) and Samuel Huntington (1996). The former's *The End of History and the Last Man* is widely understood (quite likely incorrectly) as an expression of Western triumphalism. After the fall of communism, it is claimed, no other serious ideological rivals to Western-style democratic liberalism remain. History will "end" in the sense that the great existential questions concerning the organization of the state and economy, the role of religion in public life, education, the family, and much else, will have been settled. Politics in the retail sense will of course continue, but little will be at stake. As Charles de Gaulle once supposedly remarked, legislators will merely haggle about the "price of bread." Importantly for our concerns, Fukuyama argues that the Western model will also take hold in non-Western settings, as it already had by the time he wrote *The End of History* in countries such as Japan, South Korea, Taiwan, and (possibly) India. While non-Western societies and governments might bridle at certain Western cultural imports, they would have to admit that the Western liberal regime was the only game left in town, so they had better get in while they could.

Huntington's *The Clash of Civilizations* offered a rather gloomier and less Western-centric interpretation of the drift of global politics. The world was not going to be brought closer together by globalization, the breakup of the Soviet Union, and the end of communism. On the contrary, the Cold War had held the demons of nationalism and religious fanaticism in check for decades. Once it was over, these demons would burst forth with renewed ferocity, causing the world to coalesce into ten or eleven different civilizations based on shared cultural values, some likely to be irreconcilably hostile to others. Skirmishes and wars would break out along the "fault lines" of civilizations, reined in—if at all—by dominant "core states" such as Russia (for Orthodox civilization) and China (for Sinic civilization). Modernization would be recognized for what it was: a ploy by the West to export its own institutions and culture, thus covertly displacing and weakening other civilizations. Consequently, the only sensible thing for any civilization to do would be to cling ever more tenaciously to its own culture and religion (and that includes the West, which should return to Christianity, eschew multiculturalism, and stop thinking that its values are universally valid).

Spirited arguments have been waged about both the meaning of terms like "modern" and "modernization" and their empirical applicability to non-Western countries and/or civilizations such as Islam. For the most part, scholars by now have distanced themselves from the view that a "modern" society is one that has the entire package of institutions characteristic of the United States, Great Britain, or France. Advocates of a multiple modernities approach worry that a detailed portrait of modernity (say, to include political democracy, secularization, urbanization, a market economy, rational-legal authority, advanced science and technology, and a welfare state) would set standards that non-Western countries could not meet, and likely would not want to meet. Instead, they emphasize more abstract characteristics such as "reflexivity" and "autonomy." They are right to do so; however, they have been so intent on underscoring the differences between modern and traditional societies that they have fallen into another trap: treating modernity as though it were a homogeneous historical period, distinct from traditional society but internally undifferentiated. By that standard, a society would be either modern or traditional. Thus, for example, one scholar has argued that the Soviet Union embodied an "alternative form of modernity" (Arnason 2002: 79), while another has contended that India is "indisputably modern" (Graubard 2002: xi). In effect, then, modernity is treated as a threshold. Once it is crossed, a country joins the ranks of the world's modern societies and there is no turning back.

In this essay, I will argue instead that modernity itself must be subdivided into waves or phases along a temporal, rather than a geographical, continuum. In other words, modernity is a "moving target." As noted, classical modernization theorists tended to assume that modernization is a process that necessarily reaches completion once certain criteria have been met: industrialization, urbanization, secularization, institutions of social security, etc. (Gilman 2003: 1–2). But in fact, the process never ends and the criteria change as time goes on. "Modern" cities of the 1960s or 1970s, such as Lille, France, or Syracuse, New York, have been left behind by a changing economy, automation, and offshoring. Meanwhile, once-sleepy places like San Jose, California, or Kuala Lumpur, Malaysia, have surged ahead and now are on the cutting edge of 21st-century modernity. Sometimes, cities and regions that were epicenters of earlier phases of modernity "reinvent themselves" and find niches in the most modern sectors of the global economy of today: San Francisco, Barcelona, and Shanghai serve as examples.

By the same token, we should avoid labeling an entire society or country as "modern" and instead think of modernity as a kind of archipelago. The most modern localities are spread out over the globe, and often in closer contact with one another than they are with their own hinterlands. Sometimes they appear to be islands in a sea of traditional society and/or earlier iterations of modern life. Bangalore, India, the headquarters of Infosys, is surely a model of state-of-the-art information technology. Yet a few miles outside the municipality farmers cultivate their fields much as they have for thousands of years—mentally and technologically almost in a different world from the young computer scientists in the metropolis.[1] Likewise, the University of Michigan is one of the world's great institutions of higher learning. Yet just a few miles away are crumbling heavy-industrial cities such as Flint and of course Detroit. In 1950 the latter had a population of 1,850,000, but by 2015 had fallen to just over 677,000. Detroit today has about 70,000 abandoned buildings and 90,000 vacant lots. In some neighborhoods, nature is reclaiming those properties as trees and shrubs poke through roofs and windows. A few residents are said to have reverted to hunting as a way of making a living, shooting raccoons and other wild animals and eating or selling them (New York Times 2013; Sterling 2009).

Thus, modernity is fragile. It is not as though a society or economy can rest on its laurels after having reached certain statistical milestones such as a high literacy rate, a robust industrial base, or well-developed infrastructure. A society must keep up with its more innovative and advanced counterparts or risk falling behind, eventually slipping back into a sort of semi-modern status. Below we will look at several examples of countries, especially Argentina, that have experienced that slippage and see why it happened. The United States is not immune from this fate. Even President Donald Trump remarked that, compared to the Gulf States or China, the United States' ancient, dysfunctional infrastructure makes us virtually a "third world country." In fact, some parts of the United States—Appalachia, the Mississippi Delta, backcountry Alaska— always have lagged behind the level of modernity achieved by more advanced regions.

To sum up the argument presented so far, multiple modernities research has focused on varieties of modernity that have emerged in different societies across the globe, especially in the Far East (what we might call "geographical" or "horizontal" modernity). The point has been to show that countries near or past the threshold of modernity need not converge on a single, "Western" model. But, if the previous observations are correct, we must also contend with disparities in modernity across time ("vertical" versions of modernity). That is, a certain stage of modernity begins to crystallize and in a matter of decades or longer gradually assumes a complete and fully developed form, economically and technologically, but also in respect to values, norms, institutions, and culture. Then, driven by a variety of forces—technological and economic change, pressure from outside (colonialism, war, trade, etc.), cultural shifts—that phase of modernity is superseded by another. In the process, many people and the institutions and practices to which they are accustomed gradually get bypassed. Although these people still may regard themselves as fully modern and in no sense behind the times, their way of life becomes less and less viable. In a sense they are marooned in a phase of modernity that is in decline and often fight desperately to hang on to it, culturally, economically, and politically. This is the point at which the phenomenon of populism rears its head.

It is worthwhile to sketch out the general features of these earlier phases, because even brief descriptions will make it clear that populist movements are fighting not so much against modernity per se as against the *next wave* of modernity, which they sense poses a threat to their way of life.

Some influential scholars argue that the United States was the first truly modern country. As Gordon Wood remarked, America after the Revolution was "the most liberal, democratic, and modern nation in the world" (cited in Heideking 2002: 219). And it was so even before many of the transformations we associate with modernization had begun. Wood (2009: 2) notes that "this transformation took place before industrialization, before urbanization, before railroads, and before any of the technological breakthroughs usually associated with modern social change." While a strong case could also be made for revolutionary France (Habermas 1967: 57–61, 75–78), the young American republic—especially by the Jacksonian era— was more thoroughly democratized, down to the grass-roots level, than was France during the revolutionary period, with the obvious and glaring exception of the institution of slavery.

Alexis de Tocqueville's *Democracy in America* offers an intriguing look at social and political life in the United States during the years that the new republic was completing the transition from elite-dominated federalism to mass democracy. For Tocqueville, the principle of equality was the source from which most other aspects of American thought and behavior could be derived. The American colonies, especially in New England, had never really been "traditional" societies. By the time of the Revolution they had developed their own social arrangements in which the old hierarchies of English origin had been greatly reduced in importance. To Tocqueville, in a country such as the United States, democracy was the natural and obvious—indeed the only—principle on which to build political authority, since its traditional sources (aristocracy, monarchy, religion) largely had been superseded. And, by the 1820s, the United States indeed had become democratic in many of the familiar ways: universal suffrage for white males, the rise of modern mass political parties, hotly contested elections, a free—if highly partisan—press, and an independent judiciary.

In economic life the United States was a land of small property owners, including both farmers and tradesmen. The availability of cheap land on the frontier evidently helped maintain that equality, as landless Americans and immigrants from Europe often moved west to buy property or squat on new homesteads. The social and political equality that Tocqueville encountered was thus matched and perhaps to some extent conditioned by the relative equality of fortunes. In short, America was leading the way into a "world altogether new" in which equality was a "providential fact" that could not be stopped but only guided (Tocqueville 2000: 6–7).

By the same token, the psychological impact of equality in America was profound. In terms of the theory of modernity, the lack of permanent, stable social distinctions left each person master of him- or herself, fostering what Tocqueville calls "individualism": a "reflective and peaceful sentiment that disposes each citizen to isolate himself from the mass of those like him … [H]e willingly abandons society at large to itself" (Tocqueville 2000: 482). Political participation in local affairs provided the antidote to that individualism and the isolation it encouraged by drawing people out of themselves and engaging them in the common affairs of their townships. Tocqueville lavishes attention on the salutary effects of political participation in small-town and rural settings, not so much because it is efficient, but because it deflects tendencies toward what, in our time, is called "mass society." Of course, there was a price to be paid for mass political participation. As Fukuyama has argued, it abetted a system of clientelism, in which political parties, after winning an election, swept out all the old officeholders and replaced them with their own supporters, a recipe for amateurish and corrupt government (Fukuyama 2014: 134–148). To summarize, America in the early 19th century and indeed until after the Civil War (1861–1865) was the most modern country on earth in *some* respects and seemed to Tocqueville to anticipate Europe's future. But as yet it lacked the kind of professionalized civil service and strong, competent state that was emerging in Prussia and elsewhere in Europe. Efforts to create such a state, such as those undertaken by Alexander Hamilton, ultimately were defeated—at least temporarily. The triumph of a "Hamiltonian" state would have to await the second and even the third wave of modernization (cf. Croly 1963).

In the aftermath of the Civil War, a second phase of modernization began; the creation of the basic infrastructure of an industrial economy: railroads (the biggest and most powerful of the new corporations), telephones and telegraphs, electrification, highways (soon to be used by automobiles), petroleum to fuel the burgeoning economy, dams for irrigation, publicly owned water and sewer systems (Chicago was already hooked up by 1856), and housing for millions of new urbanites. As we know, parallel developments were taking place in Germany, England (with its much earlier start), and eventually France and Italy. In our context, what matters are the political and social changes wrought by the second wave of modernization,

As Richard Hofstadter has argued, America harbored an "agrarian myth" that farming was the only honest, noble, and virtuous way of life, and the only one suitable to shore up the social foundations of a republic such as the United States (Hofstadter 1955: 23–59). Consequently, while the rise of modern industry offered opportunities for impoverished rural folk to find jobs in cities, it also undermined the egalitarianism and widespread property-ownership that Tocqueville had found in the 1820s. At that time, most Americans preferred a laissez-faire economic system because they feared that centralized regulatory institutions (such as the Bank of the United States, dismantled by President Andrew Jackson) would create monopolies that favored the wealthy. But, by the second half of the 19th century, monopolies (often called "trusts") were forming due to the "natural" evolution of business enterprises in fields such as railroad-building, oil refining, and mining. The fact that a relative handful of wealthy individuals now controlled the labor of millions "presented a challenge to traditional republican thinking, wherein freedom and liberty were tied to the economic security and independence that accompanied owning one's property or… the means of one's livelihood" (Woodard 2016: 115). Farmers were especially hard-hit by recurring bank failures and "panics" that drove down commodity prices and led to foreclosures. The railroads made things worse by overcharging them to ship grain and livestock from rural areas to urban distribution centers such as Chicago.

Not unexpectedly, the economic pre-eminence of the great corporations translated into raw and ruthless political power. The oligarchs bought and sold state legislators, governors, judges, and even United States Congressmen and Senators. Montana was pretty much owned by the Anaconda Copper Company. By 1905, two-thirds of the US Senate was controlled by the railroads (Woodard 2016: 129), partly because senators were then selected by state legislatures. In short, the United States lacked an effective, modern, professionalized bureaucracy that might have been able to rein in the power of the giant corporations. That, indeed, was very much the point of Herbert Croly's desire to achieve what he called "Jeffersonian ends" (democracy and fairness for the little guy) by "Hamiltonian means" (formidable state power).

These abuses provoked two kinds of responses. First, from about 1900 until 1914, the country experienced the Progressive Era, which legislated the beginnings of modern regulatory and anti-trust institutions that formed the institutional framework for the third wave of modernization from Franklin Roosevelt's New Deal (1932–1941) through Lyndon Johnson's "Great Society" (1963–1968). We shall return to it soon. The second response was what Americans call "populism," an uprising of farmers and some early labor unions that found political expression in the creation of the People's Party in 1892 and then in the elections of 1896 and 1900, when the Democratic Party nominated the populist champion, William Jennings Bryan, for president. At its best, American populism was a left-leaning movement that made reasonable demands, including the direct election of US Senators, the breakup of monopolies, and debt relief for farmers (through the free coinage of silver).

But there was another side to the American agrarian movement, more reminiscent of the phenomenon we know today from Europe and now the United States as "right-wing" populism. Its spokesmen typically denounce "elites" as "enemies of the people"; they mistrust pluralism and prefer instead to govern by and through the "will of the people"; and they practice a form of identity politics that excludes their opponents and critics as not really belonging to the people at all (Müller 2016: 2–3). Even leftist American populism sometimes displayed these tendencies, especially when the issue of immigration was at stake. In California, politicians and labor leaders who denounced the power of the railroad monopolies also denounced the Chinese immigrants who largely had built the railroads. Populist attacks pictured the work of these immigrants as a kind of slave labor similar to plantation slavery in the South, this time exploited by monopolies to impoverish real Americans. By 1879 they had managed to put a referendum on the ballot that called for the complete exclusion of all Chinese from the state of California. Passing by a margin of 150,000 to 900 votes, the measure led to at the national level to the Chinese Exclusion Act of 1882 (Limerick 1987: 263–264), which lasted in some form until the 1960s. A few decades later, Williams Jennings Bryan turned up in Tennessee as an attorney prosecuting John Scopes for teaching evolution in a public school in violation of that state's Butler Act, symbolizing the turn of populism away from political and economic causes and toward religious, anti-scientific ones.

The point of this exposition is to show that populism is not inherently anti-modern. Instead, it expresses the desire to hang onto an earlier form of modernity that has been superseded by the relentless development of productive forces and their impact on social relationships of all kinds. Populists in the 1890s in the United States wanted to preserve the rural America they had grown up in, in which independent farmers and merchants could earn a decent living and small towns could continue to thrive. The America of the age of Jacksonian democracy, then the most modern country in the world, was their touchstone of what a modern economy and society should look like. To them, the dawning age of monopolies, corrupted politics, mass immigration, and economic dependency seemed not an advance but a return to a kind of feudalism or even slavery that, they believed, still characterized much of Europe and the Far East.

In some ways the American pattern is anomalous. In Europe, especially in England, the development of modern industry and finance, and the extension of market relationships to land and labor preceded even the modest beginnings of electoral reform (the Reform Act of 1832 in Britain enfranchised about 20% of adult males), the disestablishment of the Anglican Church, and the handover of politics from a narrow, landed elite first to the middle classes and then the entire population. In Germany (or, more accurately, Prussia) the construction of the modern state began in response to defeat at the hands of Napoleon's armies and involved the creation of a modern bureaucracy. Although it was staffed almost exclusively by members of the nobility, the bureaucracy was known for its honesty and competence. And, of course, it was the paradigm of the "rational-legal authority" depicted by Max Weber (1968: 150–166) in the early 20th century.

At the risk of oversimplification, we might say that the first two phases of modernity were switched in the United States and Europe. Americans expanded democracy and equality before the development of adequate state capacity. Consequently, the US in the 1820s and 1830s evolved into the "clientelistic" political system noted already, one in which jobs, contracts, and political patronage were the currency of the realm, and the triumph of one political party over the other at the polls meant that all officeholders from the previous administration would be replaced by political appointees. Not until 1883, via the Pendleton Act, did the United States install a modern merit-based bureaucracy that could stand comparison with that of Prussia/Germany. There, state capacity was well developed by the latter part of the nineteenth century, as were the foundations of the modern university system, scientific research, etc., while political democracy, individual rights, and equality lagged behind. For example, Prussia, by far the most important state in the German Federation, still had a three-class voting system that gave the top third of taxpayers (about 5% of the population) much greater political influence than the two tiers below them. Nevertheless, well before full democracy arrived in Germany in 1919, the labor movement had gotten organized and laid claim to the loyalty and support of the ever-increasing class of industrial workers. In fact, by the eve of World War I, fully a third of the German electorate habitually voted for labor's chief political representative, the Social Democratic Party. Otto von Bismarck, German chancellor for thirty years in the late 19th century, made it a top priority to win over or at least neutralize the nascent working class. As part of that strategy, he and the Reichstag put in place social insurance programs that would arrive in the United States only many decades later: health insurance in 1883, accident insurance in 1884, and disability or old-age insurance in 1889 (Neumann & Schaper 2008: 28). Hence, paradoxically, the first efforts to tone down untrammeled capitalism in Germany were inextricably bound up with Bismarck's campaign against the Social Democrats and their affiliated unions.

In the United States, the third wave of modernization commenced during the Progressive era, continued in a more militant spirit under the New Deal, and persisted until about the mid-1970s. Its hallmarks were, during the Progressive era, the creation of the many of the agencies, departments, and boards that still exist today and regulate the economy: the US Forest Service, the Bureau of Reclamation, the Federal Trade Commission, the Federal Reserve System, the anti-trust division of the Justice Department and many more. To these, the New Deal added the Securities and Exchange Commission, the National Labor Relations Board, the Social Security Administration, and others now defunct, such as the Work Projects Administration and the Civilian Conservation Corps. It also encouraged a more Keynesian approach to economic matters, including a commitment to deficit spending in times of recession.

The Great Society witnessed the inauguration of Medicare (state-sponsored health insurance for the elderly), Medicaid (health insurance for the very poor), and—in the 1970s—the beginnings of environmental regulation under the Environmental Protection Agency. It should be noted that, throughout this reform era, the rationale for regulation of the economy was often disputed. Some key figures, such as Theodore Roosevelt, Herbert Croly, and Franklin Roosevelt, wanted to empower a modern, high-capacity "big" government as a counterweight to the power of huge corporations. Others, such as Woodrow Wilson and some New Dealers, resisted this aspect of modernization and wanted to return the United States to what it had been in its earlier years: a land of small producers, small towns, and competitive markets without cartels and monopolies. Trust-busting was to be their chief weapon in the battle against a non-competitive economy. Here again, the goal was to return to an earlier era of modernity, not to traditional society.

In brief, the third wave formed the world in which many older Americans came of age. It enabled the United States to start catching up with Europe in terms of social protections afforded to citizens and in capacity-building for the administration of the myriad new laws and programs passed by Congress. But, we should recognize that Europe was not standing still during this era. In Great Britain, for example, the Labour Party implemented many of the recommendations of the famous and highly popular Beveridge Report shortly after World War II, including its crown jewel, the National Health Service, which goes far beyond the United States—even after the adoption of Obamacare—in providing medical care for every citizen. The Federal Republic of Germany built on the foundations laid in the Imperial era by Bismarck, gradually extending social insurance to more groups and with greater generosity of benefits. The latter included family allowances, long-term care for the elderly, a model apprenticeship program, and—Social Democracy's major achievement—the scheme of co-determination, in which workers' representatives sit on corporate boards of directors (Neumann & Schaper 2008: 29–37).

The social backdrop to this third wave of modernization was the vast expansion of the middle class and the improvement of living standards even for blue-collar workers, lifting many of them into at least the lower middle class as well. These economic improvements transpired fairly quickly in the United States after World War II, but even more rapidly in Europe, especially Germany, Italy, and France, which saw sustained and rapid growth for what the French call the "Glorious Thirty" years. In part, rising living standards were a function of that growth itself and the productivity gains that made it possible. But they also owed much to the ability of unions to increase wage levels through collective bargaining and successfully push for higher minimum wages or industry-wide pay scales even for non-union workers. Finally, economic improvements reflected better and more widely available education, which sooner or later got transmuted into innovation. This, too, was indirectly a result of a greater commitment of funds to public purposes, for example the construction of new universities and the maintenance of low tuition rates. To some observers, the third wave of modernization seemed as though it might be the last one. Modernization theorists in the 1950s and 1960s envisaged gradual progress in the affluent West and faster progress in the developing world, but no qualitatively new and wrenching changes.

Because the reforms enacted during the third wave of modernization were generally well-received, they did not trigger massive populist opposition, at least not at first. But they did foment an undercurrent of suspicion and hostility to the more redistributive aspects, especially in the United States. The tenor of the opposition to third wave modernity is well summed up in Richard Hofstadter's phrase, "the paranoid style in American politics." Opposition to this wave—we can call it the modern welfare state, for convenience sake—tends to fashion a narrative in which betrayals, conspiracies, foreign intrigue, and plots by "others" against American liberties figure prominently. It is interesting to listen to Hofstadter's words, because, although he was writing a half-century ago, his portrait of the "paranoid" critics of the welfare state perfectly captures the mentality of right-wing populism today, in the age of Donald Trump and the Tea Party:

The modern right wing ... feels dispossessed: America has largely been taken away from them and their kind, though they are determined to try to repossess it and to prevent the final destructive act of subversion. The old American virtues have already been eaten away by cosmopolitans and intellectuals; the old competitive capitalism has been gradually undermined by socialist and communist schemers; the old national security and independence have been destroyed by treasonous plots ... Important changes may be traced to the mass media [and the villains are now] eminent public figures like Presidents Roosevelt, Truman, and Eisenhower.

*(Hofstadter 1967: 23–24)*

In the United States, at least, the third wave of modernization has evoked protests both from people stuck in the first wave (e.g., from declining rural areas and small towns) and the second wave (businesspeople confronted by increasing regulation from the welfare state's many agencies and departments and who resent the power of organized labor; taxpayers who believe that their tax dollars go to undeserving recipients in the form of "welfare"). To some extent, their hostility is understandable. Rural America and the farm economy generally have been in a crisis since the Seventies, when crop prices fell so low that farmers could not pay their mortgages, let alone afford seed, fertilizer, equipment, and other factors of production. Despite some temporary improvement, rural economies continue to struggle. In a similar vein, countless small towns have been hit by the advent of big-box stores located in other, larger towns; the decampment of banks, schools, and government offices; and the withering away of local ownership. In short, Main Street is getting boarded up as big corporations and internet commerce sap its vitality.

The fourth wave began roughly in the 1970s as chronic inflation, lagging economic growth and high unemployment called into question the role of government in steering the economy and of labor in setting wages, and ushered in a more neo-liberal set of policies, not just in America but even in Germany, Spain, England, and other European countries. At the same time, those years witnessed the slow decline of the manufacturing economy of the second and third waves as well as the emergence of the industries that dominate the 21st century and now count as truly modern: information and medical technologies, financial services, robotics, and tourism. Left behind were "rustbelts" from the English Midlands and northern France to the upper Midwest in America—places that once were the heart of third-wave modernization, along with their demoralized and embittered inhabitants. It is here, of course, that we encounter the intersection of "multiple modernities" and right-wing populism.

We soon will come back to that intersection. But, to reiterate the broader point of this analysis: because modernity is a moving target, multiple modernities exist on a temporal continuum, the ultra-modern city or industry of today may become the rustbelt of tomorrow, unless it manages to reinvent itself. Employees who once had cutting-edge skills will be laid off and forced to seek new kinds of (often poorly paid) employment. They did not change; the world changed around them—and not only in an economic/technological sense, but also in respect to values, norms, and laws. Populism is thus the "voice of modernities past" struggling to maintain the kind of world their inhabitants know, understand, and in which they can hope to succeed. Incidentally, there are of course those who oppose modernity per se and wish to return to or retain a traditional society, but they are few: for example, the Amish, Benedictine monks, and many indigenous peoples the world over.

There has been much speculation about what the fourth wave world will look like, since as yet its outlines are not entirely clear. According to some scholars, Western societies will become much more unequal than they are today (cf. Piketty 2014; Milanovic 2016) as the accumulation and investment of wealth tends to favor those who already have wealth as opposed to those who hope to obtain it by dint of work and saving. On the other hand, international inequality, especially between the West and Asia, will decrease as societies in the latter continue growing at a rapid clip. Furthermore, the nature of work will continue to change as machines replace low- and even medium-skilled humans. Some observers of the auto and trucking industries forecast that self-driving trucks and cars will be on the road within five years, which will eventually result in two million "big-rig" truck drivers in the US alone losing their jobs, not to mention innumerable cab and delivery truck drivers. And, we can already see in the Uber phenomenon a tendency for employees in the sense we once knew them to be replaced by independent contractors only loosely affiliated with the company for which they ostensibly work. Finally, there is no reason to think that globalization will cease. Jobs will continue to be outsourced to whatever location seems to offer the best combination of low labor costs, decent infrastructure, and cost-effective transportation to the point of sale. In short, prospects look bleak for the less educated lower-middle classes of the Western world, the "great losers" of globalization (Milanovic 2016: 20).

All of these trends spell trouble for the institutions of third wave modernity that helped to establish and sustain the affluent societies in which older Americans and Europeans grew up. Because labor union bargaining power and density has declined so much according to OECD data—less than 11% of Americans belong to unions, and less than 12% of French workers do (McCarthy 2017)—the unions will not be able to preserve their great 20th-century achievement: delivering a middle-class lifestyle for their members. Although older members may continue to enjoy high pay and job security until they retire, while the newly hired will earn considerably less and be more subject to dismissal. In the United States and Great Britain, especially, years of tax revolts, privatizations, and freezes on public spending at all levels of government have made it ever more difficult for agencies to do their jobs, from monitoring and reducing air and water pollution to collecting income taxes and catching tax evaders. In Europe, national administrative systems are not under attack to this degree, but the "Eurocracy" in Brussels has become the scapegoat for mass immigration (actually the remit of national governments) and— as we shall see—the target of right-wing, Euroskeptical right-wing populists nearly everywhere. In short, it is not hard to foresee the gradual dismantling of the welfare and regulatory state that many of us have relied on for our entire lives. That may be the most worrying trend as we enter the fourth wave of modernization.

If the analysis given thus far is correct, then we should conceive of populism in our time as the effort of people who inhabit earlier versions of modernity to hang onto the normative, political, and technological core of the lives they have always led. We should expect the strongest support for populism to come from older people, especially those whose jobs and way of life are or were linked to economic forces that have been outstripped by new technologies and new institutional arrangements, but who can still remember when things were different. Moreover, we should not be surprised if the voter base of populist parties construes its struggle in moral terms as well: as a battle against the breakdown of traditional norms, gender roles, values, religious convictions, social discipline, and sometimes ethnic-religious identity. Finally, support for populist candidates and causes most likely would come from areas outside the archipelago of fourth-wave modernity: rural areas, small towns, and declining industrial cities. Again, adherents of populist causes don't think they have changed; it is the world around them that is changing, and—they believe—always for the worse. Finally, we should expect a high correlation between levels of education and votes for populist candidates, with the less-educated opting for the latter. This is understandable, since many less educated people improved their standard of living in the second- and third-waves of modernization, but in the fourth wave are the most vulnerable to competition from even less well-educated migrants, outsourcing, and automation or robotization.

Let us examine the profiles of right-wing populist supporters and the kind of electoral appeals they make in some recent cases that have been well researched. First, if we take the Brexit vote in Great Britain as representative of populist demographics, then the expectations outlined above were largely confirmed. The strongest correlation between support for "remain" and "leave," respectively, was education level: 66% of those educated to a level no higher than a high-school diploma voted for leave, while 71% of voters with a higher education degree voted for remain. Also, 75% of voters between 18 and 24 years of age preferred remain, while 61% of voters over 64 chose leave. The strongest support for Brexit in England came from areas outside London, especially in the Midlands and North (Politico 2016). London itself, a highly diverse and modern global city, voted overwhelmingly to remain (although, tellingly, large industrial cities like Sheffield and Birmingham opted to leave). It is worth recalling that, before Margaret Thatcher become prime minister, manufacturing provided 18% of the British economy. By 2010 it supplied only 10%, leaving millions of former manufacturing workers economically adrift and with no love for free trade or the EU, which many believed had cost them their jobs (Judis 2016: 95).

Turning to the case of France, the 2017 contest between Emmanuel Macron and the populist National Front leader, Marine Le Pen, illustrates the same divide. Macron, it is said, appealed to the "optimistic France, to those who are doing reasonably well and who believe that the younger generation will do even better

(Goldhammer 2017: 23–24). His campaign advocated a "different kind of politics—a politics attuned to the modern world" (Goldhammer 2017: 24). By contrast, Le Pen tried to mobilize the "losers" in fourth wave modernization, attacking many of its soft targets: the financial community, "the system," the "Uberization of society," and "savage globalization (Economist 2017b: 47). Her chief areas of strength were in the old industrial towns of the north and in areas of the south such as Provence-Alpes-Côte d'Azur, with many small towns and large numbers of immigrants. In fact, already by 1995 the National Front had cut into the old left-wing voter base. One-third of its support that year came from those who had previously voted for the Socialist François Mitterrand (Judis 2016: 103). By contrast, Le Pen lost the city of Paris, achieving only 10% of the vote in the 2016 presidential election. As one scholar put it, Le Pen appealed to a "lost golden age of a happy, organic society." But she did not merely conjure up a rural idyll; instead she also "associated it with the heyday of heavy industry, when factory workers could earn a decent wage and aspire to a middle-class life" (Bell 2017). In our terms, she appealed to those who looked to lose out in the transition from the third to the fourth phase of modernity, while Macron was making headway among wealthier and better educated French citizens who had better prospects in the new economy: "Macron's margin of victory over Marine Le Pen grew larger as the average income and average level of education in a community rose—as the average percentage of working class voters declined" (Edsall 2017).

Polling and election studies of other European countries also bear out the expectations outlined above. In Belgium, the VB (Vlaams Belang), a populist party appealing to Flemish nationalists, performs best among male, blue-collar workers with low levels of formal training (de Lange & Akkerman 2012: 30). In Austria the FPÖ, a highly successful populist party once led by Jörg Haider, enjoyed considerable electoral success because it "had given voice to groups that had not felt represented by the elites…, sections of society that felt excluded" (Fallend 2012: 123).

If we analyze the shocking election victory of the populist candidate Donald Trump in the US, we find that the profile of his voter base closely resembles those of Le Pen and the Brexit supporters. On the whole, Trump voters are older, less educated and somewhat poorer than average (half of Trump's primary election voter base earned less than $50,000 a year). They were the most pessimistic about the direction of the economy of all the voters in the primary elections: 48% said the economy was "poor," far more than supporters of Ted Cruz and John Kasich did. Moreover, during the primaries 67% of the Trump supporters said that free trade was bad for the United States, again a much higher figure than that for other candidates (Judis 2016: 75).

It also is illuminating to look at the reasons for Trump's narrow victory in three rustbelt states: Wisconsin, Michigan, and Pennsylvania. Had Hillary Clinton won those states, she would be president today. We have an insightful analysis of the Wisconsin case by Katherine J. Kramer, who carried out in-depth interviews in rural areas and small towns in that state. She distilled her experiences into the argument that voters in those places were motivated by a "politics of resentment." The classic populist appeal pits the "people" against the "elites," and it is the one Trump made all across the country. But in these three states, it paid off handsomely, as rural voters, responding to Trump, shifted their discontent with supposedly elitist cities (Milwaukee and Madison) into anger at the elites in far-off Washington. To some extent, the enthusiasm of rural voters for Trump simply extended a long-term defection of rural voters away from Democrats and toward Republicans. Nevertheless, as recently as 2008 rural Wisconsin counties voted strongly for Barack Obama against John McCain (Kramer 2016: 13). The drift toward Republicans has a great deal to do with the politics of resentment, because, as Kramer writes, "rural places have been experiencing a long, slow death for decades … [R]ural economies are fighting a losing battle" (Kramer 2016: 94). Farmers and small-town dwellers in Midwestern states like Wisconsin have endured economic trouble ever since the 1970s and many blame it on uncaring elites who adopt policies that help cities but harm the rest of the state. Indeed, they did not even identify Wall Street as the villain behind the Great Recession of 2008; rather, they pinned the blame on "government" (Kramer 2016: 173). The Wisconsin story was repeated in many other states as well. As David Graham (2017: 24) comments, "it was rural America that carried Donald Trump to victory … The gulf between urban and nonurban voters was wider than it had been in nearly a century. Hillary Clinton won 88 of the country's 100 biggest cities, but still went down to defeat." Here is a classic case of populist politicians exploiting the resentments of citizens whose lives and experiences are in some ways reminiscent of first wave modernity: small town dwellers accustomed to grass roots democracy but now faced with ruin due to vast, impersonal forces emanating from distant cities run by people unlike themselves (or so they think). They do not oppose modernity as such. They just want it to benefit them, too.

At one time, the word nationalism had relatively positive connotations, especially when applied to the efforts of suppressed nationalities to break out of multiethnic empires such as the Austro-Hungarian, Russian, and Ottoman. But today, populist politicians such as Nigel Farage, Marine Le Pen, and Donald Trump have managed a hostile takeover of the entire concept, stripping it of its associations with progressive politics and using it to justify mercantilism ("America First"), possible exits from the EU or Eurozone ("Brexit"), and of course various proposals to build walls to keep immigrants out. What happened? Essentially, the fourth wave of modernity gave us a world in which more and more decisions had to be made at levels of government higher than the nation-state, from the EU to NAFTA, the WTO, the IMF and other trans-national institutions. They were established not to sidestep or frustrate national-level democracy, but to solve specific problems that nation-states could not solve on their own any longer (e.g., banking crises, obstacles to trade, migration flows, or threats to the global Commons). Moreover, the fourth wave swept in newer, more cosmopolitan and tolerant values, predisposing the residents of the archipelago of ultra-modern cities and regions to regard immigration and multiculturalism as normal and desirable—indeed indispensable to the kinds of economic activities characteristic of such places (finance, IT, elite higher education). In short, nationalism has evolved into a codeword for policies that allegedly would resurrect the declining second- and third-wave economic bases of Europe and North America, and even the first-wave of small-town, grass-roots democracy, however idealized.

Contemporary right-wing populists claim that earlier forms of modernity can be revived if the "correct" policies are pursued. In the United States such policies are advocated by some of Trump's present and former advisers, such as Stephen Bannon, all under the rubric of "economic nationalism," an idea that has found echoes in Europe's right-wing populist scene as well, where Heinz-Christian Strache speaks of "Austria First" and Marine Le Pen proposes to build a virtual wall around France by withdrawing from the Eurozone, holding a referendum on leaving the EU, and placing severe limits on immigration. The goal of the Trump administration, or at least one of its influential factions, is not simply to reduce immigration and adopt frankly mercantilist policies; it is to destroy what Bannon calls the "administrative state" that arose during the third wave of modernization. In effect, Bannon and his associates (the so-called "alt-right") want to wage war against rational bureaucracy, procedural rules, and the power of experts and educated public opinion to define the agenda and make policy. And, of course, they have made every effort to vilify the press and "objective" journalism, branding the latter as the "opposition" and "enemy of the people." Trump himself has threatened to try to revoke NBC's broadcasting license because he dislikes what that network has reported about him and his administration.

Trump's many lies are well-documented.[2] To be sure, lying in politics is nothing new. What is unprecedented is that a presidential candidate and now President of the United States consistently would tell such bold-faced whoppers (Barack Obama, who was not born in the United States, wiretapped me; Ted Cruz's father was complicit in the murder of John F. Kennedy) and get away with it, because his populist supporters disdain the press as part of the liberal elite and thus inherently untrustworthy, and prefer to take what Trump says at face value rather than credit the mainstream media for its careful fact-checking and determination to challenge his falsehoods. Of course, not all media are "mainstream" in this sense. Fox News, Breitbart, and right-wing talk radio repeat or even originate many of these lies. When Trump is called out for his untruthfulness, he typically replies that he "read it on the internet," i.e., on right-wing websites with little regard for accurate reporting.

What would happen if such populist policies were followed consistently for a considerable period of time? Is it really feasible to turn back the clock and restore an earlier phase of modernity? Are multiple modernities possible along a temporal or vertical axis as well as across geographical and cultural zones? We have ample empirical evidence to consult in evaluating the likely outcome of applied populism. In the United States, as previously noted, populists helped to enact some sensible and needed reforms. Yet they also had a hand in enacting Prohibition and in the Scopes "Monkey Trial," which made it difficult to teach evolution in public schools for decades, thus stifling the progress of biology as a science. But the People's Party never actually governed. There are many other cases in which populists did govern and enacted an economic-nationalist, mercantilist, anti-elitist agenda: Mexico from the 1930s (the Cárdenas era) to 1980s; Brazil under Vargas in the Thirties; Myanmar from the 1960s until recently. But Argentina is probably the most notorious case, for populists have ruled that country intermittently from the 1940s until last year and have left their imprint on public policy for many decades.

To paraphrase Simon Kuznets's famous statement, "There are four types of countries: developed, underdeveloped, Japan, and Argentina" (Acemoglu & Robinson 2012: 384). Argentina's history confirms the argument made earlier that countries can get "stuck" in a certain phase of modernization without being able to move on to the next. When that occurs, their economies drift into obsolescence and their relative economic status declines. Unlike other Latin American countries Argentina by the 20th century enjoyed a booming economy and high standard of living:

> Between 1870 and 1913 Argentine exports were the fastest growing in the world, increasing at a rate of 6% per annum; at the end of the nineteenth century per capita GDP was about the same as that of Germany, Holland, and Belgium, and higher than that of Austria, Spain, Italy and Sweden.
>
> *(Fukuyama 2014: 275; see also Williamson 2009: 459)*

However, by 1978 its per capita GDP was only a sixth of Switzerland's and a fifth of Canada's, countries that were once more or less its economic peers. In other words, Argentina breezed through second-wave modernization. As we shall see, it did not successfully negotiate the third wave, even though many of the elements necessary for that transition were present.

The prosperity that led observers to compare Argentina to Canada, Australia, and sundry European countries derived mainly from agricultural products and livestock grown on huge landed estates and eventually exported. Until the 20th century the landed oligarchs controlled its politics. By 1914 Argentina enacted universal suffrage, which enabled other social classes gradually to wrest power away from the *estanciero* elite. But mass democracy also brought with it instability and the bane of Latin American politics, the military coup, which occurred in 1930 and again in 1943, the latter led by a young colonel named Juan Domingo Perón. Perón fashioned a nationalist, populist program that won the support of both right and left, the labor movement, and of course many elements of the military itself. He organized a corporatist state somewhat along the lines of Mussolini's Italy in which labor unions were offered a relatively privileged position in exchange for their loyalty. But it was Perón's charismatic authority, demonstrated in mass rallies reminiscent of those staged by Mussolini and later populists like Hugo Chávez of Venezuela, that held the movement and country together.

Perón's populist economic program was geared to subsidizing local manufactures, with the ultimate aim of weaning the country off imported finished goods from Europe and the United States. Those policies seemed to work for a while, but eventually the state fell into debt, popular support waned, and even the Church disapproved, all of which led to Perón's ouster in 1954. His economic mismanagement had lasting and disastrous consequences: "In effect Perón had converted the state into a machine for producing budget deficits, trade imbalances, and chronic inflation" (Williamson 2009: 471). For that reason, one might expect that Argentine citizens would have been glad to be rid of him, but so powerful was his attraction (and that of his first wife, Eva) for working-class Argentines, that Perónism has become deeply entrenched in the country's political life. Perón himself returned for an encore in 1973 and then, after his death, his second wife Isabel also took a turn governing the country. More recently, Argentina's economic woes, including debt default, hyperinflation, and austerity, were abetted by two latter-day Perónist politicians, Néstor and Cristina Fernandez de Kirchner, who governed the country from 2003 to 2016. The latter won notoriety, in classic populist fashion, for corrupting the statistical agency in Argentina that measures and publishes reports on inflation and other economic indicators. So extreme was her manipulation that she was censured by the IMF for causing "inaccuracy" in statistical reporting (Economist 2017a: 34). She also specialized in protectionist trade policies and huge fiscal deficits. Her statistical manipulation certainly reminds one of Donald Trump's contempt for allegedly "rigged" jobs reports during the campaign and reports of the low number of attendees at his inauguration, which he claimed falsely to be the biggest ever. It appears to be an article of faith among populists that elites, including those who present statistical reports, are inherently untrustworthy; hence, their facts and figures can be dismissed or even manipulated whenever convenient. Truth has no defenders in the populist camp. It is hardly surprising that an anonymous journalist called Trump a "Peronist on the Potomac" (Economist 2017a: 29).

The lesson of Argentina's decline is that populism does not solve real problems, at least not in the long run, because its policies represent an incoherent mixture of clientelism, dreams of economic self-sufficiency, protectionism for non-competitive national firms, subsidies for well-connected industries, amateurish administration, bloated state employment rolls, and clumsy meddling in fields that should be the remit of trained professionals. But it also confirms the argument that there are indeed multiple modernities along a time line. Argentina was modern—at least in terms of its economic performance—by 1900. It no longer is, because it could not manage the transition to the honest, rational governance, broad-gauged social welfare, and highly productive industry characteristic of third wave modernity, let alone the innovative, market-oriented, and IT-influenced fourth wave.

The continuing influence of Perónism in Argentina suggests what might happen if the United States and/or Great Britain were to have a more or less permanent populist movement dedicated to restoring the kind of society, culture and economy that those two countries enjoyed in the Fifties and Sixties. We can already read the tea leaves as Trump and his minions dismantle regulatory bodies such as the Environmental Protection Agency that attempt to rein in pollution and climate change or else dismiss the scientists who once worked for it. In effect, Trump has touted coal—the classic second wave fuel—as America's energy source of the future. By the same token, we can foresee what might become of Great Britain once it has left the European Union and must surmount obstacles of cost and red tape to sell its goods in Europe. Britain used to sell about half of all exports to EU countries, so the loss or diminution of those markets will deal a severe blow to its entire economy. The most advanced part of that economy is, of course, the financial sector headquartered in London. It is not yet clear how many banks will be leaving London for new locations in Dublin, Frankfurt, Paris, and other EU cities, but it appears that the number—and concomitant job losses—could be high. In short, Britain is risking the reality of a genuinely modern, competitive economic sector in favor of the phantom of a return to the heavy-industrial economy that once made cities like Birmingham and Sheffield wealthy, but that is in decline nearly everywhere.

There is thus a powerful economic case to be made against populism. Countries—or even regions and cities—that have tried some or all of its signature policies have not remained prosperous and successful. Instead, they have lapsed into stagnation, clinging to some earlier phase of modernity that becomes increasingly marginalized and untenable as time goes on. In a geographical or spatial sense, modernities certainly are multiple, and that is something to be celebrated. But the "ghost of modernities past" can become a snare and a temptation that populists are able to exploit for their own self-interested and nefarious ends.

Where does this brief overview of the disastrous effects of populism in Europe and the Americas leave us? We began with efforts by Eisenstadt (2002), Wittrock (2002), Göle (2002), Giddens (1990), and many others to say what the core of modernity is. Their conclusions converged on the insight that modern societies differ from traditional ones in certain fundamental ways:

> Central to the cultural program [of modernity] was an emphasis on the autonomy of man … [and] emancipation from the fetters of traditional political and cultural authority… Such autonomy implied, first, reflexivity and exploration; second, active construction and mastery of nature, including human nature.
>
> *(Eisenstadt 2002: 4–5)*

In opposition to the ancient orders, an "intensive reflexivity" developed that envisioned the possibility that there could be multiple "core transcendental visions" (Eisenstadt 2002: 4) In short, autonomy and a certain utopian impulse, a hope or expectation that the world could be a very different and better place, characterized modernity's first dawning (Eisenstadt 2002: 4–5).

If one wants to explain how modernity emerged from the matrix of traditional society, this seems like a good starting point. But now, after we have passed through several successive waves of modernity, we are able to see more clearly that modernity is an ongoing enterprise, not a finished product, and that it makes us as much as we make it. No doubt, autonomy, reflexivity, and agency are necessary conditions for modernization to begin and be sustained over time. But they are not enough. In fact, certain societies in which modernization got off the track were precisely the ones in which human agency and autonomy perhaps were valued more highly than they should have been. Some of the most disastrous experiments in natural and social engineering in the 20th century were carried out by leaders who believed that human will and utopian visions could triumph over mere facts and natural or economic laws. Think of Pol Pot in Cambodia, who intended to create a perfect society—modern in his understanding—by killing all educated citizens and emptying the cities. Or Stalin, who attempted to transform Soviet agriculture by forced collectivization and, in the process, may have killed 5 million people while actually reducing agricultural output. Nor should we omit more contemporary dictators such as Robert Mugabe in Zimbabwe, who unleashed the worst hyperinflation since Germany's in 1923. Or Hugo Chávez and Nicolás Maduro of Venezuela, whose arbitrary policy-making and gross mismanagement have turned what was once one of South America's wealthier countries into one of its more impoverished, where the shelves in supermarkets often have no food to sell anymore and citizens are fleeing to other countries. These cases have a lowest common denominator: The rulers seemed to think that they could reshape their respective societies at will, paying little attention to "objective" limitations, perhaps by inspiring or terrorizing their populations into redoubled efforts to remake conditions in the desired image.

In light of these and other experiences—when modernization succeeds and paves the way for its own next phase, vs. when it fails—it becomes clear that modernization is a trial-and-error process in which certain principles, institutions, practices, and personnel gradually have come to be regarded as indispensable, even if people don't like them very much and prefer to imagine a world in which we could do without them. I want to call these "constraints." They do not exactly describe an iron cage in a Weberian sense, but at least a space in which institutions from politics to academia, to the media, must operate. Some of these institutions and practices include:

- The authority of natural science in areas in which there is consensus and the data support certain conclusions.
- The "laws" (for lack of a better word) of economics, granting that they do not always lead to indisputable conclusions but do set the limits of rational policy-making.
- The role of experts in most fields, especially when it comes to complicated, technical ones such as law, accounting, education, environmental protection, and banking oversight. Again, there can be and usually is debate within the community of experts. The bandwidth of policy-making is broad. But the point is that a modern society is one that is guided by expert opinion in most areas.
- Bureaucracy in Max Weber's sense of a hierarchical arrangement of offices with a clear chain of command in which positions are filled on the basis of merit rather than personal loyalty to a leader or party.

- The existence of an educated public in which issues of politics, culture, science, etc. can be aired and debated. Of course, there may be fairly strict limits on what can be discussed and how (cf. China or Singapore), but no modern society can entirely eliminate public discussion. The role of the public sphere also implies the presence of a trained corps of journalists to sift, evaluate, and present clearly the questions to be considered.
- The importance of procedures and "due process." Indeed, political scientists Wolfgang Merkel and Sasha Kneip regard procedures—which, following Vivien Schmidt, they call "throughput"—as a key component of democratic legitimacy (Merkel & Kneip n.d.). We should and normally do regard decisions as legitimate if they have been reached via legally mandated, agreed-upon procedures and norms.
- Tacit acceptance of the criterion of truth as the basis for clarifying, defining, and choosing policy options on the part of most citizens. There can and should be debate about what the truth is, but in a modern society it is not—or should not be—acceptable to tell blatant lies with the intention of making them widely accepted as true.

If we consider what populist governments and/or leaders have actually done or said, we notice that these constraints are regularly flouted. We have already mentioned the ways in which Mrs. Kirchner in Argentina manipulated economic statistics. But surely Exhibit A on this point are the statements and decisions made by candidate and later President Donald Trump and his appointees. For example, in his first few months in office, Trump pulled the US out of the Paris Accord, calling global warming a hoax, despite the fact that there is virtually unanimous scientific consensus that it is occurring and is caused by human activities such as burning fossil fuels. Likewise, in May of 2017, the Environmental Protection Agency, led by climate change denier Scott Pruitt, fired nine members of its 18-person Board of Counselors, scientists who normally advise the agency on policy, and later replaced them with coal and oil industry personnel. He also ordered that climate change data be removed from federal websites. Finally, he claimed that Trump's new pro-coal policies had created 50,000 new jobs in that sector, when the *entire* US coal industry supports only 51,000 jobs. In fact, only 1,300 positions have been added. After being challenged on this whopper by reporters, his aides confessed that he "misspoke" (Thompson 2017). At the same time, the Department of the Interior, under Ryan Zinke, suspended 200 advisory boards which normally would have enabled citizens to make recommendations on natural resource management (Wiles 2017). Congress has also done its part to keep science out of political decision-making. For example, there have been many important studies done of major environmental disasters such as oil spills. But now House Bill 1431 forbids the EPA from using any data that cannot be reproduced. Since oil spills and similar disasters are one-off events, by their very nature scientists cannot "reproduce" the data they have gathered on them and thus cannot use it to make policy (Thompson 2017).

Even without actually doctoring statistics, Trump and his minions also deliberately have created false impressions among American citizens. For example, he constantly stressed during his campaign that terrorists were roaming America killing innocent people and that there was a vendetta against police among (though he did not say so directly) African-Americans. He portrayed cities as hotbeds of out-of-control crime, when in fact there has been a long-term decline in violent crime in the United States. Trump has also claimed that he would have won the popular vote during last year's presidential election if not for three million or so fraudulent votes cast—presumably many by illegal immigrants who somehow posed as citizens. In 2017, he even empaneled a Presidential Advisory Commission on Election Integrity under Kansas Secretary of State Kris Kobach, who for years has made similar claims about his own state, but who has found no evidence that large numbers of people voted illegally there.

Still, the goal of a right-wing populist such as Trump is not so much to defend misstatements and lies by marshalling facts in their support as it is to create an environment in which they circulate on social media and in tabloid newspapers, where there are essentially no standards of objective truth, so they gradually can seep into the public consciousness—or at least that portion of it in Trump's camp—as if they were indeed matters of fact. Of course, Trump is not the only far-right politician to banish facts and truth-seeking from his kingdom. In the weeks and months leading up to the Brexit referendum, the Leave forces floated a figure for the level of Britain's EU payments 100% higher than it actually was, and suggested that it would be enough to cover shortfalls in that country's National Health Service Budget (Sherer 2017: 38).

In sum, one of populism's hallmarks is the rejection of elites, but that is only part of the story. The elites being pilloried on both sides of the Atlantic are often those, such as journalists and scientists, who try to supply accurate information and generally those who point out the limitations under which leaders must operate: laws, regulations, norms, institutions, and sometimes even physical realities. The dismal outcomes of so many populist regimes arise in the long run from their disdain for those constraints. The first hazy outlines of the fourth wave of modernity are indeed disheartening, so it is easy to understand why so many would like to return to agrarian simplicity (the first wave), libertarian, unregulated capitalism (the second wave), or the welfare state wedded to peak industrialism (third wave). But we are much more likely to cope with all the changes in the offing if we carry on informed, fact-based public debates about what is likely to happen and to fashion intelligent public policies that respect the constraints noted above. When policy-making flows from fantasy, wishful thinking, voluntarism, and lies, the outcome is usually abysmal.

## Notes

1  I therefore would reject the claim of Graubard (2002: xi) that "India is incontestably modern." Some cities, regions, and institutions in India are indeed modern, but they are parts of the archipelago of modernity.
2  The Pulitzer Prize-winning website Politifact (www.politifact.com) has rated 70% of Trump's statements as completely or partly false.

## References

Acemoglu, D. & J. Robinson. 2012. *Why Nations Fail: The origins of power, prosperity, and poverty*. New York: Crown Business Books.

Arnason, J. 2002. "Communism and Modernity." In S. Eisenstadt (ed.), *Multiple Modernities*. New Brunswick, NJ: Transaction Publishers, pp. 61–90.

Bell, D. 2017. "Le Pen's Long Shadow." *The Nation*, April 24–May 1, pp. 27–34.

Croly, H. 1963. *The Promise of American Life*. New York: E.P. Dutton.

de Lange, S. & T. Akkerman. 2012. "Populist Parties in Belgium: A case of hegemonic liberal democracy?" In C. Mudde & R. Kaltwasser (eds.), *Populism in Europe and the Americas: Threat or corrective for democracy?* Cambridge: Cambridge University Press, pp. 27–45.

Economist. 2017a. "A Peronist on the Potomac." *The Economist*, February 18, p. 29.

Economist. 2017b. "The Rage Against Macron." *The Economist*, May 6, pp. 46–47.

Edsall, T. 2017. "The End of the Left and the Right as We Knew Them." *The New York Times*, June 22. Available at www.nytimes.com/2017/06/22/opinion/nationalism-globalism-edsall.html?em.

Eisenstadt, S. 2002. "Multiple Modernities." In S. Eisenstadt (ed.), *Multiple Modernities*. New Brunswick, NJ: Transaction Publishers, pp. 1–30.

Fallend, F. 2012. "Populism in Government: The Case of Austria (2000–2007)." In C. Mudde & R. Kaltwasser (eds.), *Populism in Europe and the Americas: Threat or corrective for democracy?* Cambridge: Cambridge University Press, pp. 113–135.

Fukuyama, F. 1992. *The End of History and the Last Man*. New York: The Free Press.

Fukuyama, F. 2014. *Political Order and Political Decay: From the industrial revolution to the globalization of democracy*. New York: Farrar Straus & Giroux.

Giddens, A. 1990. *The Consequences of Modernity*. Stanford, CA: Stanford University Press.

Gilman, N. 2003. *Mandarins of the Future: Modernization theory in Cold-War America*. Baltimore, MD: Johns Hopkins University Press.

Goldhammer, A. 2017. "On the March in France." *The Nation*, July 17, pp. 23–24.

Göle, N. 2002. "Snapshots of Islamic Modernities." In S. Eisenstadt (ed.), *Multiple Modernities*. New Brunswick, NJ: Transaction Publishers, pp. 91–118.

Graham, D. 2017. "Red State, Blue City." *The Atlantic*, March, pp. 24–26.

Graudbard, S. 2002. "Preface." In S. Eisenstadt (ed.), *Multiple Modernities*. New Brunswick, NJ: Transaction Publishers, pp. vii–xiv.

Habermas, J. 1967. "Naturrecht und Revolution." In J. Habermas, *Theorie und Praxis*. Neuwied am Rhein: Luchterhand, pp. 52–88.

Heideking, J. 2002. "The Pattern of American Modernity from the Revolution to the Civil War." In S. Eisenstadt (ed.), *Multiple Modernities*. New Brunswick, NJ: Transaction Books, pp. 219–248.

Hofstadter, R. 1955. *The Age of Reform*. New York: Vintage Books.

Hofstadter, R. 1967. *The Paranoid Style in American Politics and Other Essays*. New York: Vintage Books.

Huntington, S. 1996. *The Clash of Civilizations*. New York: Touchstone Books.

Judis, J. 2016. *The Populist Explosion: How the great recession transformed American and European politics*. New York: Columbia University Press.

Kramer, K. 2016. *The Politics of Resentment: Rural consciousness in Wisconsin and the rise of Scott Walker*. Chicago, IL: University of Chicago Press.

Limerick, P. 1987. *The Legacy of Conquest*. New York: W. W. Norton & Co.

McCarthy, N. 2017. "Which Countries Have the Highest Levels of Labor Union Membership?" *Forbes*, June 20. Available at www.forbes.com/sites/niallmccarthy/2017/06/20/which-countries-have-the-highest-levels-of-labor-union-membership.

Merkel, W. & S. Kneip. n.d. "The Idea of Democratic Legitimacy." Unpublished manuscript.

Milanovic, B. 2016. *Global Inequality: A new approach for the age of globalization.* Cambridge, MA: Harvard University Press.

Müller, J. 2016. *What is Populism?* Philadelphia, PA: University of Pennsylvania Press.

Neumann, L. & K. Schaper. 2008. *Die Sozialordnung der Bundesrepublik Deutschland.* Bonn: Bundeszentrale für Politische Bildung.

New York Times. 2013. "Anatomy of Detroit's Decline." *The New York Times*, December 8. Available at www.nytimes.com/interactive/2103/09/12/US/detroit-decline.

Piketty, T. 2014. *Capital in the Twenty-First Century.* Cambridge, MA: Belknap Press.

Politico. 2016. "How Brexit Vote Broke Down." Available at www.politico.eu/article/graphics-how-the-UK-voted-eu-referendum.

Sherer, M. 2017. "Can Trump Handle the Truth?" *Time*, April 3, pp. 32–39.

Sterling, B. 2009. "Urban Detroit Racoon Hunter Predicts Imminent Cannibalism." *The Detroit News*, April 9. Available at www.detroitnews.com/apps/pbes.dl/article.

Thompson, J. 2017. "The Trump Administration's False Coal Stats, Explained." *High Country News*, June 8. Available at www.hcn.org/articles/epa-chief-pruitt-dispenses-false-coal-job-stats.

Tocqueville, A. de, 2000. *Democracy in America.* Chicago, IL: University of Chicago Press.

Weber, M. 1968. *Soziologie, Wirtschaftliche Analysen, Politik,* ed. J. Winckelmann. Stuttgart: Alfred Kroner Verlag.

Wiles, T. 2017. "Where Trump Has Weakened Public and Scientific Input." *High Country News*, May 17 issue. Available at www.hcn.org/articles/trump-administration-weakens-scientific-and-public-input/prin.

Williamson, E. 2009. *The Penguin History of Latin America.* London: Penguin.

Wittrock, B. 2002. "Modernity: One, None, or Many?" In S. Eisenstadt (ed.), *Multiple Modernities.* New Brunswick, NJ: Transaction Publishers, pp. 31–60.

Wood, G. 2009. *Empire of Liberty.* Oxford: Oxford University Press.

Woodard, C. 2016. *American Character.* New York: Penguin Books.

**PART II**

# The EU and China: Diverse identities and political prospects

# 5

# MODERNITY, MODERNIZATION, AND THE NEW AUTHORITARIANISM WITH CHINESE CHARACTERISTICS

*Xinning Song*

Modernization and modernity have different meanings in Chinese. Modernization (*xiandai hua*) mainly refers to economic development and industrialization, while modernity (*xiadai xing*) is a broader concept that also includes certain social, political and ideological perspectives. Throughout China's quest for modernization and modernity during the last 175 years of its history, authoritarianism has played an important role. Authoritarianism is always a debatable idea. The Chinese understanding of the phenomenon differs considerably from that of the West. According to Juan Linz, authoritarianism means limited political pluralism. The foundations of its legitimacy rest on emotion, minimal social mobilization, and informally defined executive power with often vague and shifting prerogatives (Casper 1995: 40). For many Chinese, authoritarianism is a form of government that lies somewhere between totalitarianism and Western-style liberal democracy. In their quest for modernization and modernity, the Chinese learned first from Europe and the United States and later from the Soviet Union, but all such Western-derived models failed until 1978, when the country launched the reforms that opened up its economy. Throughout modern Chinese history, authoritarianism with Chinese characteristics (i.e., different styles of authoritarianism) has played a crucial role in promoting modernization and modernity. And that generalization continues to be true even in contemporary China.

## The development of modernity and authoritarianism in China

More than a century ago, the Chinese began looking for ways to modernize and eventually enter the era of modernity. After the Opium Wars of 1840–1842 and 1856, when China was defeated by Western powers, the country's leaders realized that its condition of backwardness had to be combatted. During the later years of the Qing Dynasty, two steps were taken to modernize China, or at least bring it to the threshold of modernity.

The first step was to learn how to use Western technology, but precisely in order to restrict its influence (*shizhi changji yi zhiyi*). From the 1860s to the 1890s in China, a drive to Westernize, known as the "self-strengthening" movement, was launched. Its goal was to acquire Western military and industrial technology, introducing into China and ultimately establishing Chinese enterprises to manufacture it.

The second step was to undertake constitutional reform and modernization. This was done during the Hundred Days' Reform in 1898. As the Westernization movement proceeded apace, Chinese elites still concentrated on the "Chinese classics as the substance and Western ideology as the usage" (*zhongxue weiti, xixue weiyong*). In the wake of the first Sino-Japanese War in 1894–1895, the Chinese realized that Western technology alone would not be sufficient to modernize China and that the country's institutional system and ideology also would need to be reformed. The main objective of the Hundred Days' Reform was to establish a European-style constitutional monarchy. Although it failed to achieve that goal, it did set a precedent for Chinese modernization and modernity in the 20th century.

After the collapse of the Qing Dynasty during the 1911 Revolution, China became a republic. Both the revolutionary government in the South and the warlord-dominated governments of the North set about introducing constitutional systems, with the exception of Yuan Shih-kai's restoration of the monarchy (83 days in 1916). In February of 1913, the National Assembly announced and then held the country's first elections. The Nationalist Party—Kuomintang (KMT) or Guomindang made up largely of former revolutionaries—won a commanding majority of seats. Parliament was tasked with producing a permanent constitution, the Draft Constitution of October, 1913, which for the first time employed the term "popular sovereignty." Sung Chiao-jen, the main organizer of the KMT's electoral victory, advocated lodging executive authority in a cabinet responsible to parliament rather than in the president.

Yuan Shih-kai's four years in power (1912–1916) had serious consequences for China, ones that long have been debated by Chinese intellectuals. Yuan's initiative, as well as his subsequent defiance of constitutional procedures and eventual dissolution of parliament, also set precedents that were later repeated. Many people in China were disillusioned by the republican experiment; China may have been a republic in name, but arbitrary rule based on military power was the political reality. The country was becoming fractured into competing military satrapies—a process captured by the expression "warlordism."

This early period of political struggle led the Chinese to re-think their economic and political system. China did witness the emergence of an intelligentsia, many members of which were educated in Japan, Europe, and the United States. This educated elite occupied important positions and became a modernizing force in society once they had returned from their periods of study abroad. Their writings and teachings were destined to exert a powerful influence on future generations of students. By 1915–1916 there were said to be nearly 130,000 new-style schools in China with more than four million pupils in the urban areas. In 1919, the May 4th

Movement was launched, led mostly by young students. The movement was triggered by the so-called Twenty-One Demands issued by the Japanese government to China during World War I and later by negotiations for the Treaty of Versailles which was supposed to end that war Two Western concepts acquired increasing popularity in China: science ("Mr. S.") and democracy ("Mr. D."). The May 4th Movement thus represented a new beginning in the long struggle to modernize China and/or bring it fully into the modern era. It sought not merely to build a stronger economy but also to adopt a Western-style (i.e., democratic) political system, although a variety of justifications for doing so were offered.

From 1916 to 1928 China went through what has become known as the warlord period. The warlord governments in the north continued trying to introduce constitutional rule, supported in that effort by the European and Northern American legal experts. In 1919 the Duan Qirui government put forward a Draft Constitution of the Republic of China (the Eight-year Draft). In 1923 President Cao Kun published a Draft Constitution of the Republic of China (Cao Kun Constitution). Duan Qirui returned to power in 1925 and put forward yet another Draft Constitution of the Republic of China (the Fourteen-Year Constitution).

The most influential theoretical justification of Chinese constitutionalism came from Sun Yat-sen's theory of five-power constitutionalism, as outlined in various speeches and essays written from the 1910s through the mid-1920s. His arguments were powerfully influenced by Western philosophy, yet they also displayed many uniquely Chinese characteristics. Dr. Sun advocated a hybrid model of government combining the traditional Western separation of powers into three branches, but with two additional branches of government drawn from Chinese history: the Examination Yuan and the Control Yuan. According to Sun, the traditional model of Western constitutionalism tended to vest too much power in the legislative branch. Sun also criticized Western electoral systems on the grounds that they were designed to ensure that the wealthy would be elected and that most executive appointments would end up entangled in nepotism. The division of the five powers would not only avoid autocratic dictatorship but also increase governmental efficiency.

Once the KMT had unified China in 1928, it adopted the principles enshrined in Sun's theory of the five powers, but only on paper. The National Assembly approved the Provisional Constitution during the Political Tutelage Stage of the Republic of China on May 5, 1928; the document came into force on June 1. Sun Yat-sen's Three People's Principles and Five Powers scheme became the intellectual basis and organizing approach of the Provisional Constitution. On May 5, 1936, the national government published the Draft Constitution of the Republic of China (May 5th Draft Constitution), but it was never approved by the National Assembly due to the Japanese invasion. There were revisions of the Draft Constitution in 1938, 1943 and 1946, in which both the KMT and the Communist Party of China participated, as well as other public figures. The Constitution of the Republic of China was passed by National Assembly on December 25, 1946, and published by the national government on January 1, 1947.

During first half of the 20th century, government in China was in a state of constant flux. The National Party (KMT, formally established in 1919) ruled for a time, then cooperated with the Communist Chinese Party (the CCP, established in 1921) from 1924–1927 and again from 1937–1946. At other times the parties were in conflict and fought two civil wars (1927–1937 and 1946–1949). After the National Party unified China in 1928, the national government adopted the Western model of a constitutional system. In its revolutionary base area, the Communist Party followed the Soviet model.

The unification of China after 1928 was actually only nominal, because semi-warlordism persisted in various provinces, such as Sichuan, Guizhou, and Shanxi. Mr. Chiang Kai-shek as the Chairman of the KMT, President of the national government, Chairman of the Military Commission, and Commander in-Chief, was the most powerful politician in China. Due to political cleavages, the existence of hostile forces (the Communist Party), and tendencies toward separatism in some regions, Chiang opted for an authoritarian style of governance, and in this he was supported by most of the Western powers, especially the United States. By contrast, the Communists criticized him as a warlord, feudalist, and dictator.

## Mao's Soviet-style "authoritarianism with Chinese characteristics"

Unlike other leaders, Mr. Mao Zedong as the leader of Communist Party of China had no experience abroad. Before the establishment of the People's Republic of China (PRC) he was quite receptive to the political philosophy and political system in the United States. On July 4, 1944, an editorial in the *Liberation Daily* entitled *Congratulations on the National Day of the United States: A Great Day to Fight for Liberal Democracy*, written by Mr. Hu Qiaomu, Mao's political secretary at the time, stated that "The Communist Party of China and other democratic forces would be partners of the democratic United States and successors to Sun Yat-sen's Three People's Principles. We expected to get support from the democratic United States" (Hu 1992: 130–133).

In September of 1945, when a British journalist asked Mao Zedong about the concept and definition of liberal democracy in China, Mao answered as follows:

> A liberal democratic China will be a country with universal suffrage, equal and secret elections to central and local government posts, and officeholders will be responsible to the people who have elected them. It will realize the three people's principles of Sun Yat-sen, "for the people, by the people, and of the people" (the principles of Abraham Lincoln), and the Four Freedoms of Franklin Roosevelt.
>
> *(Mao 1996: 27–28)*

Although Mao did not like America's foreign policy or its China policy, he always praised the American domestic democracy when he met in the 1940s with foreign journalists in Yanan, Northern Shaanxi. After April of 1949, when the People's

Liberation Army captured Nanjing, the capital of the Nationalist government, the CCP decided to invite John Leighton Stuart, the US Ambassador to People's Republic of China, to Beijing to meet the new leadership. But the State Department of the United States decided not to have any contact with the Communists.

Initially, Mao Zedong was not especially friendly to the Soviet Union, on account of the bad experiences he had there while working with the Comintern in the 1920s and 1930s and with Stalin in 1940s. But several factors led Mao and his Communist colleagues to shift from the Western to the Soviet model. First, there was the hostile policy of the United States and its allies towards the new China after 1949. Second, the CCP was grateful for the considerable support it received from the Soviet Union, especially during the first half of the 1950s. Third, the unstable situation within China played a role. And finally, we must not overlook Mao Zedong's aspiration to be the great leader of the world revolution.

During the initial period of the PRC, Mao Zedong followed the principles of the new democratic revolution and favored democratic arrangements. After 1956, however, when the CCP launched its socialist revolution, both external threats and internal debates within the socialist camp sharpened. Meanwhile, domestic political and economic problems were becoming more serious. Mao implemented Leninist and Stalinist principles within the party and developed his own style of authoritarianism in China.

Mao Zedong held the most important positions in the party and government both before and after the establishment of the People's Republic. Mao was the Chairman of the provisional government of the Chinese Soviet Republic in 1931 and 1934. He was the Chairman of the Central Military Commission of the CCP in 1935, and the Chairman of the Politburo and Secretariat of the CCP in 1943. And he was the Chairman of the Central Committee of the CCP from 1944 (the 7th Plenary Session of the 6th National Congress of the CCP) until his death in 1976. He was the first Chairman of the Central People's Government of the new China in 1949 and the President of the State of the People's Republic of China in 1954 during the first plenary session of the first National People's Congress. In 1959, Liu Shaoqi replaced Mao as the President of the State of the People's Republic.

The authoritarianism of Mao Zedong diverged from that inherent in the Soviet model. Mao's brand of authoritarianism had three notable characteristics. First, democratic centralism was practiced within the party. Democratic centralism means that all the political decisions reached by the party through its democratically elected bodies are binding upon all party members. During Mao's era, there were free discussions on most of political and economic issues within the Communist Party at both the central and local levels. Criticism and self-criticism were important principles. Although Mao wielded absolute power in China, he strongly emphasized the importance of criticism. He made many mistakes in domestic policies, such as the Great Leap Forward movement. In the later 1950s and early 1960s, he also practiced self-criticism, admitting his own mistakes. The main purpose of the so-called "Congress of Seven Thousand People" (the enlarged working conference of the Central Committee of the CCP) in 1962 was to correct the mistakes of the Great Leap Forward. Mao openly criticized himself for his lack of experience and knowledge in economics affairs, and assumed direct and indirect responsibility for the errors committed by the Communist Party. He emphasized again the importance of democratic centralism, arguing that the principle was applicable not only to the Party itself but the whole country. In weighing the relationship between democracy and centralism, he put democracy first: "It is impossible to have correct centralism without democracy. Without it there would be no correct centralism … Our centralism is centralism based upon democracy" (Mao 1999: 295–296). After the Congress of Seven Thousand People, Mao in fact retreated to the second rank of the CCP's leadership, while Liu Shaoqi and Deng Xiaoping advanced to the first rank.

Second, there was a centralized system of governance. Although Mao talked a lot about assigning greater importance to democracy than to centralism, the latter remained essential to Chinese governance. Also, in his speech before the Congress of Seven Thousand People, he set two limitations upon democracy. One limit had to do with party discipline: The minority must be subordinate to the majority, and the lower echelons of the Communist Party should be subordinate to its Central Committee. The other limit was that no secret group should be formed (Mao 1999: 297). While Mao had no official position in the government after 1959, he nevertheless remained the dominant force in the Party until his death. He was the person who made the final decisions despite the fact that he was officially in the second rank of the leadership.

Relations between the central and local governments constituted another key factor in the centralization of governance. In a speech to the enlarged conference of the Politburo on April 25, 1956, Mao addressed ten major relationships, including the relationship between the center and local authorities. According to Mao, China should grant a bit more power and independence to the local level, allowing it to assume greater responsibility, while still consolidating the central unified leadership. His remarks can be paraphrased as follows: China should not centralize power excessively, as the Soviet Union had done. Instead, we should study the experiences of the capitalist countries even though China has a totally different political system. We need a strong, unified central power as well as unified planning and discipline. No one should be allowed to destroy this united power structure. At the same time, he said, we must give full play to local initiatives (Mao 1976: 1). But clearly, Mao believed that centralism was more important than local initiative. He reminded his colleagues of their blunder during the first phase of the People's Republic when they established a grand regional system in China. In order to maintain unified central power, Mao implemented another policy during this era: a rotation scheme for the major military commanders-in-chief.

Third, we must not forget Mao Zedong's personality cult, which reached its zenith during the Cultural Revolution. Mao acquired his unchallenged personal authority in the Chinese Communist Party in 1945 during the 7th National Party Congress of the CCP. He was elected as the Chairman of the Politburo, Chairman of the Secretariat, and Chairman of the Central Committee of the CCP. Mao Zedong's thought was also enshrined in the Party's constitution. Before 1956 Mao was on record as opposing cults of personality. In fact, he thought that one of Stalin's chief mistakes was to encourage such hero worship, and accordingly Mao warned the Chinese to learn from that error (Mao 1956: 1). Yielding to Mao's decision, the revision of the Party Constitution that was carried out during the 8th National Party Congress in 1956 deleted any reference to Mao Zedong's thought. But after 1958, opposition to personality cults was regarded as a challenge to Mao's authority. By then, Mao had assimilated another lesson from the Soviet Union: Without a personality cult that he could rely on, Nikita Khrushchev was removed from power.

The Cultural Revolution of the late 1960s saw the peak of Mao's personality cult. Mao was regarded as the Great Teacher, Great Leader, Great Captain, and Great Helmsman. Everyone should be loyal to him and Chinese people even prayed every day that he would enjoy a long life. Mao did not particularly like or subscribe to this cult, but he came to see it as a necessary political tool.

## Deng Xiaoping's new modernization and authoritarianism

In 1978, just two years after Mao Zedong's death, China initiated reforms to open up its economy and society. This was the so-called "second revolution," a new modernization process led by Mr. Deng Xiaoping. Deng belonged to the first generation of the CCP leadership. He joined the Communist Party in 1924 and became the Secretary-General of its Central Committee in 1928–1929. He was elected to the Central Committee of the CCP in 1945. After 1949, he served as a vice premier; he became Secretary-General in 1954, and in 1955 he was selected as a member of the Politburo, to be elevated to its Standing Committee in the following year. During the Cultural Revolution he lost his positions, but in 1973 he was rehabilitated by Mao Zedong and named vice premier and member of the Politburo. He was appointed vice chairman of the CCP's Central Committee, vice premier of the Chinese government, and Chief of the General Staff of the PLA in 1975. He lost all his positions again in 1976 when the "Gang of Four" and Hua Guofeng temporarily assumed power in China after Mao's death.

The definitive end of the Cultural Revolution brought Deng back into power. He resumed all his posts in the party, government, and PLA in July, 1977. He was elected vice-chairman of the CCP's Central Committee in August of that year, and Chairman of the Chinese People's Political Consultative Conference the following March. Deng resigned as vice premier in 1980. He was elected to the Standing Committee of the Politburo and chosen to be Chairman of the Military Commission of the Central Committee and the first Chairman of the Central Advisory Commission in 1982 (at the 12th National Party Congress), and Chairman of the Central Military Commission of the CCP in 1983 (at the 6th National People's Congress). He resigned the post of Chairman of the Military Commission in November of 1989 and, in 1990, stepped down from his post as Chairman of the

PRC's Central Military Commission. Deng Xiaoping never held the number one official position in either the Communist Party or the Chinese government. But in reality, he was the supreme leader after the Mao era passed. Revered along with Mao as part of the first generation of CCP leadership, he belonged to the core of the second generation of leadership of the CCP and the PRC. More importantly, he is credited with being the chief architect of China's reform and opening.

Deng Xiaoping's design for that reform and opening had two main components. The first of these was to unleash the market economy as the engine of China's modernization, above all in the fields of industry, agriculture, science and technology, and national defense (the so-called "four modernizations"). The second concerned China's internal governance, especially the leading role of the Communist Party. In 1982, during the 12th National Party Congress, Deng Xiaoping described his vision for China as "socialism with Chinese characteristics." Many people interpreted this vision as an embrace of neo-authoritarianism: Deng seemed to be endorsing a form of capitalism led by the Communist Party of China. That model incorporated the following features.

First, it prioritized economic development. In this view, the primary task of the post-Cultural Revolution Communist Party was to rescue the Chinese economy, which was collapsing after ten years of disorder. Deng Xiaoping advocated slogans such as "Development is the absolute principle," and "Let some people get rich first." These words were well-received by a majority of the Chinese people, no matter whether they were conservatives or liberals. Economic modernization became everyone's overriding objective. Political reform could wait until economic reform and economic development had succeeded. That set of priorities became a matter of broad consensus.

Second, Deng's program was non-ideological. Mao Zedong had been regarded as a romantic revolutionary leader strongly committed to an ideology. By contrast, Deng Xiaoping exhibited much more pragmatism. As early as 1962 he advocated a view that is widely known as the "cat theory": No matter whether the cat is white or black, it is a good cat if it can catch mice. In 1976 Mao Zedong criticized him precisely for holding that position. In the early 1980s the cat theory became one of the most popular slogans in China and later in the world. Deng Xiaoping also propounded a theory known as "crossing the river by touching the stone." It encouraged the Chinese to experiment with a variety of methods, regardless of ideology, that promised to promote economic development. Deng's least ideological slogan was, "no argument." As he himself explained: "No argument is my innovation. No argument means we will be buying time and doing more real things. The point of the slogan is that we should carry out reforms and breakthroughs without arguing about them" (Deng 1993: 375). In other words, the Chinese should not debate about whether a given reform measure is socialistic or capitalistic. We should carry out all of our reforms under the rubric of "socialism with Chinese characteristics."

The third feature of Deng's neo-authoritarianism involved seeking a balance between the Communist Party and the government. Like Mao and other party members, Deng Xiaoping supported the principle of democratic centralism, but he cared more about the ruling position of the Communist Party. On the one hand, his reform and opening proposal required ideological emancipation; on the other, the Cultural Revolution had sown widespread ideological confusion. How was the leading role of the CPC to be consolidated? Deng Xiaoping decided to include leadership by the party as one of the four fundamental principles of the Chinese constitution, and insisted on ideological unity, as expressed in the statement that "every Party member should be consistent with the Central Committee ideologically." At the same time, Deng argued that the CPC should be able to assert and improve its leadership by making sure that it functioned within the framework of the Chinese constitution. In 1987, the nature of the division of labor between the Party and the government was put on the agenda and was regarded as the next crucial step in political reform.

Fourth, Deng wished to limit political reform to reform of the administration. He realized that the Chinese political system was ill-suited to accommodate market reforms. There were wide-ranging debates in China on how to define and how to implement political reform. Because maintaining the ruling position of the party was his first priority, Deng supported reforms mainly in administrative rather than political matters. His innovations included a term-limit system for the president of state, the prime minister, the president of the National People's Congress, and other officials. In 1982, the first village elections were held. Then, beginning in the 1980s, examinations were instituted to select civil servants, judges, and other public officials. Deng Xiaoping himself resigned the chairmanship of the Central Military Commission and officially retired from public life in 1989. He was the first leader of the Chinese Communist Party to do so.

In contrast to the authoritarianism of Mao Zedong, Deng Xiaoping's version combined a cult of personality with a commitment to rule by the party. He held absolute personal authority in the Communist Party, the Chinese government, and the Chinese military. He was the number one person in China at the time even though he did not occupy the official number one position. From 1980 on Deng held no formal post in the government, and he officially retired in 1989. But he continued to hold a tight rein over the Communist Party, and succeeded in dismissing two general party secretaries in 1987 and 1989. Like Mao Zedong, as a politician he was not challenged by the Chinese people, but many of the concrete items of his reform program and policy of opening, especially the political ones, were debated within China.

## "Socialism with Chinese characteristics" in the new era, and Xi Jinping's authoritarianism

Subsequent Chinese leaders, such as Jiang Zemin and Hu Jintao, did not deviate from the main strategy of Deng Xiaoping. Due to their lack of personal charisma and a political legacy, they were not regarded as authoritarian leaders in the sense that Mao and Deng were. Mr. Xi Jinping belongs to a new generation of leadership of the Chinese Communist Party, since he did not enter the country's central power structure until 2007 and became the top leader only in 2012.

As Xi Jinping declared during the 19th National Party Congress in October, 2017, China is entering a new era in modernization and modernity, because the country basically has achieved the four modernizations. It has become the second largest economy in the world, with extremely strong industrial, agricultural, technological, and military capabilities. China's new target is to become an economically more powerful and modernized country by achieving a fifth modernization, pertaining to its system of governance.

After Xi Jinping came to power in 2012, a tendency toward recentralization was evident. He not only took over the supreme positions in the Party (Secretary-General), the state (President of the State), and the army (Chairman of the Military Commission of the Central Committee of CCP and Chairman of the Central Military Commission of the People's Republic of China), but also headed most of the so-called "leading groups" in China. In the wake of the Party National People's Congresses of 2018, some of those groups were renamed "leading committees." Xi Jinping now commands the most important of those groups, such as those devoted to national security, comprehensively deepening reform, comprehensive law-based governance, finance and economics, cyber-security and informatization, foreign affairs, and relations with Taiwan. The functions of many of those groups are governmental in nature rather than party-based. Nowadays, Xi is widely regarded as the most powerful politician both in China and indeed the entire world.

There is little resistance to Xi Jinping's recentralization or authoritarianism, for the following reasons:

1.   The consensus view shared by both intellectuals and ordinary citizens is that China needs strong leadership.
2.   Xi Jinping has strong personal sources of power.
3.   Xi Jinping has outlined new policies for comprehensively deepening reform.

Below we briefly examine these three reasons.

### The consensus view that China needs strong leadership

During the twenty years after Deng Xiaoping's death, China never enjoyed such leadership. The Hu Jintao/Wen Jiabao period (2002–2012) was seen as having displayed the weakest leadership in the history of the People's Republic. The saying intended to capture the drift of that era is, "taming the river by nine dragons." It means that the nine members of the Politburo's Standing Committee all had their own personal agendas and rarely consulted with one another. Another saying from that period was that "no government decree can go beyond Zhongnanhai," meaning that no one really followed the rules and orders issued by the central government. The era was also one in which corruption afflicted both the government and army.

## Xi Jinping's personal sources of power

Xi's power emanates first and foremost from his family. His father, Xi Zhongxun, was among the first-generation leadership of the CCP and the PRC. He joined the Communist Youth League in 1926 and the Communist Party in 1928, and was one of the major leaders of the revolutionary base in northern Shaanxi. After the establishment of the PRC he served as minister of propaganda in 1950 and became a vice premier in 1959. Having run into problems with Mao Zedong in 1962, he was demoted to a position as the head of a local factory. Once the reform era began and China started to open up, Xi Zhongxun was chosen to govern Guangdong Province in 1978 before his elevation to membership in the Politburo of the CCP in 1982. From 1980 to 1993, he was also vice president of the National People's Congress.

The second source of Xi Jinping's personal power is his work experience. A middle school pupil when the Cultural Revolution started, he was sent to the countryside in northern Shaanxi Province in 1969. In 1974 he joined the Communist Party and soon became the party secretary of the village where he worked. He was the worker-peasant-soldier student at Tsinghua University from 1975 to 1979. After graduation he worked for three years at the Central Military Commission as the secretary of General Geng Biao, the secretary-general of the Commission. Subsequently he headed Zhengding County in Hebei Province from 1982 until 1985, Fujian Province from 1985 to 2002, Zhejiang Province from 2002 to 2007, and Shanghai in 2007. From 2008 to 2012, he was China's number two leader, elected to the Standing Committee of the Politburo and chosen to be vice president of the state. In reviewing his experiences, one notices that Xi has been a Communist Party leader at all levels of the party organization as well as in numerous governmental institutions.

Xi Jinping's final personal power source resides in his anti-corruption campaign. Corruption is regarded as the malignant tumor of the Communist Party. After coming to power in 2012, Xi defined the anti-corruption campaign as his highest priority in the effort to strengthen party discipline across the board. From December of 2012 to October of 2017, more than 200 corrupt Chinese officials above the deputy-minister level were apprehended and punished, including members of the Standing Committee of the Politburo of the CCP, several former vice chairmen of the Central Military Commission, and a former vice president of the Chinese People's Political Consultative Conference (CPPCC), as well as some former ministers and PLA generals. According to a report by Wang Qishan, once a member of the Politburo's Standing Committee and Secretary of the Commission for Discipline Inspection of the CCP's Central Committee, more than one million government officials at different levels were being punished for corruption as of October 31, 2016, all having been apprehended since the 18th National Party Congress in 2012 (Wang 2016: 1–4). The Chinese Communist Party had talked about anti-corruption campaigns for many years, yet many Chinese had believed that without strong leadership a real anti-corruption campaign would be impossible.

## Xi Jinping's new reform policies

After 40 years of reform and opening, China is embarking upon a new stage of development. Those decades enabled China to become one of the most powerful countries in the world, not only economically but also politically and militarily. At the same time, China faces more internal and external problems internally. How to continue and deepen the reform and opening is the major task facing the current leadership.

Xi Jinping's new strategy for further development differs from that of Deng Xiaoping and successors such as Jiang Zemin and Hu Jintao. The core element of so-called Xi Jinping Thought is that China should cultivate "socialism with Chinese characteristics" for the new era. It requires that the "principal contradiction" must be redefined. In China, the (re-)definition of the principal contradiction is a way in which the leadership can indicate the main problem and task awaiting attention by the Communist Party. In 1981, Deng had defined the principal contradiction as that between the "ever-growing material and cultural needs of the people" and the country's "backward social productivity." By this, he meant that the major problem of Chinese society was to satisfy economic needs so as to ensure sheer survival; hence, the main task of the Communist Party was to grow the economy. In order to do that, development was deemed to be absolutely the top priority. At the 19th National Party Congress in October of 2017, Xi Jinping offered a new definition of the principal contradiction in China: that between "the people's ever-growing need for a better life and unbalanced and inadequate development." By this, Xi means that the main problem in Chinese society is not simply to guarantee that people will survive but to help them attain a better quality of life—politically and socially as well as economically. Thus, the main task of the Communist Party is to seek balanced and adequate development under a system of law-based governance and social justice. Xi's redefinition also means that the principal objective of reform and opening is not primarily to enable some people to get rich, but to promote shared prosperity for everyone.

Xi also has stipulated that the new development plan, extending to the middle of the 21st century, will proceed in two stages. In the first stage, encompassing the years 2020 to 2035, China is tasked with completing its socialist modernization, building upon the foundations created by a moderately prosperous society. In the second stage, from 2035 to 2050, China is supposed to develop into a great modern socialist country, one that is prosperous, strong, democratic, culturally advanced, harmonious, and beautiful. The concrete goals for each stage include bolstering the rights of the people to participate and to develop; reinforcing law-based governance; introducing the rule of law throughout the country, government, and society; launching a more modern social governance system; and much more.

Another aspect of Xi Jinping's strategy involves the "fifth modernization," i.e. the modernization of governance. The main task of Deng Xiaoping's reform and opening was to carry out the four modernizations. The first three modernizations and then the modernization of defense were achieved by generations of the

Chinese leadership, including Xi himself during his first term (2012–2017). In November of 2013, during the 3rd Plenary Session of the 12th National Party Conference, Xi designated the improvement and development of the socialist system with Chinese characteristics and the modernization of the governance system and capabilities as the overall objective of comprehensively deepening reform. In his address to the Central Party School on February 17, 2014, Xi emphasized that "we have to adapt the total process of national modernization, improving the level of scientific ruling, democratic ruling, and law-based government." According to him, the modernization of governance refers not only to the improvement of state capacities but also enhancing the capacity for law-based management of the political as well as the economic, social, and cultural realms. Last but not least, it relates to the ability of the Chinese people to run their own affairs (Xi 2014: 1) Deng Xiaoping's reform and opening mainly concerned economic growth and the survival of the Chinese people, in addition to the survival of the CPC. By contrast, Xi Jinping's comprehensive deepening reform is more focused on ensuring better lives for the Chinese people, coupled with better performance by the Party.

## Conclusion

Throughout the history of Chinese modernization and modernity, we can see that authoritarianism always has been an option for ruling elites in China, especially after a period of chaos or weak leadership. Chiang Kai-shek drifted toward authoritarianism after unifying China in 1928, but with the support of Western powers that were keen to pick a winner to compete with communism. Mao Zedong embraced authoritarianism in an effort to deal with internal and external challenges emanating from both the United States and the Soviet Union. Deng Xiaoping put political authoritarianism in the service of economic development. Finally, Xi Jinping's authoritarianism is designed to meet numerous far more complex domestic challenges and to increase China's power in world affairs.

The Chinese process of modernization and modernity followed a path of learning from the West, and then from former Soviet Union, but those efforts to copy others all failed. Communist leaders such as Deng Xiaoping and Xi Jinping have tried and are still trying to find a Chinese way to economic development and good governance. But China still has a long way to go to realize its ambition.

## References

Casper, G. 1995. *Fragile Democracies: The legacies of authoritarian rule*. Pittsburgh, PA: University of Pittsburgh Press.
Deng Xiaoping. 1993. "Reform and Open-up is a Great Experiment." In Deng Xiaoping, *Collected Works of Deng Xiaoping*. Beijing: People's Publishing House, p. 375.
Hu Qiaomu. 1992. *Collected Works of Hu Qiaomu*. Beijing: People's Publishing House.
Mao Zedong. 1956. "On the Historical Experience of the Dictatorship of the Proletariat." *People's Daily*, May 4.

Mao Zedong. 1976. "On the Ten Major Relationships." *People's Daily*, December 26.

Mao Zedong. 1996. "Answers to the Question of Campbell." In The Party Literature Research Centre of the Central Committee of the CPC (ed.), *Collected Works of Mao Zedong*, vol. 4. Beijing: People's Publishing House, pp. 27–28.

Mao Zedong. 1999. "Speech at the Enlarged Working Meeting of Central Committee." In The Party Literature Research Centre of the Central Committee of the CPC (ed.), *Collected Works of Mao Zedong*. Beijing: People's Publishing House, pp. 295–296.

Wang Qishan. 2016. "Comprehensively Strengthen Party Discipline and Enhance the Political Base of the Ruling Position of the Party." *Qiu Shi Journal* 23: 1–4.

Xi Jinping. 2014. "Improvement and Development of the Socialist System with Chinese Characteristics and Carrying Forward the Modernization of the Governance System and Governance Capacity." *People's Daily*, February 18.

# 6

# THE POLITICAL IDENTITY OF THE EUROPEANS AND THE CHALLENGES OF THE TIME AFTER MODERNITY

*Furio Cerutti*

Time matters in politics. This is clearly the case when one considers the time required to make and implement decisions. But it also applies to the ability, or inability, of political actors to perceive the flow of time: the end of one epoch and the beginning of a new one, the latter characterized by the emergence of new problems and new groups.

In respect to the epoch we are living in, or—as I shall suggest –the one that we are leaving behind, the existence of multiple paths to modernization seems to be a widely acknowledged, non-controversial fact. But in order to grasp the confusing complexity of this matter, we need more precision in our language. In the first section below, I will therefore try to clarify what we mean when we speak of modernity and modernization.

Having thus defined my frame of reference, I shall explain how the political identity of Europeans relates to modernity, and how this identity is essential to the legitimacy of the European Union.

Lastly, I will return to the question of modernity in a more philosophical key, which includes the dimension of the future. I shall argue that the modern pattern of politics is coming to an end due to its inability to provide adequate governance for our globalized planet. This statement holds true in particular with regard to a few global, potentially life-threatening challenges that humankind has brought upon itself. In the era to follow modernity, the legitimacy of a polity will be evaluated largely based on its ability to address those challenges, above all those emanating from nuclear weapons and climate change. When it comes to meeting those challenges, Europe may have unique opportunities.

This is admittedly a complex, perhaps cumbersome agenda. The reader is likely to wish to get to the main floor or *piano nobile* as quickly as possible: that is, the one on which Europeans actually live. But a serious grand tour of the building must begin with its basement, in which the pillars sustaining the entire edifice can be seen.

My starting point is to acknowledge that, in both the academic and the political debate in Western countries, the notion of the modernization process as one exclusively guided by the European and (later) American road map has lost credibility. The normative idea that in order to modernize a country must follow that road map likewise has fallen on hard times. The research efforts the results of which Shmuel Eisenstadt (2000) systematized many years ago under the rubric of "multiple modernities" by now have been endorsed by many historians, sociologists, and philosophers. On another track, the belief that modernization based on industrialization and urbanization must lead to democratization also has been disproven by developments in countries whose economic and social modernization has failed even to enhance respect for citizens' fundamental rights and the rule of law. Since the wide scholarly debate on these issues cannot possibly be charted here, I shall look instead at real political processes, which do indeed speak a very clear language, even though facts always need to be interpreted. For example, the inward-looking, if not isolationist, posture of the Trump administration and its rejection of any so-called globalist temptations can be read as an abandonment of the effort to universalize the American paradigm of modernity. To be sure, even the pretense that one could accomplish such a goal was discredited by the failure of every attempt to create a new world order based on the post-Cold War "Washington Consensus," especially efforts toward that end made under the presidency of George W. Bush (2001–2009).

Does this failure mean that we are now in an unproblematically pluralistic world, in which many paths to modernization—also called "modernities"—coexist in a peaceful and indifferent reciprocity of recognition and toleration? On the one hand, the answer seems to be yes: Hardly any country today is willing to risk escalating tensions or launching wars for the sake of imposing its own model on others. Countries may go to war, but typically they do so either for less ideological reasons, such as national self-assertion, or through miscalculation,[1] which of course would be catastrophic in the nuclear field. On the other hand, the multiplicity of paths to modernization is surrounded by a certain conceptual fog, which I would like to dispel as far as possible. My first suggestion is conceptual and terminological, aimed at establishing a distinction between modernity and modernization, in contrast to the usual tendency to conflate those terms.

## Modernity and modernization

By *modernization* let us understand a set of processes taking place in all sectors of society (though not necessarily with the same speed) characterized by enhanced and frequent innovation, functional differentiation, and on-going rationalization, resulting in a higher net efficiency of the productive and administrative system in both the private and public sectors. Those processes have taken place equally in countries with predominantly market economies (e.g., the UK and US) and those that rely, or relied, heavily on state intervention (e.g., the USSR and Nazi Germany). Moreover, if we look at the political side, we find that these same processes occur under both liberal and authoritarian regimes. Although modernization creates conditions conducive to a higher standard of living for citizens, it does not by itself lead to such a favorable outcome. The crucial factor is how the social product is distributed among classes and groups, an element having much to do with the political, legal, and cultural circumstances under which modernization occurs. To put it in classical Marxian terms, the progress of the productive forces, which leads to increasing wealth in a given society, does not by itself determine whether its members will achieve greater well-being and autonomy, nor does it decide which groups will prosper and which will not. Instead, the outcome depends on how and whether the relationships of production and distribution—in a word, the power relations—are reshaped (Marx 1859).

It is on these grounds that I propose to stop using "modernity" as a synonym for "modernization" (i.e., the outcome of this process) and to reserve it for the civilizational, social, legal, and political formation in which a technical, organizational, and administrative logic of modernization is embedded. From this it follows that the several stages of the modernization process[2] can be embedded in *modernities* as different as the liberal and democratic or the authoritarian and even the totalitarian ones, or in regimes that either do or do not respect and promote the autonomy of the individual. Personal autonomy, in any case, underlies a stable and legitimate political order: or at least as stable as it gets in the realm of politics, where conflict and change are essential elements.

Given these assumptions, the next step is to highlight the specific features of European modernity, which also lie at the heart of the present European identity. The concept of the "modern" was invented by Europeans intellectuals in order to define their attitude towards antiquity. Indeed, the very idea of considering one's own collective life in historical perspective was specifically European and in time was applied even to the Holy Scriptures, one of the roots of European civilization along with the Greek and Roman cultures. In sixteenth-century Tuscany, Giorgio Vasari, the first historian of art, defined the painting of his contemporaries from Leonardo da Vinci onward as *"maniera moderna"* (Vasari 1550). A century later, French literati engaged in the famous and politically laden *querelle des anciens et des modernes*, which found resonance in other countries as well. Modernity came to be seen, particularly during the Enlightenment period, as a new era in the history of civilization, characterized by a positive attitude towards individual autonomy, independence from external (religious and/or ideological) authorities, equal respect for all citizens/humans, bottom-up or contractual associations establishing the polity, and critical respect for the scientific exploration of the universe inspired by curiosity. Technical and industrial modernization accompanied Europe's progress towards modernity, but the latter esteems civilizational, ethical, and political values and aims, which modernization does not. The intertwinement of modernization and modernity is a complex and tricky phenomenon, in which the ideal features of European modernity as described above have been twisted or corrupted time and again by hubris in the transformation of nature, the steadily growing destructiveness of our weaponry, and the distortion of the qualities of individuals inside what Max Weber termed the "iron cage" of modern work. Two additional poisons generated by the will to dominate nature and society are racism and colonialism, arising from a modernization process not restrained by modernity's universalistic values and principles. The grounding fathers of Critical Theory, Max Horkheimer and Theodor W. Adorno, dubbed this poisoned intertwinement a "dialectic of Enlightenment" (Horkheimer & Adorno, 1947). But the attitude to self-criticism, a distinctive feature of the European mind that came to maturity in the nineteenth (Marx and Nietzsche) and twentieth centuries, already had surfaced at the beginning of the modernization process—for example, in the Dominican friar Bartolomé de las Casas's condemnation of the horrors perpetrated by Europeans in the Americas (de las Casas 1550).

Nowhere was this dialectic easier to grasp than in the deeds of the modern state, which took shape mainly in the seventeenth and eighteenth centuries in the great kingdoms of France, Britain, Austria, and Spain as well as in the *ius publicum europaeum*, the legal net binding them together after the Westphalian Treaties of 1648.[3] The corresponding international order lasted until 1914 before collapsing in the two world wars. The foundering of that order made room for the attempt to build a new and different structure of interstate relations in the form of the United Nations. Such was the *political* modernity born in Europe, with all its accomplishments and downsides; many of its features, particularly the organization of the state, later spread across the world with local adaptations. To anticipate, I shall argue in the final section of this chapter that the modern political order has become incapable of grappling with new challenges in a way comparable to what the modern state did with the challenges of the early post-medieval period. But let us first look more closely at some specifically European developments.

## The political identity of Europeans and the project of modernity

What has this discussion to do with European identity?

To answer that question, we first need to know what exactly we are talking about, since "identity" is a notoriously treacherous word. In my view, we are dealing neither with a hodgepodge of every possible component (social, cultural, religious, personal) of identity, nor with a monster from the past—impossible to modify—that shapes and controls the minds of present-day human beings. Rather, we will focus on *political* identity as the ongoing process in which a nation, party, or a movement defines and redefines the values, principles, and goals it wants to pursue. However, we should not neglect to consider the memories and symbols that such nations, parties, or movements recognize as their own. We call "identity" what the citizens have on their minds, not what a philosopher or politician tells them to acknowledge as the glue that holds them together. "European identity" is an inevitable, but perhaps confusing, abbreviation for "the political identity of the Europeans." That expression, in turn, by now refers primarily to the citizens of the European Union.[4]

As is the case especially with fledgling polities, European identity contains a strong normative element, one that gives rise to a project. It is not simply what Europeans think of themselves at any given moment, as we might suppose when consulting the Eurobarometer. It also refers to what they hope and intend that Europe should become with regard to its citizens' beliefs, ties to their respective countries, and relations with the rest of the world. The bedrock commitment that enables at least a majority of Europeans to share the values of liberal and social democracy for the common polity is their positive attitude toward and acceptance of difference, diversity, and peacefully regulated conflict. The cooperation and integration of 28 countries would not have been possible without these basic attitudes. In the wake of World War II, i.e., since roughly 1945, Europeans finally learned the lessons of the continent's tragic twentieth-century history. Taking a longer time span into account, one that would include Hitler and Napoleon before him, it has become clear that Europe cannot be unified by the sword, but only by the word: that is, by the many (sometimes far too many) words set forth in treaties, international conferences, and parliamentary or diplomatic discussions. Or, if we prefer to consider more sophisticated discourses, we might cite the words rooted in an intellectual tradition that dates back at least to the Renaissance, the Enlightenment, and the rise of socialist thought. Oddly enough, this tradition developed alongside, and in spite of, the many wars fought among Europeans peoples. Unfortunately, that tradition proved too weak to prevent the peak of destructive racism represented by the Shoah. Developments since 1945 have given the European polity as well as its citizens the peaceful and tolerant character that is appreciated by other countries. Nevertheless, those developments and the intellectual scaffolding that supports them do not help make its decisions either timely or well-defined.

But is this political identity of the Europeans a reality, or only an intellectual blueprint? The notion that the EU exists and has sway in the life of the people used to be confined to elites, but is now much more widely shared (68% feel like citizens of the European Union, while 31% do not). The increased salience of the EU to its citizens likely has arisen because the Union has played a major and visible, if not often felicitous, role in the management of issues of large concern to everyone, such as immigration, food safety, disaster relief, and the economic and financial crisis that emerged after 2008. During the last seven or eight years, those same factors have diminished the citizens' trust in the EU to 42% (Union-wide), against 47% who do not trust it. Those statistics match up neatly with opinions about the EU's image. A high percentage (37%) of respondents say they are neutral about the image of the Union, while 40% see it positively and 21% see it negatively.[5] The degree of citizens' identification with the Union, which—unlike the nation-state—remains a voluntary association, and their approval of its policies and performance are very much subject to the ability of its leaders and institutions to provide peace, the recovery of prosperity, and correct answers to challenges like immigration. And yet another factor influences their responses as well: a feeling on the citizens' part that the results achieved on matters such as peace and prosperity reflect a type of regime corresponding to the model(s) of good governance that they themselves have in mind. Both political and civic dimensions come into play here. The definitive abolition of the death penalty and the active pursuit of gender equality and non-discrimination based on a person's sexual orientation are constitutive elements of European identity, not just of European law. It should go without saying that laws (including the Treaties and EU ordinary laws and regulations) and political debates (in which principles and goals are discussed and embedded) are valuable sources for studying the political identity of the Europeans, in addition to the more commonly employed opinion surveys and other tools of social scientific inquiry. To sum up, while nothing is ever definitive in politics, that statement holds especially true for a fledgling post-national polity, one that is not a state in the traditional sense and is existentially threatened at times by phenomena like the resurgence of nationalism and protectionism or the rise of populism. The latter poses the greatest danger to present-day democracies and in particular the European experiment, because it assails the legitimacy of representation and undermines constitutional limits to power.

Legitimacy, political legitimacy: This is what explains the importance of political identity in Europe as well as elsewhere. In any type of regime, but especially a liberal democracy, institutions and leadership cannot be regarded as legitimate unless a substantial majority of citizens believes that it makes sense to live together under the same principles and goals, however numerous the manageable differences between actors might be. In the EU the problem of legitimacy is particularly complicated due to the fact that the allegiance of citizens is split between the Union and its member states. Regardless, we might initially want to read the uncertainty or even paralysis of European governance that has characterized entire periods after the 2008 crisis as indicating a retreat of the political identity of the Europeans. The same can be said of the present drift of the Visegrád countries (Poland, Hungary, Slovakia, and the Czech Republic), and more recently of Austria, toward defining themselves as "illiberal democracies" as well as Christian bulwarks against Muslim immigration. These trends amount to the rise of a "Fortress Europe" identity. The broad support for such a defensive mentality offers evidence that the struggle over identity is not a sideshow distracting attention from more substantial (e.g., economic) conflicts. Instead, it appears to be an independent and major factor in political life (note that there is no immigration from Muslim countries to the Eastern EU-member states, but debates over identity persist there nevertheless). Furthermore, a slim majority of Britons, always opposed to integrating their British identity into the European one, voted in 2016 to pull their kingdom out of the Union.

It is clear that the political identity of the Europeans changes in response to crises, and varies in time and place; yet through all that it remains a hot topic of cultural debate and political struggle. To be sure, democracies—even if older and located in traditional nation-states—do not escape these oscillations, which are only natural in a free society. Nevertheless, quarrels over identity can endanger the very existence of a "federative" union of states such as the European Union, even though it is not a "federal" United States of Europe and is unlikely to become one any time soon. In any case, as far as it stands and grows, the political identity of the Europeans, including the words, values, and attitudes that inform it, embodies the spirit and the project of European modernity. This project includes the ability to engage in self-criticism and accept revision: skills learned during the late 19th and early 20th centuries, during which the very intellectual legitimacy of modernity—the *Legitimität der Moderne,* as Hans Blumenberg (1985) put it—was contested by Nietzsche, Heidegger, and far-right thinkers.[6]

## New threats, new politics?

The vagaries of European politics and identity-formation suggest that we should regard the close relationship between this identity and the project of European modernity as a token of the continent's maturity in the face of unresolved problems. But that is not the only reason to draw such a conclusion. If, as I shall argue, we are leaving political modernity behind, the coincidence of those factors does not suffice to bolster Europeans' pride in themselves or their readiness for times to come. Let us examine the different structures of the two eras we are comparing.

Political modernity in Europe—the era lasting from the Westphalian Treaties of 1648 to the outbreak of the Great War in 1914 or, more definitively, the end of the Second World War in 1945—was based on a plurality of sovereign states, each claiming to provide for the safety and well-being of its citizens. In more general terms, political modernity as configured in Europe was based on the following principles and circumstances:

- Moderate challenges. In the worst case, what was at stake in human conflicts were the lives of individuals and/or the freedom of a people.
- Technology as a morally neutral tool.
- The unfolding of armed conflicts in a narrow time horizon and a stable civilizational environment. (Even after World War II, it still was possible to rebuild cities, industries, and stable societies in 10–15 years, the shadow of the Cold War notwithstanding).
- A disjunctive system of external security provided by the single state (i.e., I feel more secure if you feel less so).
- The principle of *salus reipublicae suprema lex* (the safety of the commonwealth as the supreme norm).

Let us turn the page: we ourselves—not just our offspring, and not just in Europe—are already living in a very different world. At the end of modernity, we are confronted with:

- Anthropogenic threats that are global and lethal: global because they are capable of hitting everyone on Earth and can be sensibly addressed only by the near totality of political actors; lethal because they endanger the survival of civilization itself (understood here as consisting of agriculture, trade, communication, and the legal framework enabling those activities) without which human life as we know it would become difficult if not impossible.[7]

- Technologies that have evolved far beyond the status of mere instruments. Indeed, it has become morally problematic partly because it can generate products such as AI or human biotechnology that, if misused for the aim of domination, would enter the list of man-made lethal challenges.
- The need to consider in our decision-making the welfare of human beings who will live in the distant future, since we already possess some scientific knowledge of what our actions or omissions might inflict upon them (see below).
- A global commons such as the atmosphere that must be preserved or lost as a whole (see below).
- A world in which *salus reipublicae* is possible only within *salus humani generis*.
- The insufficiency of the state as a provider of security, even while being at the same time a creator of utter insecurity. Thus, the modern "security dilemma" as defined in international relations theory culminates in a nuclear balance of terror.

As mentioned previously, one important change in the political decision-making context that has emerged in the time after modernity[8] is the new and enhanced role of "the future" for policymaking. No longer simply a scenario conjured up by the utopian visions of poets and prophets, the future—or rather the scientific, verifiable knowledge of it—has become available to decision-makers to an unprecedented, though still limited, degree. This observation holds true primarily in the case of projections concerning three potential disasters: global warming, lesser damages to our environment both globally and locally, and the foreseeable physical, medical, and economic consequences of a nuclear exchange. However, there are other, non-lethal challenges, the future impacts of which can be forecast with a high degree of probability. An important case of this kind concerns the future of social security, notably its financial and demographic sustainability. This issue matters because social security measures constitute a pillar of public support for liberal democracy.

The growing importance of the future and of scientific prognoses about it highlights the renewed relevance of futurology for policymaking. The salience of predictions underscores the importance of reinforcing the links between science and politics against the disdain of populists and their efforts to distort or dismiss it. It also redefines the relationship between politics and moral or legal normativity in a way that is different from their prevailing separation in European modernity. To be clear, if we propose to take upon ourselves (say) the economic and mental costs of redefining our way of producing and consuming in a carbon-free manner, we need to develop moral and philosophical reasons for doing so, thus motivating our solidarity towards generations of the far future. But such reasons and motivations are far from self-evident or uncontested; they need to be subjects of debate. Self-interest, however enlightened it may be, will never provide an adequate foundation for solidarity with the unborn.

All things considered, at the interface between political modernity and post-modernity a change seems to be occurring in the very definition of politics. Politics in general and modern politics in particular (let us call it Politics #1) were dominated by conflicts among groups, countries, and parties over scarce and divisible goods, both material and relational, such as territory and prestige. But it appears that in our era a different type of politics (Politics #2) is emerging, which we may characterize as an *activity aimed at saving and managing the global commons not only for the inhabitants of the present but also in behalf of future generations.* This emerging bipolarity of politics is neither a wish nor a normative statement, but rather a conceptual innovation made in the attempt to interpret real processes. Initiatives such as the Paris Climate Accord can be understood only as results of the changing attitude underlying Politics #2. Unfortunately, nothing similar is happening in the area characterized by the other lethal threat, the existence of nuclear weapons, of which proliferation is only an aggravating side-effect. Only the replacement of the unreliable deterrence regime by a commitment to general disarmament, accompanied by a robust enforcement regime, would signal real progress. But we are very far from achieving anything that approximates such an outcome.

Politics #2, the indicator of post-modern times, is obviously not destined to replace the adversarial politics we all know too well. Any utopianism is misplaced in the face of unprecedented man-made threats that can be called challenges only insofar as they are introduced into our political agenda. The two models of politics will coexist, sometimes colliding and sometimes compromising with each other. And Politics #1 will often attempt to strangle Politics #2 in the cradle, as we have recently seen with the Trump administration's withdrawal from the climate agreement. Due to its post-national structure, lack of a nuclear arsenal,[9] and laudable record in climate policy, the European Union is in a good position to further Politics #2 or to bring about acceptable compromises, provided it can summon up enough political will to play a more active role. The struggle against nationalist populism and the energetic reaffirmation of the original European identity are decisive in this regard (Cerutti 2008).

To the extent that post-modern Politics #2 is able to survive and flourish, it has the potential to open up a new terrain of dialogue and cooperation even among countries and cultures whose "multiple modernities" with regard to the underlying models of good governance and the limits to be set on political power differ in seemingly irreconcilable ways. Cooperation in efforts to counter lethal threats to humankind, especially in behalf of future generations, can coexist with clear statements of differences in the conception and practice of governance. This is the case despite the fact that recent domestic developments in China and Russia seem poised to sharpen rather than downplay those differences. The convergence of the EU and China with reference to climate policy could set a good example of how cooperation on ultimate issues might work in spite of divergent notions of governance.[10] But at the same time, the destiny of modernity depends on making nuclear war impossible. Here, we cannot yet discern any light at the end of the tunnel, while new and unexpected concerns keep emerging.

## Acknowledgment

This chapter is dedicated to the dear memory of Zhu Liqun of China Foreign Affairs University. She remains unforgettable to her friends and colleagues from both East and West.

## Notes

1 See the speech given by nuclear scientist and policy-maker Ernest J. Moniz (2017).
2 On globalization and modernization, see the contribution by Lewis Hinchman to this volume (Chapter 4). See also Cerutti (2014).
3 See the classical account of the rise of European public law given by Schmitt (2006).
4 My notion of European political identity is explained in Cerutti (2008).
5 All these figures are from Eurobarometer (2017).
6 On the value and meaning of freedom in the European tradition, cf. Martin Chung's contribution to this volume.
7 My notion of global and lethal challenges comes close to Qin Yaqing's "transnational threats," as described in Chapter 9 of the present volume. But it is restricted to those—nuclear weapons and global warming, notwithstanding their different dynamics—that can endanger human civilization as a whole, similar to the threats to life and limb that Thomas Hobbes saw as the motives inducing individuals to leave the state of nature and take refuge in the polity. For further discussion see Cerutti (2007).
8 For that time I am otherwise using the term "post-modern" with a hyphen in order to distinguish it from mainstream postmodernism, a school of thought that has contributed poorly to the understanding of what happens at the end of the modern era.
9 The French phrase *force de frappe* could be "Europeanized" and used as a bargaining chip in worldwide disarmament negotiations.
10 On the primary role of multilateral institutions, see Chapter 9 in this volume by Qin Yaqing, who insists on the need to make them capable of managing the global commons, and Chapter 7 by Mario Telò.

## References

Blumenberg, H. 1985. *The Legitimacy of the Modern Age*. Cambridge, MA: MIT Press.
Cerutti, F. 2007. *Global Challenges for Leviathan: A political philosophy of nuclear weapons and global warming*. Lanham, MD: Rowman & Littlefield.
Cerutti, F. 2008. "Why Political Identity and Legitimacy Matter in the European Union." In Furio Cerutti & Sonia Lucarelli (eds.), *The Search for a European Identity*. London: Routledge, pp. 3–22.
Cerutti, F. 2014. "Two Global Challanges to Global Governance: A Philosophical View." In Zhu Liqun, F. Cerutti, & Lu Jing (eds.), 全球治理: 挑战与趋势 [*Global Governance: Challenges and trends*]. Beijing: 社会科学文献出版社 (Social Science Academic Press), pp. 1–15.
de las Casas, B. 1550. *A Short Account of the Destruction of the Indies*. Available at www.colum bia.edu/cgi-bin/cul/resolve?AUL4333.
Eisenstadt, S. 2000. "Multiple Modernities." *Daedalus* 129(1): 1–29.
Eurobarometer. 2017. "Standard Eurobarometer 87." Available at http://ec.europa.eu/comm frontoffice/publicopinion/index.cfm/Survey/getSurveyDetail/instruments/STANDARD/ surveyKy/2142.
Horkheimer, M. & T. Adorno. 1947. *Dialectic of Enlightenment*. New York: Seabury Press (1972 reissue).

Marx, K. 1859. "Preface." In K. Marx, *A Contribution to the Critique of Political Economy*. Available at www.marxists.org/archive/marx/works/1859/critique-pol-economy/preface.htm.
Moniz, E. 2017. "Ernest J. Moniz Addresses Global Nuclear Risks." Available at www.belforcenter.org/index.php/publication/ernest-j-moniz-addresses-global-nuclear-risks.
Schmitt, C. 2006. *The Nomos of the Earth in the International Law of the Jus Publicum Europaeum*. Candor, NY: Telos.
Vasari, G. 1550. *The Lives of the Artists*. Oxford: Oxford University Press (1991 reissue).

# 7

# MULTIPLE MODERNITIES IN A MULTIPOLAR AND MULTIREGIONAL WORLD

## Some conditions for an interregional dialogue

*Mario Telò*

### Addressing multiple modernities through a multidisciplinary dialogue

Political science and European Union studies must go beyond a unidirectional multidisciplinary approach—in effect, a dialogue with economics, which favors functionalist theories—and rediscover the philosophical, historical, cultural, and territorial dimensions of politics as alternatives to technocratic governance. But a more historically-minded version of multiple modernities would also stand in marked contrast to the theories of the "hyperglobalizers" and the "new medievalists" (Gamble 2014).

However, this new multidisciplinary approach—more open to the cultural, territorial, and historical dimensions of politics—should not be confused with traditional "geopolitics" (a state-centric discipline) or with the view of regional civilizations as mutually exclusive (Huntington 1996). Instead, following Fernand Braudel's *"longue durée"* approach (Braudel 1958) and historical institutionalism (Hall & Taylor 1996; Steinmo *et al.* 1992; Scharpf & Schmitter 1995), we should examine the relevance of national and regional institutional legacies in the context of larger territorial entities, such as macro-regions. The version of historical inquiry recommended here also has the virtue of offering alternatives to exclusive national populism, on the one hand, and traditional cosmopolitanism, on the other. Finally, it enables us to distinguish clearly between cultural and political identity at the regional level (Cerutti *et al.* 2011).

### Deepening the definition and the current dynamics of "regions"

Why do "macro-regions" (or simply "regions") matter? The international multidisciplinary literature of the last 50 years distinguishes between economic regionalization and political regionalism. It defines regionalism as a structural feature of increasingly multilevel global governance. By "region," the scholarly literature understands more than just the regional dimension of economic and trade regionalization. Instead, it conceptualizes the multidimensional and institutionalized cooperation among neighboring states and societies, diffused across every continent. To understand the full meaning and trajectory of such cooperation, one somehow must include its historical and cultural background. Rather than representing simple functional differentiation within the same model of globalization and modernity, each region displays its own distinctive path to modernity, combining divergences and convergences with alternative paths.

We also can distinguish between region and regionalism. A deeper definition of regionalism would portray it as a region including policies, politics, and incipient polities. Over the last 30 years, scholars have made progress in that direction, as a comparison of the following statements makes clear:

(A)   "Regionalism means that a limited number of states, linked by geographic proximity and reciprocal complex interdependence" integrate their development (Nye 1968).

(B)   "Regionalism is a various and multi-dimensional institutionalized set of multilateral cooperation among interdependent neighboring states and societies" (Telò 2014).

Our approach to regionalism also includes a certain degree of "regionness": that is, the historical and cultural background of regional entities as Björn Hettne (2008) originally put it. The concept of "cognitive regionalism," based on constructivist literature and underlining the increasing weight of identity needs, shared perceptions, and feeling of common belonging, also can enrich our understanding of the phenomenon (Acharya 2013; see also Chapter 9, this volume).

The development of regional cooperation among neighboring countries on every continent is driven both by endogenous and exogenous factors. Enumerating those factors may help answer two crucial questions: Why is regionalism resilient over time, and what current challenges does it face?

(A)   **Endogenous drivers** (Gamble & Payne 1996; Hettne et al. 2001; Fawcett & Hurrell 1995; Milner & Mansfield 1997; Telò 2014) include:

- Trade interests, economic lobbying, and social factors, and the role of transnational civil society networks and cities in better framing their global networking (Bhagwati 1992; Baldwin 2001).
- Political factors, as when states seek to recapture their declining or lost sovereignty (endangered by globalization), strengthen their capacity to prevent regional conflict, or support domestic democratic consolidation.

Taken together, these developments help to explain the diffusion of a bottom-up regional cooperation, parallel to democratization, during the Eighties and Nineties on every continent. ASEAN, MERCOSUR, the EU, and SADC represent some of the more successful examples. Contemporaneous academic literature defined this wave as "new regionalist" to underline the distinction between it and the top-down regionalism that prevailed during the decades of US hegemony.

(B)   **Exogenous drivers** include the globalization process and the end of the bipolar world. But, in addition, we are witnessing structural and enduring causes of regionalism, accompanied by some serious challenges:

- Challenges associated with global governance, efficiency gaps, and legitimacy deficits in global multilateral organizations like the UN, WTO, IMF, and FAO. Does improved regional cooperation complement alternative paths to liberalization and improved governance efficiency and legitimacy?
- Challenges related to the global power system. Does the end of the bipolar world in 1991 and the rise of the multipolar system provide space for the emergence of new regional actors, especially given current political uncertainty and unpredictability?
- Challenges stemming from cultural globalization and the top-down model of Western global modernity. These forces often provoke a fundamentalist or exclusivist identitarian backlash. Under what conditions can regionalism offer a third way: a liberal version of communitarianism/republicanism that mediates between the American model of modernization, on the one hand, and exclusivist nationalism or ethnic/religious localism, on the other?

## The impact of economic and political-military multipolarity on regionalism

The world clearly has become multipolar following the failure of the George W. Bush administration's efforts (2001–2008) to replace the bipolar power structure that collapsed in 1991 by a unipolar, US-centered system. Of course, multipolarity is only a descriptive concept. As such, it is not in principle hostile to regional and global multidimensional and multilateral cooperation. However, in some cases, it is reshaping regionalism in a variety of ways, both instrumental/hierarchical and non-multilateral. Two questions arise here.

First, as the power players in an increasingly multipolar world seek greater security, is the emerging "military multipolarity" affecting regionalism? The hard power and military dimension of that kind of diversity shows an asymmetrical multipolarism. Let us look first at defense budgets, summarized in the following table, as an indicator of power shifts.

**TABLE 7.1** Defense budgets of selected countries

| Country | Defense budget | Percentage of GDP | Remarks |
|---|---|---|---|
| USA | $611,186,000,000 | 3.3% | This sum amounts to almost 50% of global defense spending. |
| China | $215,176,000,000 | 1.9% | Contrary to conventional wisdom, the gap between China's defense budget and that of the USA is increasing every year. |
| Russia | $69,245,000,000 | 5.3% | This sum entitles Russia to be considered a military as well as an energy power. |
| India | $55,923,000,000 | 2.5% | Increasing. |
| France | $55,745,000,000 | 2.3% | Decreasing since 1989. |
| UK | $48,263,000,000 | 1.9% | Decreasing since 1989; however, the looming Brexit may affect its defense posture and budget. |
| Japan | $46,126,000,000 | 1.0% | $48 billion in 2018, increasing in the context of the regional balance of power. |
| Saudi Arabia | $44,243,000,000 | 1.3% | Increasing. |
| Germany | $41,067,000,000 | 1.2% | Decreasing since 1989. |
| Italy | $27,934,000,000 | 1.5% | Decreasing since 1989. |
| Brazil | $23,700,000,000 | 1.3% | Increasing. |
| Spain | $14,893,000,000 | 1.0% | Decreasing since 1989. |

*Source:* SIPRI (2016).
Note: Figures given in constant 2015 US dollars.

On this particular point we may conclude that in the context of the current asymmetrical multipolarity, it would be premature to talk about an emerging new bipolarism (US/China). Therefore, plenty of room still exists for autonomous players, whether states or regions. However, power politics, on the one hand, and fragmentation, on the other (Haass 2008), risk affecting the multilayered institutionalization of international life, including regional cooperation.

Second, how does the economic dimension of global power shifts bring about relevant asymmetrical gains, convergence, and divergence in the context of the current "great transformation"? Since 2007–2008, shifts in global economic power have been quite dramatic. The emerging economies are on the way to overtaking some of their Western counterparts, thus reversing a century of domination. The economic and financial crisis that began in those years accelerated this *"longue durée"* process (in the understanding of the French historian Fernand Braudel, 1958), with extremely destabilizing social and political consequences for Western domestic politics. Populism—to cite but one example—has long-term, structural economic causes. Brexit, the election of Donald Trump, and the onslaught of the extreme right in Europe are just a few of its consequences. In theoretical terms, populism should be studied through historical institutionalism, since that approach can capture the complexity and variety of its forms based on the framing effect of turning points. Economic and political changes are provoking a new "great transformation" comparable to the one described by Karl Polanyi (1944) in respect to the first half of the 20th century. The emergence of a multipolar world and the persistent economic crisis may be seen as critical junctures that are launching a new era (Telò 2016; Telò, Sapir, & Sassoon 2017).

In this new era, the economic dimension of capitalist diversity within the changing globalized economy shows both competition and complementarity among various socio-economic models, such as the following.

- *China*: An example of export-led state capitalism modified by increasing focus on the country's domestic market (public debt, high financial interdependence with the US and trade interdependence with the EU). China now will have to face the challenge of carrying out the domestic reforms addressed by the 19th Congress and the Xi Jinping speech.
- *The EU*: A social market economy centered on the Eurozone. It now confronts the challenge of strengthening centralized Eurozone governance while addressing decentralized domestic reforms.
- *The US*: Neo-liberal capitalism with a recent protectionist trend and unpredictable economic future because of contradictory Federal Reserve Board and administration objectives.

The varieties of capitalism increase when we consider the respective models of India, Brazil, and South Africa, variously combining openness and protection and other distinctive national/regional ways.

Let us draw a few conclusions from what has been said. Contrary to the conventional wisdom of the first two decades after 1991, the globalized economy is not characterized by increasing convergence. Asymmetrical gains, competition, and diversity all matter within the enhanced globalized economic interdependence. The global institutional framework has adapted partially to the new conditions, yet often remains deadlocked (e.g., the WTO); is moderately resilient but unable to reform (e.g., the IMF and the UN Security Council); and although it appears somewhat more multilayered than in the past (various regional organizations and interregional arrangements), yet is also partially divided and competitive (e.g., US protectionism and alternative multilateralism, as in the AIIB).

## The cultural dimension of regional "cultural identities"

The cultural dimension of the critical juncture we have been discussing deserves special emphasis. How is that aspect of regional integration affected by a form of multipolarity characterized by major power asymmetries and economic diversity, as depicted above?

The various cultural legacies interact with the new dialectic between global modernity and the regional revolt of losers, victims of the "globalization malaise" (Berger 2016). The populist wave in Western politics is not merely the outcome of cynical manipulation by nationalist leaders. The middle and working classes are often handicapped by global shifts of economic power, as figures show; they express dissatisfaction by rebelling against elites, whom they consider to be guilty of openness to globalization and its consequences (trade and migration flows) and mobilize in favor of protectionism, inward-looking nationalism, and other illiberal trends.

Populist parties and leaders channel the upheaval against globalized elites, particularly in the West. The so-called "populist explosion" (Judis 2017) fosters exclusive communitarianism (cf. Chapter 1, this volume), while heightening feelings of common belonging and stoking defensive identity concerns. Is Judis right to emphasize, in contrast to the hyper-globalizers, the shift from multiple modernities toward exclusive regional civilizations and identities? Is the coming scenario even more fragmented towards micro-identities than the one forecast by Huntington (1996)?

First, we should distinguish between cultural and political identities (Cerutti 2017). The concept of "cultural identity" is both controversial and fragile (Jullien 2017). According to cultural fundamentalists, there is an apparently long-term trend towards strengthening "cultural identities" as exclusive forms of self-definition, including at the regional level. What is serious in this thesis? What is changing?

- By manipulating discourse about "Asian values" versus "Western values," Dr. Mahathir Mohammed, Malaysia's longest-serving leader, was influential enough to justify the exclusion of an important trading partner, Australia, from ASEAN. True, when we consider the softer and more inclusive RCEP (ASEAN + 6), this exclusive approach seems to be on the way out, since the broader trade bloc now does include Australia and New Zealand. However, in Southeast Asia we are witnessing a renewed upsurge of the exclusive identity approach, revived by Myanmar's violation of human rights of Muslim Rohingyas.
- The European People's Party's rhetoric portrays the "EU as a Christian club" that should exclude Turkey and other non-Christian applicant countries on religious grounds. However, such xenophobia seems dated. Membership negotiations with Turkey have stalled not because Turkey is non-Christian, but because of the authoritarian Erdoğan regime's lack of respect for human rights and democratic values. And yet, a remnant of this exclusive Christian identity approach may be resurgent on a smaller scale: Witness the illiberal Hungarian regime led by Premier Orbán, the violations of the rule of law by Polish leader Kaczyński and the newly formed right-wing coalition under

Austrian Chancellor Kunz. Ironically, these outbursts of populism are happening at a time when Pope Francis strongly argues in favor of a somewhat more ecumenical Christian identity.

- ALBA, a regional organization created in 2004 by Hugo Chavez, the late President of Venezuela, emphasized South American revolutionary unity against the imperialist "gringos." For a while, ALBA exerted influence over various countries. But when Venezuela's government began its slide into dictatorship under Nicholás Maduro, it became increasingly isolated, having been suspended from MERCOSUR. Now its anti-imperialist rhetoric appears self-serving and outmoded. However, both left-wing and right-wing populist discourses of exclusion are emerging in Brazil and other countries (cf. Chapter 3, this volume).

These forms of manipulation of diffused needs for shared belonging by the losers in the globalized economy have been revived in a stronger and more vocal form during the last decade. The national protectionist message delivered by Donald Trump is worrying both because it vitiates the claims to political leadership by the United States and because it tarnishes the country's image and moral authority. On some continents, Trump's isolationist message and actions risk undermining the credibility of the Western alliance and jeopardizing the West's traditional contribution to universal values. Defending policies that favor "America first," building walls against immigrants from Latin America and Arab countries, discarding previous multilateral commitments, and abandoning the free trade approach to international commerce all will have *longue durée* consequences, such as reviving and strengthening anti-Americanism and anti-Western movements while exacerbating backlashes focused on exclusive identities elsewhere in the world.

## Global continuity and discontinuity: In the context of the unpredictable epoch that lies ahead, what can be said about the evolving features of regionalism?

The institutionalization of international life continues, even progressing at regional, interregional and global levels, where it is supported increasingly by civil society networks and civic participation. However, there is evidence that implementation deficits and legitimacy gaps are developing in the global institutional network. The newly emergent major historical junctures alluded to above are affecting regional and multilateral cooperation. In this context regionalism is becoming much more ambiguous than before.

On the one hand, democratic regionalism—the best framework we have for understanding the convergence and cooperation characteristic of multiple modernities—is expanding on every continent as a structural feature of increasingly-multilayered global governance. By some accounts, we will have more multidimensional regionalism in the world of the 21st century than we did during the 20th. Moreover, in certain cases (e.g., the EU, ASEAN, MERCOSUR), democratic regionalism looks rather impervious to economic and political crises even when it confronts factors that might lead to disintegration.

On the other hand, new competitive, instrumental, and authoritarian regional/ interregional arrangements are emerging. While it is true that such arrangements (e.g., BRICS) seem to be compatible with the principles of regional cooperation, some member countries tend to prefer a hierarchical and instrumental understanding of regional cooperation. Many examples confirm this interpretation. For instance, Russia's President, Vladimir Putin, has assembled a Eurasian Community dominated by his own country: Saudi Arabia has launched the Gulf Cooperation Council (GCC); and Venezuela, as previously noted, has spearheaded ALBA. Regionalism is currently becoming a more variegated and ambiguous feature of the global changes wrought by post-free-trade liberalism. In other words, regional and interregional trade arrangements are driven by alternative political/security objectives and factors rather than by economic rationality. Competitive regionalism leads to hierarchical spheres of influence in the Westphalian style while potentially sparking political and/or military conflicts of the sort we see in Ukraine (provoked by the Eurasian Community) or in Qatar (backed by the GCC). Competitive regionalism supports non-democratic domestic practices. It is exclusive and hierarchical rather than open and multilateral. In some cases, the concept of "counter-multilateralism" may be applicable (Keohane & Morse 2015).

## The crisis of the concept of "the West"

The changes occurring within the West are particularly ambiguous. Under Barack Obama, the United States seemed bent on crafting large-scale arrangements with its allies aimed at achieving greater security and geopolitical interregionalism, such as the Transatlantic Trade and Investment Partnership (TTIP) and the Trans-Pacific Partnership (TTP). By contrast, since Donald Trump's election in 2016, the US has tilted toward policies of protectionism and trade wars expressive of its more inward-looking nationalism. Obama evidently hoped to reinvigorate the Western community in a geopolitical form, even expanding it to include Japan in the Pacific area, thereby creating a trilateral trade and security bloc. The TTIP was seen by many as a sort of economic version of NATO, while the TPP was supposed to be an "all but China" alliance. Those efforts were rolled back by Trump, who initiated dramatic changes in American policy. "America first," Trump's campaign and policy slogan, combines national protectionism with arrogant transactional bilateralism. It expresses hostility toward every kind of regional and global multilateral arrangement, regime, or organization, including NAFTA, the EU, the TPP, and the TTIP. A trade strategy document presented by the Trump Administration to Congress at the beginning of March, 2017 stated explicitly that "it is time for a more aggressive approach." That document was meant to justify violations of existing trade and security arrangements, the weakening of international organizations, trade wars, and the sharpening of political and cultural conflicts.

Within a very competitive and unstable global context, the new approach taken by the American government aggravated the unpredictable behavior of other players, such as North Korea and Russia, in spite of the resilient role of international community organizations. American actions and the responses that they evoked have multiplied the factors leading to trade wars and political instability.

Does the consequent tendency toward a new transatlantic rift mean that a crisis of the West is impending? The sea change initiated by the Trump administration is not just about abandoning the long-established position of the US as global leader. The president's "America first" rhetoric openly flouts a core tenet of the multilateralism, as announced by Woodrow Wilson in 1919 and pursued with greater success by Franklin D. Roosevelt in 1943–1944. There are parallels to this "go-it-alone" position in the United Kingdom as well.

As is well known, the UK in June of 2016 opted to leave the European Union after 40 years of membership in that body, choosing instead to craft its own trade agreements. Almost two years later, the UK seems to be searching desperately for new ways of engaging with the rest of the world as an individual country. The rhetoric of "taking back control" is in line with Britain's tendency to yearn for the 19th century's "splendid isolation," gazing inwards, protecting its turf, and adopting an antagonistic rather than cooperative position toward other nations. The pro-Brexit discourse about the supposed revival of national sovereignty is associated with the illusory Victorian ideology of "Global Britain."

The evolution of the United States and Great Britain toward nationalism to some extent reflects unique circumstances in the Anglo-Saxon world. However, the trend has met with fierce resistance within both countries. Moreover, it is clear that an alternative political cycle has been playing out in France and Germany since 2017, one that may presage further regional integration. The EU's de facto joint Macron/Merkel leadership may usher in four or five years of stability supported by the economic growth that has followed European Central Bank President Mario Draghi's expansionary "quantitative easing" policy. The US is dismantling cooperation, fostering trade wars, stoking new conflicts, and exacerbating cultural cleavages. Meanwhile, although the EU looks self-confident and assertive, it also increasingly appears to stand alone as a Western defender of multilateralism, cooperation, openness, and peace. That explains why the current discussion about a "decline of the West" has nothing to do with the self-flagellating thesis propounded by Oswald Spengler in the aftermath of World War I.

What is at stake here is a serious split between two alternative approaches to global governance (Habermas 2004) based on alternative versions of modernity expressed in a series of dichotomies: deregulated capitalism (combined with trade protectionism) versus a social market economy; support for the death penalty and racism versus social cohesion and welfare for all; NRA-based ideas of domestic security versus public security policies; nationalism versus international bridge-building and cooperation; the exacerbation of conflict and disputes (including those with friends) versus openness and inclusiveness; the "clash of civilizations" versus global dialogue among multiple modernities.

Furthermore, the general trend towards nationalism that has emerged within the Anglo-Saxon world is antithetical not only to the social market economy, but also to regional cooperation as such (including within NAFTA and the EU) and the multiple multilateral approach of the continental EU. The transatlantic rift, the crisis of the concept of "West," and American policies and attitudes all are pushing Europe and democratic regional organizations generally toward a difficult dilemma: either accepting decline or looking for new ways to be an international actor through enhanced politicization.

## The Chinese strategy: navigating between nationalism and multilateralism

China is taking advantage of the withdrawal of the United States, notably by promoting Asia-Pacific regionalism and adopting a shrewd, proactive, multiple-regional strategy. In effect, Trump is making not America but rather China great again!

The multiple China-centric (de facto) arrangements, institutions, and programs confirmed by the 19th congress of the CCP in 2017 are extremely relevant even if they do raise problems. These include:

- The "Belt and Road" initiative, a huge double interregional project in conjunction with Europe, to be funded by the investment of a trillion dollars.
- The Asian Infrastructure Investment Bank (AIIB) with 84 members, technically at top level and operating according to multilateral rules. De facto, however, the AIIB competes with the IMF and with other regional lenders, such as the Asian Development Bank.
- Strengthening the Shanghai Cooperation Organization (SCO) in Central Asia, an organization that inevitably will compete with the Eurasian Community.
- China-centered, six-party talks on Korea (arguably with insufficient attention to the costs of failure).
- The Regional Comprehensive Economic Partnership (RCEP), a proposed trade agreement among countries that produces 29.5% of global GDP. It is equivalent to the ASEAN + 6 group (Japan, South Korea, China, Australia, New Zealand, and India) and will be an alternative to the shaky TPP, now kept alive through the efforts of Japan and Australia.
- Commitment, at least on the rhetorical level, to interregionalism and various kinds of multilateralism, including the Asia-Europe Meeting (ASEM) and partnerships with Africa and South America.

The Chinese understanding of multilateralism is framed by Chinese ideas and approaches, and much research needs to be conducted on this issue. In the current competitive context, China's neighbors have become more proactive as well. The reaction of India, in spite of its inclusion in ASEAN + 6, is instructive: Together with Japan, it has launched a new "Road of Freedom." Japan, in parallel with its inclusion in ASEAN + 3, participates in trilateral cooperation with South Korea and China and signed a second-generation trade arrangement with the EU at the end of 2017.

## Interregionalism and cultural dialogue

What is the best institutional framework for fostering intercultural dialogue? Multidimensional interregional relations are shaped by both democratic and hierarchical actors. Democratic regional organizations, even if not similar to states, are developing institutional and political identities framed by regional treaties—in some ways comparable to constitutions—that support democracy, human rights, and the rule of law. Examples include the ASEAN Charter for ASEAN, the Treaty of Lisbon for the EU, and the Asunción and Ouro Preto Treaties for MERCOSUR.

Of course, global charters such as the one discussed by Thomas Meyer in Chapter 1 of this volume, the 1966 UN International Covenant on Social and Political Rights, remain highly relevant as well. However, regionalist literature is correct in stressing that regional charters are more efficient and legitimate than global charters and less likely to be discredited by the remoteness of their goals, their too-distant global organization, and their cosmopolitanism. For those reasons, most people tend to see them as examples of wishful thinking and utopianism. The declining centrality of UNESCO and other UN cosmopolitan institutions emphasizes the need to focus on new and improved forms of cooperation—especially regional forms, since they are better designed to accommodate divergent economic, cultural, and political approaches to globalization.

Moreover, we should take into account the resilience of transnational social networks and ties that grew up parallel to economic globalization (cf. Meyer 2014 for a critique of Samuel Huntington). Umberto Eco's understanding of "transcultural relations" (Eco 2007) supports the view that there is a kind of complementarity between bottom-up cultural ties and the new multilateralism. Both include exclusive national and regional identities.

One finding of our research suggests that there may be an alternative understanding of cultural dialogue, less focused on its two traditional forms (interstate and global) and more concerned with the following features that seem well suited to encouraging interregional dialogue.

(A)   The balance between the internal cohesion of a regional actor and its external openness influences its capabilities (Caffarena 2014). In the current competitive context, some models of modernity may include strong internal cohesion policies on the one hand (similar to those of the Roman Empire with its open concept of "citizenship"; cf. Telò 2018), while hampering relations, including trade, with the outside world (the Roman "Limes"). Switzerland provides an excellent example of internal cohesion accompanied by barriers to the outside world. Traditionally, the Swiss have deepened their model of internal democracy by holding frequent referenda, while protecting it against high levels of immigration and resisting solidarity commitments to the EU and global governance. Balancing the requirements of the domestic modernity model against those of greater global openness is the main challenge within a world characterized by multiple modernities.

(B)   Cultural openness does not mean entertaining the superficial illusion that diverse cultures can or should be merged. We find useful the philosopher François Jullien's concept of "*Altérité*" as an alternative to "cultural identity" (Jullien 2017): It is the first step toward a true dialogue between alternative understandings of modernity, aiming to produce and jointly construct the "*commun*." Beyond a merely functional convergence via economic and trade ties and their linguistic equivalent ("Globish"), the dialogue should start by underlining the "*Écart*": that is, *taking critical distance from one's partner.* Concretely, it might mean convening colloquia and open conferences like the ones promoted by the Macau IEEM while multiplying translations as a precondition for a deeper communication. *Écart* implies a willingness to address explicitly (instead of hiding) the divergent conceptual and philosophical foundations of different civilizational backgrounds even while seeking common ground. To cite just one example, the concept of "durability" builds bridges between the EU and China, whereas the Western concept of human rights lacks linguistic equivalents in Mandarin. In this context, the concept of "cultural identities" is replaced by the concept of "cultural resources."

(C)   If we choose the method of holding colloquia that follow *Écart/Commun* principles to initiate cultural dialogue, eventually we must face a crucial question: whether classical—and indispensable—political concepts such as sovereignty, power, the rule of law, and human rights gradually will and should become elements in the shared political language of humankind itself. Accordingly, parallel to the synchronic dimension of multiple modernities addressed by Meyer in Chapter 1, the diachronic dimension, from Westphalian politics to revised Westphalian politics, should be part of the common dialogic agenda (see Chapter 6, this volume). We will focus the concluding paragraph of this chapter precisely on the analysis of this essential question.

(D)   The argument presented so far emphasizes the role of regional and interregional dialogue as the proper global institutional framework for a dialogue among multiple modernities that is capable of transcending the traditional dichotomy between cosmopolitanism and interstate relations. In other words, this article has argued for a set of multidimensional "hybrid interregionalist ties"[1] that will bring forth a "post-revisionist" knowledge strategy. The latter will offer an alternative both to the traditional Eurocentric approach and more recently disseminated Europhobic views (Fawcett et al. 2015).

Interregional relations are increasingly based on reciprocal, fair, multidimensional partnerships (including cultural ties) and dialogues; however, such relations would never succeed without openness in trade. Trade is also a social construction (Wendt 1999). What trade arrangements are needed in the 21st century? Trade can no longer progress through mere free trade agreements alone, because it is also a matter of social and cultural dialogue. Only through "second generation" commercial arrangements that feature effective market regulations, high standards for environmental controls, social concerns, and public procurement, as well as permanent conflict-resolution mechanisms, can trade encourage and frame intercultural dialogue.

In order to conceptualize the new ways of upgrading international trade relations to a complex and rich cultural dimension (beyond globalism, realism, and cosmo-politanism), the concept of dialogue not only should stress the inadequacies of current global-level discussions but also should highlight the enhanced impact of relevant variations among the political cultures of the dialogue partners on inter-regional relations. Some examples are as follows:

- US interregionalism, which includes the Free Trade Area of the Americas (FTAA), Asia-Pacific Economic Cooperation (APEC), and also the TTP and the TTIP, even if Trump is trying to dismantle them.
- EU interregionalism, which includes APC, Asia-Europe Meeting (ASEM), the Asia-Europe Foundation (ASEF), EU-CEPAC, the EU-Canada Compréhensive Trade Agreement (CETA), and the Barcelona Process.
- Chinese interregionalism, which features China-Africa summits, the Belt and Road initiative, and the Regional Comprehensive Economic Partnership (RCEP).
- ASEAN interregionalism, which embraces ASEAN +6, RCEP, and ASEAN-MERCOSUR.
- MERCOSUR interregionalism, which includes the India-Brazil-South Africa Dialogue Forum (IBSA), CEPAC, and MERCOSUR-Africa.

Stories of both success and failure should be assessed in a detailed and critical way. Why is the record mixed in so many cases? Are alternative trends in global governance emerging? What about the distinctive impact of the different political cultures of the main partners?

## Predicting the changing global context: Two scenarios

The global system is evolving. Having moved beyond the historical legacy of 70 years of the Western liberal order, the world is now headed for a post-hegemonic discontinuity as the current critical juncture indicates (see Chapter 9, this volume). Inevitably, the previous network of regional and interregional arrangements will be affected. Several scenarios for global governance are possible.

According to realist literature, the most likely of these will be a combination of fragmentation, protectionism, relativism, and power politics. In this scenario, there will be multiple modernities, but they will be susceptible to a shift toward cultural intolerance or fragmented identities and/or relativism. Its main feature would be the downgrading and/or disintegration of regional organizations within a multipolar, post-hegemonic would. Multiple modernities would evolve towards relativism, while a protectionist, nationalist, competitive brand of modernity comes to the fore. Within such a dangerous, conflict-laden scenario, democratic and peaceful actors increasingly will face difficult dilemmas:

- Regionalism/interregionalism would stand at a crossroads. It might disintegrate due to a bias in favor of contingent/instrumental cooperation, or it might wither away under the pressures of hierarchical power politics/spheres of influence and internal disintegration.
- An authoritarian, top-down, fiercely competitive regionalism and interregionalism could set the stage for an increasingly fragmented, conflictual system of global governance. Democratic regionalism, as practiced in the EU, would risk falling victim to this twofold trend. With a weakened EU might come intensified trade wars and political conflicts, inward-looking nationalist policies, and the recrudescence of old-style spheres-of-influence politics. Trade wars would be the prelude to political and even military conflicts in the context of a revived "Thucydides trap" (Allison 2017).

Is an alternative global governance scenario likely to emerge? What about the evolving democratic regional organizations in this new, highly competitive setting? ASEAN, MERCOSUR, the EU, and similar entities have little choice but to deepen their integration and enhance their political unity if they wish to survive. They are experiencing a difficult transition due to both internal and external challenges. Disintegrative and integrative tendencies are currently besetting each regional organization. However, there is evidence of resilience and the revival of what we called in the 1990s the "new regionalism." Here we find cooperation within a region on account of territorial proximity, but one that also is expressed in demands for a new combination of common (anti-nationalist) protection and openness in the discourse of some segments of the regional leadership. The main comparative research question thus becomes: Is there any common trend that might lead out of the crisis and fragmentation, even if it is merely inchoate?

According to our hypothesis the answer is yes, provided that a more explicit political dimension in favor of an alternative version of modernity emerges. But this would entail the victory of the movement to pool and share the national sovereignty of the member states, combining cooperating inter-governmental bodies with supranational institutions and rules. What forms might such a creeping supra-nationality take?

## Consequences for regional politicization in the context of the politicization of global governance challenges: The case of the EU

Although every democratic regional entity faces similar policy dilemmas, the case of the EU represents in some ways a unique policy paradox. In the EU's experience, no autonomous socio-economic and cultural model is possible without a single currency. Yet no single currency can endure without a stronger institutional framework for economic governance.

In spite of its unique situation and historical experiences, the EU might learn a few lessons from ASEAN. First, the latter can point to a recent positive record of creeping supra-nationalism operating both through and beyond the usual intergovernmental framework. Its advances are evident in the Charter of 2008 and a 2003 environmental policy cooperation regime called the "Transboundary Haze Pollution Agreement." Second, the EU could learn from ASEAN how to implement the usually successful practice of drawing concentric circles around the association's hard core: the more thoroughly integrated ASEAN 10, which decided to build a "community" based on the three pillars of economics and trade, political cooperation and security policy, and socio-cultural collaboration.

The circles ringing the hard core ten are: "ASEAN + 1" (with China); "ASEAN + 3" (with China, Japan, and South Korea); "ASEAN + 6" (referred to above); and the "ASEAN regional forum" (in which the EU, the US, and Russia also have been invited to participate). Are such concentric circles realistic in the case of the EU? In the EU's jargon, the appropriate definition is "differentiated integration." It is just this sort of differentiated integration that was championed by the EU Council of Rome (Declaration of March, 2017). In fact, a scheme of five concentric circles as the evolving architecture of the European Continent has been drafted already and soon will take effect. It will involve the following elements:

- Consolidating and democratizing the 19-country Eurozone by deepening economic governance (e.g., through a Eurozone-level finance minister plus a separate Eurozone budget and parliament).
- Creating hard cores of "9 +": "enhanced cooperation" (article 20) or "structured cooperation" (article 46). Enhanced cooperation on European defense matters was approved in October, 2017.
- Deepening the EU 27, and possibly enlarging the Union to include several applicant countries, by perfecting the single market and adopting a common commercial policy based on the democratic legitimacy provided by the European parliament.
- Developing, as an alternative to enlargement, special and flexible relationships with external countries such as the UK, Ukraine, and Turkey, but also perhaps Georgia, Armenia, Azerbaijan, and other neighbors, in the context of a new, Eastern and Southern neighborhood policy.

Far from being utopian, this scenario is to a large extent already on the horizon and may allow the EU not only to cope with Brexit, the disintegrating effects of the Trump election, and the crisis of the West, but also to assume responsibility for defending essential Western values like democracy-promotion, human rights, economic and trade openness and multilateralism, as advocated by Angela Merkel in 2017.[2]

## The main institutional and theoretical issue at stake: Toward a more binding global governance?

Democratic regionalism is becoming ever more political, a necessary evolution in a dangerous world. But it will succeed only if it operates in and through a new, expanded and deepened, more legitimate and efficient multilateral network shaping convergence and cooperation. There will be no new regionalism without new forms of multilateralism. In marked contrast to the illusions of the old "EU normative power" approach (Manners & Lucarelli 2006) of the 1990s and early 2000s, we should not expect the multilateral governance described here to be modeled on the EU. Instead, it should be pluralist and open to alternative cultural approaches to justice and good multilateral governance (see Chapter 9, this volume).

Specifically, various regional/interregional arrangements could provide building blocks and intermediary stages towards a post-hegemonic, pluralist and multi-layered form of global governance. New, bottom-up dynamics could be complementary to the WTO, IMF, UN and other global organizations. In spite of unpredictable nationalist trends and other factors of instability, emerging multi-lateral regimes like the Paris Agreement limiting climate change (hammered out at the 2015 Conference of Parties, COP 21) and the multilateral management of terrorism, Iran's nuclear program, the Korean peninsula crisis, and other security challenges will be critical in rebalancing the trend in favor of global/regional multilateralism.

Trade arrangements are also crucial, due to their widening and deepening effects. Given the size of the partnerships, even bilateral relations eventually could develop into forms of multilateralism. For example, the EU's partnership with China could evolve in ways that support this trend. It might be possible to negotiate higher standards for investment and trade deals that build bridges between European and Chinese ideas of modernity.

Provided that it can cope with its current deficit of internal legitimacy, the EU could make notable progress toward this new multilateral scenario and thus take a major step toward comprehensive security. It should do so by combining the coordinating work of the European Commission and the High Representative for Foreign Policy while taking a broader approach to external relations and mustering the political will of a hard core of leading member states, in accordance with Articles 20 and 46 of the Maastricht Treaty.

For these same reasons, the EU and new regional organizations might do more than merely survive the threatening combination of power politics and fragmentation, of cultural arrogance and relativism. In the best-case scenario, the EU could contribute in a constructive way to a more pluralist and culturally-varied system of global governance that would accommodate a wide array of cultural approaches to multilateral and multilevel cooperation, even while asserting its more binding notion of international and transnational cooperation. Multilateralism is currently an ambiguous concept, one that can be construed in ways that are either constraining or instrumental; multidimensional/long term or contingent; ad hoc or strategic; regional/interregional or merely global. Regional entities like the EU and ASEAN as well as benevolent continental States like Brazil, China, Canada, and others could agree on convergent multilateral agendas regarding at least some common global and regional priorities, including denuclearization, climate change, and struggles against poverty, infectious diseases, criminality, terrorism, civil wars, and mass murders perpetrated by dictators.

In this innovative scenario, the central question becomes: To what extent might alternative paths to multilateralism converge, despite cultural differences, on a more constructive struggle to preserve and promote the Commons? In light of the EU's internal multilateral experience, this outcome will be possible only through a more binding (and legitimate) system of global governance. Concretely, what might that mean?

The goal of establishing a more binding system of global governance is by no means merely an arrogant notion being pushed by the EU. The framework of isolated state sovereignty, understood as a sufficient and appropriate framework for coping with a wide range of problems (e.g., environmental degradation, financial instability, nuclear proliferation, terrorism, human rights violations, internal fragmentation), has been criticized justifiably by the majority of elites on every continent. Furthermore, the sovereignty-based invocation of "non-interference in another country's domestic affairs" against any and all forms of supranational governance increasingly has been marginalized within the world epistemic community. Nevertheless, the notion of "governance beyond the state" remains controversial, partly owing to a litany of ancient and recent abuses. Under what conditions would a more binding and legitimate scheme of supranational governance be possible and desirable? We have identified five cases that can help to address those questions and point the international community in the right direction.

*First*, we can examine the political dimension of convergence in which traditional, sovereignty-enhancing multilateralism worked to good effect at the national level. The UNSC agreement on sanctions in the Korean crisis of 2017 and the winning coalition against ISIS both illustrate the enduring relevance of a Westphalian approach to global interstate cooperation. Although these outcomes remain fragile, they are working despite continuing differences of opinion (such as between the EU and China) because they accept international law as a shared framework. Relevant examples include the decision by The Hague Tribunal to reject Chinese claims to the South China Sea and the multilateral condemnation of Russian occupation of Crimea and related violations of international borders.

*Second*, we can review the evolution of economic governance. At least since 2001, a broad convergence has emerged on the usefulness of supranational trade regimes. For example, the WTO and its multilateral panels may find several member states, both large and small, guilty of violating the association's trade rules. Donald Trump currently accuses these panels of "violating national sovereignty." Furthermore, there is convergence between the EU and China concerning the failed IMF share-distribution reform and the US Senate's refusal to ratify that reform. As a consequence of such shortcomings and deadlocks at the global level, the Chiang Mai Initiative, the Asian Infrastructure Investment Bank, and the European Stability Mechanism were created. These can serve as examples of regional multilateralism. But the question remains: Will regional multilateral efforts such as these complement the Bretton Woods institutions?

*Third*, we can consider the responsibilities of the international community in the face of large-scale killings. So far, inaction and indifference toward international community intervention has been the prevalent attitude. For that reason, we should watch with interest the broad convergence that has taken place since 2005 around Kofi Annan's Responsibility to Protect (R2P) concept on the coercive use of force under Chapter VII of the UN Charter and its application during the initial phase of the Libyan crisis of 2011 (first articulated in Annan 1999). It is understandable that considerable controversy arose between the majority of the West and the BRICS about its further use in Libya, Sudan, and Syria in 2015–2016. Therefore, the epistemic and policymaking communities are studying some new compromise formulas, such as "responsibility while protecting." Proposed by Brazil in 2011 with some Chinese support, it would mean that the world community should assume responsibility to prevent human rights abuses only as a last resort, and would forbid both the misuse of the power to intervene and all efforts at regime change. The doctrine also would include monitoring and possible suspension. Some countries want to require the explicit and full consent by the host country prior to any such intervention, but that proviso would provoke a deadlock.

*Fourth*, we can point to efforts to agree on a common policy regarding climate change. In marked contrast to the discord that occurred at Copenhagen in 2009, the world welcomed convergence on the importance of state self-constraint ("*rété-nue*" in French) and a sovereignty-pooling process initiated at COP 21 in Paris. The open questions addressed at COP 22 (Marrakech, 2016) and COP 23 (Bonn, 2017) concerned what should be done about implementation-monitoring and what costs and consequences should ensue in the event of defections, whether actual (as in the case of the US) or only potential.

*Fifth* and finally, we need to develop a new concept of reciprocity revolving around enhanced mutual trust. The market-based view focuses on "specific reciprocity." Trade provides the best example, since it is free if the participants choose to engage in it, and since the prices of the goods exchanged are set by supply and demand. The problem is that individual economic transactions do not lay the foundations for long-term trust. The opposite case involves reciprocity based on "gifts." For instance, the Marshall plan, NATO assistance to Georgia, Russian aid to Abkhazia/South Ossetia and Donbas, some Western aid programs for developing countries, and possibly even China's Belt and Road initiative are based on investments by donors, without substantial financial costs to the recipient country. However, as the anthropologist Marcel Mauss (2001) has explained (in a view supported by Pierre Bourdieu) that gift economies typically entail three phases: giving, receiving, and—most relevant in our context—reciprocating. The implication is that reciprocity in gift-giving may entail long-term subordination (in political and economic terms, as a kind of subordinated model of modernity) of the actor receiving the gift vis-à-vis the donor. In short, a de facto hierarchical relationship emerges that has some similarities to spheres of influences. Diffuse reciprocity is a large, innovative, and intermediary avenue, one that is yet to be explored (Keohane 1986).

## Conclusions

Because it recognizes the dark side of multipolarity and the crisis of the West, research on a new multilateralism is far removed from utopian cosmopolitanism. Instead, its challenge is to seek new levels and forms of cooperation and understanding between the two extremes. Both democratic regional entities and benevolent states need to innovate. There is considerable room for research on the five steps mentioned above, and notably about "reciprocity" as a long-term, trust-based interplay between regional and/or state actors, among multiple modernities, and among diverse cultures. The shape of the multilateralism of the future will be influenced by the solutions provided to this crucial challenge. Although the freedom of specific reciprocity (as in trade relations) should be maintained, the long term and multidimensional side of gift-giving also entails interesting input for the future. On the one hand, people-to-people networks should support issue linkage, since exchange does not necessarily happen in the same policy field. On the other hand, a broader temporal dimension also merits consideration. The latter would be impossible without the evolution from the necessary step of the mutual *"écart"* to an enhanced, institutionalized, and multidimensional reciprocal trust.

## Notes

1 "Hybrid interregionalism" describes the multidimensional relations between (on the one hand) a regional organization such as the EU, ASEAN, or MERCOSUR and (on the other) another regional organization; a large, quasi-continental state such as China, India, the US, or Brazil; or a group of states located on two or more different continents.
2 Several times after Trump election in 2018, Angela Merkel repeated her vision of an autonomous Europe. One example (from her speech to the European Parliament in Strasbourg on November 13, 2018) may suffice to illustrate her position: "The times when we could rely on others are over. This means we Europeans have to take our fate fully into our own hands."

## References

Acharya, A. 2013. *The Making of South East Asia*. Ithaca, NY: Cornell University Press.

Allison, G. 2017. *Destined for War*. Melbourne: Scribe.

Annan, K. 1999. "Two Concepts of Sovereignty." *The Economist*, September 18, p. 49. Available at www.economist.com/node/324795.

Baldwin, R. 2001. *A Domino Theory of Regionalism*. Working Paper no. w4465. Cambridge, MA: NBER.

Berger, S. 2016. "Resilient Europe." Paper delivered at Conference of European Studies. Philadelphia, PA.

Bhagwati, J. 1992. "Regionalism versus Multilateralism." *World Economy* 15(5): 535–555.

Braudel, F. 1958. "La Longue Durée." *Annales* 13(4): 725–753.

Caffarena, A. 2014. "Couples and Trust-building in International Society: A social capital perspective." In B. Vasort-Rousset (ed.), *Building Sustainable Couples in International Relations: A strategy towards peaceful cooperation*. Basingstoke: Palgrave Macmillan, pp. 23–43.

Cerutti, F. 2017. *Conceptualizing Politics: An introduction to political philosophy*. London: Routledge.

Cerutti, F. *et al.* (eds.). 2011. *Debating Political Identity and Legitimacy in the EU*. London: Routledge.

Eco, U. 2007. "Transcultura." Paper presented at EU and India conference, Pondicherry.

Fawcett, L. & A. Hurrell. 1995. *Regionalism and World Politics*. Oxford: Oxford University Press.

Fawcett, L., M. Telò, & F. Ponjaert (eds.). 2015. *Interregionnalism and the EU*. Abingdon: Routledge.

Gamble, A. 2014. "Regional Blocs, World Order and the New Medievalism." In M. Telò (ed.), *EU and New Regionalism*. Farnham: Ashgate, pp. 25–42.

Gamble, A. & A. Payne (eds.). 1996. *Regionalism and World Order*. London: Red Globe.

Haass, R. 2008. "The Age of Nonpolarity: What will follow US dominance." *Foreign Affairs* 3(87). Available at www.foreignaffairs.com/articles/united-states/2008-05-03/age-nonpolarity.

Habermas, J. 2004. *Der gespaltene Westen*. Frankfurt am Main: Suhrkamp.

Hall, P. & R. Taylor. 1996. "Political Science and the Three New Institutionalisms." *Political Studies* 44(5): 936–957.

Hettne, B. 2008. "Security Regionalism in Theory and Practice." In H. G. Brauch *et al.* (eds.), *Globalization and Environmental Challenges*. Berlin: Springer.

Hettne, B., Inotai, A., & Sunkel, O. (eds.). 2001. *Comparative Regionalism: Implications for global development*. London: Palgrave.

Huntington, S. 1996. *The Clash of Civilizations and the Remaking of World Order*. New York: Simon & Schuster.

Judis, J. 2016. *The Populist Explosion: How the Great Recession transformed American and European politics*. New York: Columbia Global Reports.

Jullien, F. 2017. *L'Invention de l'Idéal et le Destin de L'Europe*. Paris: Gallimard.

Keohane, R. 1986. "Reciprocity in International Relations." *International Organization* 40(1): 1–27.

Keohane, R. & J. Morse. 2015. "Counter-multilateralism." In M. Telo *et al.* (eds.), *Politics of Transnational Trade Relations: The TTIP in a globalized world*. Burlington, IN: Routledge, pp. 17–26.

Manners, I. & S. Lucarelli. 2006. *Values and Principles in EU Foreign Policy*. London: Routledge.

Mauss, M. 2001. *The Gift: The form and reason for exchange in archaic societies*, 2nd edition. New York: Routledge Classics.

Milner, H. & E. Mansfield. 1997. *The Political Economy of Regionalism*. New York: Columbia University Press.

Nye, J. 1968. *International Regionalism*. Boston, MA: Little, Brown & Co.

Polanyi, K. 1944. *The Great Transformation*. Boston, MA: Beacon Press.

Scharpf, F. & P. Schmitter. 1995. *Governance in the EU*. London: Sage.

SIPRI. 2017. *Report*. Stockholm: Stockholm International Peace Research Institute.

Steinmo, S., K. Thelen, & F. Longstreth. 1992. *Structuring Politics: Historical institutionalism in comparative analysis*. Cambridge: Cambridge University Press.

Telò, M. (ed.). 2014. *EU and New Regionalism*. Farnham: Ashgate.

Telò, M. 2016. *Regionalism in Hard Times*. London: Routledge.

Telò, M. 2018. "The Past & Present of Europe's Intercultural Dialogue: Beyond a 'normative power' approach to two-way cooperation." In T. Meyer and J. de Sales Marques (eds.), *Multiple Modernities and Good Governance*. Abingdon: Routledge, pp. 101–117.

Telò, M., A. Sapir, & D. Sassoon. 2017. *La place de l'Europe dans le monde du 21e siècle*. Brussels: Editions académie en poche.

Wendt, A. 1999. *Social Theory of International Politics*. Cambridge: Cambridge University Press.

# 8

# THE CRISIS OF THE WESTERN LIBERAL ORDER AND THE RISE OF THE NEW POPULISM

*Andrew Gamble*

Since the financial crash in 2008, there has been a marked rise in nationalist forms of populism in Western democracies, which challenged the principles and institutions that have underpinned the Western international order for so long. The election of Donald Trump and the vote for Brexit in the United Kingdom in 2016 were two of the most dramatic instances of this new phenomenon, but there were many others. Populism, however, did not begin with the financial crash in 2008. While those events and the very slow recovery that followed certainly helped to amplify populism, creating conditions in which it could thrive, many existing populist parties and movements were active long before 2008. This paper first explores the roots of populism in globalization and the neo-liberal policy regime of the preceding two decades, and then discusses some of the recent manifestations of this populism, particularly in the shape of Trump and Brexit.

## The triumph of the Western liberal order

The year 1991 marked the official end of the Cold War, with the collapse of the Soviet Union and the dismemberment of the Soviet empire. Many new, independent states emerged from the wreckage. The victors of the Cold War were not slow to proclaim the advent of a new world order, the return to the "One World" of the 19th century. Francis Fukuyama called it "the end of history," meaning that the long ideological conflicts over what kind of modernity should finally prevail had been settled in favor of capitalist liberal democracy (Fukuyama 1989). Although there would still be disputes and frictions, the big questions now had been settled. There was nothing beyond capitalist markets and liberal democracies. The alternatives all had been vanquished.

For a time, this optimism seemed justified. An era of liberal peace began. With the collapse of its only superpower rival, the position of dominance held by the

United States was further strengthened. No other country could compete. There seemed to be few obstacles to the United States imposing its will and its preferences on the rest of the world. All talk of US decline, so rife in the 1980s (Kennedy 1988), quickly disappeared. The international order had become unipolar, a major watershed in geopolitics and the evolution of the international system. The United States towered over its allies as well as its enemies.

The triumph of the United States also meant the triumph of globalization and neo-liberalism. The international economy had been painfully re-constructed during the 1980s, and now everything was in place for a new era of expansion and prosperity. The 1990s saw a quickening of the pace of globalization: increasing flows of finance, trade, investment, information, and people. There were also some major new participants. China, India, and Brazil became big players in the new international economy, and helped reshape it. The new division of labor that had been emerging in the 1980s now became still more pronounced, with a great deal of traditional manufacturing shifting to China and other low-cost economies. The opportunity for American and European firms to outsource large parts of their operations remade the international order, and by helping to industrialize and modernize the world's most populous economies began a process of transition to a very different kind of international order, with potentially very different players. The effects on Western economies took a number of forms. The flood of cheap products contributed to steady economic growth by helping to remove inflationary pressure from the economy. It also led to further job losses in traditional manufacturing industries and districts. This process of deindustrialization went farthest in the Anglo-Saxon economies. It was less pronounced in some other Western economies, particularly the newly unified Germany, which clung to its model of export-led growth and fiscal conservatism despite the challenge of reintegrating East Germany.

The deepening and widening of globalization during the 1990s were aided by the consolidation of the new Western economic policy regime, which increasingly was called "neo-liberalism," although mainly by its critics. Neo-liberalism comprised many different doctrines and schools, which often conflicted. But the character of the policy regime which neo-liberal ideas helped construct and legitimate was fairly clear. It was associated with privatization of state assets, deregulation of the economy, low taxation, flexible labor markets, marketization of public services, and the weakening of trade unions. One critic dubbed it the "Washington Consensus" (Williamson 1989). Monetary policy was given priority over fiscal policy, and there was a strong drive to promote the development of the service sector—finance in particular. The neo-liberal regime encouraged the financialization of the economy, the development of financial intermediaries at every stage of the life cycle, and a vast expansion of financial services. This trend went along with a steep rise in household, corporate, and public debt as essential means to lubricate the finance-led model of growth.

Low inflation, one of the key features of the neo-liberal policy regime, was achieved less through tight monetary policy than through the impact of the immense productive power of China, India, and the other rising powers. Another by-product of the new policies was sharply increasing inequality. This was true of all countries, including the rising powers, but it was particularly marked in the Anglo-Saxon countries, where for several decades there had been a levelling trend. But from the 1980s onwards this trend reversed and, by the time of the financial crash, inequality was returning to levels not seen since before 1914 (Piketty 2014; Atkinson 2015). The trend attracted a lot of comment, but its effect was muffled by the general rise in prosperity and the economic optimism of the period. Although there were periodic financial crises, including the Asian financial crisis in 1997 and the dot com bubble collapse in 2000, they were successfully defused without wider repercussions for the international economy.

## Critics of the new world order

Despite the ascendancy of neo-liberal ideas and the increasing tendency to treat them as commonsensical, there were many critics of the new world order. All argued that political and economic realities were more complex than allowed for in triumphalist accounts of the end of the Cold War. Against the idea of there being just one modernity, critics argued that there were many different possible modernities, and many different possible forms of globalization. Against the idea of a single central order, critics argued that any stable order needed to be built on regionalist, multilateral foundations. Against the idea of a harmony between global markets and national democracy, critics pointed to the paradox associated with globalization: that it tended to undermine national democracy rather than strengthening it, and helped create the conditions for the populist backlash against globalization and the global elites who promoted it.

The idea of multiple modernities disputes the implicit assumption, widely held after 1991, that there was now not just ideological uniformity but economic, cultural, and political uniformity as well. In that view, only one world was possible, and it was just a matter of time before all nations adopted the practices, beliefs, and institutions of the Western capitalist democracies. This idea that modernity and modernization had only one destination lay at the root of many formulations of what became known as hyperglobalization. It had been formulated before, for example by theorists of modernization in the 1950s (Rostow 1960). But against the view that history had a single teleology and that everything was headed in the same direction, there always had been those who pointed out that alternatives existed, and that despite the many commonalities which different modernizations shared, their differences nevertheless were marked. There could be no simple assumption that history was linear. A monism underlaid some of the most prominent accounts of modernity, which simply assumed that the world could be made one and the differences between societies, national traditions, and historical experiences could be eradicated. But the longer that the new era of globalization has lasted, the more apparent it has become that the different models diverge and that the conceptions of modernity held, for example, by the Indians or the Chinese are quite distinct.

One of the early critics of the assumptions of the hyperglobalizers was Samuel Huntington, who predicted that although the post-Cold War era might be spared a new clash of ideologies, it would suffer instead a clash of civilizations (Huntington 1997). This line of reasoning suggested that, far from the creation of One World under the benign governance of the United States, the post-Cold War environment would find itself riven by conflicts over culture. The deep differences between the world's civilizations would provide the focus for a politics of identity that would cast other civilizations as rivals and potentially as antagonists. Therefore the United States should abandon its attempt to form the rest of the world in its own image and come to terms with a world of many civilizations, many globalizations, and many modernities. Other critics went farther, arguing that neo-liberalism and the kind of globalization project it championed was yet another utopian project, of a kind familiar from Western political history. By seeking to remake the whole world in its image, neo-liberalism accepts only its own picture of economic and political order as correct. It has a vision of a market society that has no need for politics or government. Societies, in this view, are held together by the bonds of market exchange. In pursuit of the neo-liberal ideal, social protections are dismantled and non-market institutions undermined (Gray 1998).

The new world order also was criticized by those who argued that the world was destined to be multipolar rather than unipolar. That was a temporary interlude. Talk of One World distracted attention from the real problem, which was ensuring that a multipolar world would also be a multilateral one. While accepting that a liberal international order was a desirable goal, these critics said that it needed to be constructed on regional political foundations. Global markets were not sufficient to bind it together, nor were the institutions established under US leadership at the global level. What were also required were strong regional associations between countries, pooling their sovereignty by establishing strong regional economies and regional cooperation. These would not be closed associations but the building blocks for wider international cooperation. The European Union was seen as the most advanced form of regional association, with its mixture of intergovernmental and supranational institutions. The EU, however, remained a predominantly civilian rather than a military power, a loose confederation rather than a new state. This is what made it interesting as a model, although as Mario Telò has argued the EU is better seen as an institutional laboratory rather than as a blueprint (Telò 2005). The circumstances of Europe were unique, and no one model could be appropriate for all the different regional associations around the world. The argument for regionalism stressed the importance of building institutions to encourage cooperation between countries that might in the past have been rivals or enemies, and that could ensure effective regulation of market actors, particularly large corporations and banks. This was a very different vision of world order from that held by the hyperglobalizers, who dreamed of a borderless world, the end of the nation-state, and the disappearance of politics.

A third line of criticism of the new world order has focused on the problem of trying to reconcile market capitalism and liberal democracy. That critique provides a way of understanding the rise of populist and anti-globalization movements and discourses across the Western democracies. The world system as Immanuel Wallerstein conceived it always contained a tension between the drive for ever greater economic integration of markets and production and the fragmentation of political authority among a number of competing states (Wallerstein 1976). Dani Rodrik explores this tension in relation to globalization (Rodrik 2011). The increasing interdependence of the international economy exists alongside the desire of individual countries to retain and exercise their own sovereignty, and also the need for them as democracies to retain the support of their citizens. In Rodrik's view, this circumstance creates a trilemma. It is possible to achieve any two of the three goals simultaneously—increasing economic interdependence, national sovereignty, and democratic legitimacy—but not all of them. In the first combination, economic interdependence and national sovereignty, authoritarian governments use their power to pursue economic interdependence and sacrifice democracy. In the second combination, economic interdependence and democratic legitimacy, national sovereignty and nation-states wither away to be replaced by cosmopolitan government. In the third combination, national sovereignty and democratic legitimacy, governments stay close to the wishes and interests of their citizens and take steps to limit or even reverse economic interdependence. The problem for global elites is that they are committed to the twin principles of a liberal international order and democratic national government. These were founding principles for the international system after 1945. But the question has always been, if a clash occurs between these two principles, which takes precedence? In the first three decades of the liberal international order, great attention was paid to what was acceptable to democratic electorates in each nation; national governments were accorded a great deal of autonomy; and the United States made concessions so that other states would stay within the Western alliance and be fully contributing members of the international order. The United States was so much the dominant power that it could afford to do this, and although the US never stopped pursuing its own interests or overthrowing governments that it perceived as a threat to those interests, it was often prepared to bow to its democratic allies because of the overriding need to maintain the cohesion of "the West" against the Soviet bloc. Cold War security considerations meant that its core allies (which came to include Germany and Japan) generally were treated sympathetically.

This fact began to change during the 1970s because the United States could no longer afford to bear the costs of the fixed exchange rate system that had been agreed at Bretton Woods. In cutting loose and floating the dollar, it both removed one of the main barriers to the inflation that was gathering pace and signaled the determination of the United States to give greater priority to its own needs and interests. The international system was gradually reshaped to fit these changed priorities, giving birth to a new set of policies and instruments for managing the international economy. Those policies and instruments created the framework within which all Western states had to operate, some more eagerly than others. The doctrines of neo-liberalism were important in shaping the new regime which emerged (Gamble 2014a). They included the monetarism of Milton Friedman and the supply-side economics of Arthur Laffer. Many of the new ideas became policy orthodoxy by the end of the 1980s for leading international institutions like the International Monetary Fund (IMF) and the World Bank, and—as noted—they came to be known collectively as the Washington Consensus. The latter was a package involving privatization, deregulation, low taxes, flexible labor markets, weak trade unions, and low public spending that was imposed both on countries that experienced economic difficulties and required loans to bail them out and on developing countries as a condition for dispensing foreign aid and restructuring their debts.

The same policy package became associated with globalization. The promotion of free markets around the world, and therefore the acceleration of flows of capital, goods, services, and money, became the hallmarks of this phase in the development of a new liberal international order, which after the collapse of communism in Europe now extended to all corners of the world, with very few countries remaining outside. The governance of this order was much more complex than in the past because of the degree of cooperation, the number of players, and the scale of the challenges involved, many of which (such as mass immigration, terrorism, climate change, and nuclear proliferation) were recognized as inherently transnational. One response was the proliferation of international organizations and NGOs designed to facilitate the management of these problems and secure greater cooperation between states (Slaughter 2009). To some, it appeared that a global polity and a global civil society were in the making to go alongside the global economy.

What was neglected here was the need to embed the new transnational institutions in the national democracies. The reason for that neglect had to do both with the inherent difficulty of the task and with the fact that any spare political energy was needed to build the transnational institutions. Some of the new members of the international order were not democracies and did not accept liberal principles. In the democracies, it was often hard to engage citizens with the complexities of international rule-making and standard-setting. As a result, it was easier to focus on the international networks rather than the national ones. In these ways the various global elites gradually grew more similar to one another and more detached from the citizens from whom they ultimately derived their legitimacy and authority.

There is no easy solution to Rodrik's trilemma. Cosmopolitan government rooted in a global *demos* might be desirable but seems unattainable. Economic interdependence being sustained by an authoritarian politics does not appeal to Rodrik. His preference is therefore for national sovereignty which is legitimated through democracy. This is also the demand of most of the new national populists. They are opposed to globalization and the global elites it has spawned, and they want to regain control of borders, money, and laws. They want to bring back production that has been outsourced and give priority to the national economy and the communities that depend upon it. If this means becoming much more closed to the outside world and retreating from existing levels of economic and political interdependence and cooperation, and accepting a lower standard of living, that is a choice many of them are prepared to make. The vitality of democracy and the ability of the majority opinion to be reflected in the policy of a sovereign government are what count.

## The 2008 crash

Even before the 2008 crash, the strains between national democracies and certain forms of globalization were evident. National populisms had grown out of angry responses to some of the effects that globalization was having. These effects included the outsourcing of jobs to China and India, the changing patterns of inequality and economic activity in high income countries (Milanovic 2016), and the increasing flow of migrants from poor countries to rich countries. All of these trends were supported by the neo-liberal policy regime, and many people in the rich countries benefited from them. But others did not, and these people were drawn into a backlash against the elites who were responsible for the policies. Although anti-globalization movements arose on the left as well, the ones that proved to have staying power were on the right.

The rise of populism might have been contained if the economy had continued to grow. There still would have been losers from globalization, but it would have been easier to compensate them. But with the onset of the financial crash a new period began. A complete financial meltdown was narrowly averted in 2008, and the rescue that was managed came at the price of a deep recession in 2009 and then no real recovery for close to a decade. Only in 2018 did the world economy as a whole begin to grow again, and there are still big question marks over its sustainability. This event was the most serious financial crash since 1929 in the US and Europe, but this time a slump and depression were averted through the use of every tool that policymakers could lay their hands on. Apart from bank bailouts and fiscal stimulus, such tools included some novel measures, particularly zero interest rates and quantitative easing. What were intended as short-term palliatives became embedded, and most countries still were using them ten years later. There was no quick return to normality, no bounceback from recession as had happened after every previous downturn since 1945. Instead, there was a long period in which living standards and wages were either stationary or falling, while austerity programs cut the size of public spending and reduced the size of the state in proportion to the now-shrunken economy. In the 1970s, the Western economies had suffered from inflation that was high and hard to control, allied with stagnant production ("stagflation"). Since 2008, those economies have been plagued by the opposite problem. Production, productivity, and investment are all stagnant again, but this time prices have been falling and the monetary authorities have been trying to prevent deflation of the kind that Japan suffered in the 1990s. Policymakers faced a deflationary trap characterized by declining expectations and permanently low investment. This was one reason why quantitative easing schemes were kept running for so long: to keep the banks liquid and the value of assets high.

Since 2008 the crisis has undergone four stages. The *first phase* was the banking crisis that erupted in the Anglo-American heartlands but was not confined to them (Gamble 2014b). Several leading financial institutions collapsed and many more had to be bailed out by governments. Two of the biggest banks in the United Kingdom were taken over by the government. For a sector that had been riding so high, and that had pressed repeatedly and successfully for less regulation in the two decades leading up to the crash, this represented a major setback. But because of the overriding need to shore up the banking system, governments were reluctant to push the banks too far, fearing a much more extensive collapse. For all the public opprobrium that bankers received, they escaped relatively lightly—especially compared to the 1930s, when several leading bankers had been tried and imprisoned for their role in the Wall Street crash. Bernie Madoff was one of the few who were prosecuted this time around, but despite the size of the fraud he perpetrated he was a relatively small player. It was not long before the banks were acting almost as though nothing had happened. The dependence of the economy on their services was too great. Some new regulation was brought in to try to avoid a repeat of 2007–2008 in the future, but it was much less radical than many critics of the financial sector wanted, and pressure soon was exerted to water it down and allow the financial markets to expand once again.

In the *second phase* of the crisis, attention switched to the Eurozone. Although many European banks had been caught up in the financial crash and had amassed huge liabilities, the main focus of this stage of the crisis was sovereign debt. The recession exposed the fragility of the public finances of the Eurozone, and the difficulty of dealing with its consequences when there existed a monetary union but no fiscal union (Marsh 2013). In both the US and the UK, the central bank was able to act as lender of last resort to the banking system, and the government could use its powers to make fiscal transfers to those parts of the economy that were hardest hit. But in the absence of both a fiscal union and an economic government, the Eurozone was subjected to pressures that threatened to tear it apart. In an attempt to hold the Eurozone together, a tough austerity policy was imposed to eliminate public deficits in all the member states and force them to lower their costs. The currency union prevented the most indebted countries, which included Greece, Ireland, Spain and Portugal, from devaluing their currencies, and the consequence was that these and some of the other weaker economies in the Eurozone suffered big falls in output and employment and huge pressure on their public finances. In Greece, which was the worst affected, these measures produced a political upheaval that led to the defeat of the established center-left and center-right parties and the victory of Syriza on a left-populist program. There followed a protracted standoff between the so-called "troika"—the European Commission, the European Central Bank (ECB), and the IMF—and the Syriza government over the conditions for a Greek bailout, specifically, the size of the spending cuts and tax increases that would be required for the advance of loans to stop a Greek default. The Syriza government initially chose defiance and won a referendum rejecting the terms offered by the troika on behalf of the EU, only then to give in and accept them. The majority faction under Alexis Tsipras decided that the alternative to a climbdown was leaving the euro and possibly leaving the EU, which was judged worse even than the very harsh terms on offer.

The Greek episode illustrates Rodrik's globalization paradox. The price of remaining connected and interdependent was to override Greek democracy, as expressed in the results of the referendum and the general election. The argument of the Greeks was that they should be helped by the rest of the EU, particularly by countries that were strong and rich. They wanted the EU to be the true supranational community that they thought they had joined. But the rich countries replied that it was the responsibility of every member of the Eurozone to operate within the rules of the community, and therefore countries that got into difficulty should not look to the taxpayers of other member states for bail-outs. Accordingly, they stuck to an intergovernmental interpretation of the treaties. The Eurozone survived its sovereign debt crisis in part by allowing the ECB to act as a central bank and use quantitative easing and lower interest rates to sustain liquidity within the bloc. Thus, the line was held, but at a considerable cost in the legitimacy of the euro and the wider European institutions. The example of Greece was used repeatedly by populists, who claimed that it showed that supranational institutions and agencies were prepared to impose their solutions on countries that stepped out of line. It helped fuel disengagement from the European project.

The *third phase* of the crisis, from 2013 onwards, saw still very limited recovery in the US and the Eurozone and faltering growth in some of the fastest growing economies in the world, most notably Brazil and China. In the first two phases of the crisis, international economic growth was supported by the rising powers, owing to their relative freedom from the contagion of Western financial markets. But this support was partly achieved by a very large fiscal stimulus—especially in China, where it led to some overheating in the economy and a significant rise in the debt carried by state enterprises. Falling commodity prices caused in part by the sluggishness of growth elsewhere also affected many developing economies. There was much speculation as to whether China, now the world's second largest economy, would deal with its internal debts by a very rapid deflation and the wiping out of inefficient producers or try to squeeze the debt gradually out of the system. The latter risked putting China into the kind of deflation trap that Japan had suffered after its bubble collapsed in 1989.

The *fourth phase* of the crisis began with the political shocks of 2016, the Brexit vote, and the election of Donald Trump. Until that point, the Western democracies had shown remarkable resilience. Apart from Greece, where an outsider movement had come to power in 2015, the Western democracies had seen many changes of government but no changes of regime. The national populists in particular had been held at bay. Challenges had been stifled. But this all changed in 2016. The focus of the crisis returned to the Anglo–Saxon countries, only this time in a political form. While the two events were very different, both exemplified the new national populism. In the Brexit Referendum, a key factor in the success of the Leave campaign was the United Kingdom Independence Party (UKIP), with its four million votes in the general election of 2017 and its army of supporters on the ground who helped bring out the Leave vote.

Populism is an imprecise term, at least in the way it is often used in media and political discourse. It has been ascribed to parties of both the right and the left, as well as to individual politicians. The term is vague because there is an inherently "populist" element to modern democracies. Politicians gain power by making pitches to the people for their support. The legitimacy of modern democracy depends on the ability of politicians to appeal to voters' values, identities, or material interests, and often all three. All democratic politics is populist in this sense, but to be characterized as populist a party or a politician must do other things as well. Populists are distinct from other politicians because they are anti-system and anti-establishment. They typically counterpose the "people" to the "elite," and blame the elite for all popular problems, suffering, and oppression (Mudde & Kaltwasser 2017; Müller 2016). Elites are corrupt; they do not listen; they are insulated from the people and no longer represent their concerns or their interests. Such populist discourses flourish in authoritarian regimes, often covertly. But these discourses are also an inherent feature of democracies. Populist parties in democracies are natural parties of opposition, sometimes permanent opposition. Problems arise if they win office. As anti-system parties, they are dedicated to overthrowing or at least radically overhauling the established order, displacing existing elites and remaking the state and its relationship to the people. They are not expected by their followers to become part of the elite itself as soon as they win power. If they are not absorbed by the existing elite and the "deep state," they must become the new establishment, which generally means moving in an authoritarian direction and restricting democracy, as has happened in Turkey, Poland, and Hungary.

Many of the populisms which have attracted attention in the last decade, such as the Front National in France, are not newcomers. Instead, they are long-established anti-system parties that benefited from political conditions after the financial crash and since have increased their support, although so far without managing a breakthrough. Other populist parties, such as the AfD in Germany or the Five Star Movement in Italy, are new organizations that have grown very rapidly. Because many other parties refuse to work with them, they find it difficult to enter government unless they can win a majority on their own. In some of the new democracies in Europe, such as Poland and Hungary, national populist parties have won power and are threatening the fragile institutions of liberal democracy, particularly the rule of law and human rights, which were established after the collapse of Communist rule. In other democracies, such as Austria, national populist parties have entered the government as coalition partners. There is now a national populist presence in the politics of almost every Western democracy, including Sweden and the Netherlands. Almost all of these parties are on the right. There are very few well-established left populist parties, apart from Syriza in Greece and Podemos in Spain. What unites the national populist parties is opposition to the EU and to globalization. Many advocate referendums to pull their countries out of the Eurozone and out of the EU altogether. Brexit has many admirers on the national populist right in Europe, but very few on the center right. The European elite is seen by populists as a unified bloc that has taken away national sovereignty and undermined national identity. The peoples of Europe, it is said, need to escape its yoke.

While the politics of many European democracies are being remade by the advance of national populism, its most dramatic recent manifestations have come in two of the oldest and traditionally most secure Western democracies: Britain and the United States. In Britain, the populist UKIP campaigned successfully for a referendum on Britain's membership in the EU, and subsequently was part of the Leave Coalition that delivered a narrow vote for Brexit on June 23, 2016. The UKIP managed to do so without ever having more than two members in the Westminster Parliament (both defections from the Conservatives), even though it had won four million votes in 2015 and had achieved significant representation in the European Parliament. Being on the winning side of the Brexit vote did not help its fortunes. Consumed by in-fighting, the party lost most of its votes and its Westminster representation in the general election in 2017. Nevertheless, the result of the referendum was a signal victory for the populist anti-system politics that was at the core of UKIP's appeal. It managed to incite a working-class insurrection. Predictably, no sooner had the vote been won than the party quickly turned to warning that the vote would be betrayed. The elites would cheat the people of what they had voted for. The populist insurgency had won the vote but it was still establishment Conservatives, most of whom had voted Remain, who dominated the government and Parliament. More than two thirds of MPs had voted for Remain. The percentage was even higher for members of the House of Lords.

The situation was different in the United States, where an outsider, Donald Trump, first won the Republican nomination and then went on to defeat Hillary Clinton in the Electoral College in the presidential campaign of 2016. Trump was not a professional politician but a property developer and TV reality show host. Drawing support from populist groups like the Tea Party and the far-right fringe of American politics, he built a campaign around outlandish populist claims (particularly involving smears against his opponents) and populist commitments (such as building a wall on the southern border to keep out Mexican immigrants). His tactic was always to pitch himself and "the people" against Washington and "the elites." The District of Columbia, in his telling, was a "swamp" that had to be drained. In many ways this was an old trope in US politics. The importance of state politics in the US meant that generations of politicians had run against Washington, but Trump took their grudge to a new level.

After Trump came to power on an economic nationalist, anti-immigrant, anti-globalization platform, the question became how far he would seek to deliver on it. Would he really attempt to drain the swamp and change the principles, procedures, and personnel of the federal government? In the beginning, Trump had radicals on his staff, like Steve Bannon who urged him to do exactly that. But Trump also surrounded himself with representatives of the military and the US financial and business communities, as well as with prominent members of the

Republican Party. The policies he enacted during his first year in office were mostly accomplished through executive orders, aimed in particular at scrapping government regulation of business. His one big legislative achievement was a tax package, crafted by Republicans and passed at the end of 2017, that disproportionately favored the wealthy elite, including Trump himself, but which was sold as benefiting the American middle class. Trump disengaged the US from the rest of the world as much as he could, canceling its involvement in the Trans-Pacific Partnership (TPP) and the Paris Accord on climate change. But—at least to that point—he was more cautious about delivering on his promises to fight a trade war with China or to pull out of the WTO and the North American Treaty Organization.

Trump's electoral victory was the most important breakthrough made by national populists in the decade following the financial crash. To win the presidency of the most powerful state in the international order by threatening to overturn many of the institutions and principles that had built and sustained this order since 1945 set off shock waves. Many feared that if it could happen in the United States, it could happen anywhere, and even if it was not repeated elsewhere, the victory of populists in the US could start to unravel the networks, alliances, and institutions that had maintained and deepened international cooperation. Trump's long-standing economic nationalism (Laderman & Simms 2017) and his crude "America First" slogan, an echo of the America First movement of the 1930s that sympathized with Hitler and opposed entering the World War II on the side of the democracies, alarmed many American allies, who had been used to the United States pursuing its own interests, but not at the same time disengaging from active leadership of the international order.

It is unclear at the moment whether the Trump phenomenon is a passing spasm that soon will be forgotten under a more traditional president or whether it betokens a lasting shift in international politics. If the US continues to be strongly critical and even at times contemptuous of many of the institutions which it worked so hard to establish to project its power and influence—or opts actively to disengage from them—the international order might rather quickly unravel, as other nations seize the opportunity to carve out their own spheres of interest. A return to a world of trade wars, currency wars, and stronger borders to deter immigration would be the likely consequence. Such an outcome is not inevitable, but it has become possible, especially since the financial crash and the increasing strength of national populism in so many countries. Steve Bannon has referred to national populism as the "global tea party" (Feder 2016). The movement's leaders in the US and Europe have established strong networks to share ideas, drawing inspiration and comfort from each other's successes. Anti-globalization, anti-European integration, and anti-immigration were the common themes that drew them together.

In Europe, the economy of the Eurozone, which had been so sluggish ever since the 2008 crash, began to show much stronger growth in 2017 and 2018. But unemployment remained high in many countries, and it was too early to say whether this was a lasting recovery or simply a consequence of the new policies adopted by the ECB. The shadow of the crisis continued to hang over the Eurozone and influence its politics. The euro was still not working as intended for all its members. Huge adjustment costs had been imposed on states with lower productivity than Germany, placing the legitimacy of the European project under threat. This danger has not passed. National populist movements remain strong, and although they suffered setbacks in elections in France in 2017 and the Netherlands in 2016, they are still advancing in several states, including Italy and Austria, while consolidating their hold on the Visegrád countries (i.e., the Czech Republic, Hungary, Poland, and Slovakia). The rejection of the European elite and European institutions is a powerful rallying call on the populist right. High levels of immigration and high numbers of asylum seekers remain potent issues. Thus, while the threat has been contained so far, there is a continuing risk.

In the last few years the growing potential for national populism to destroy the Western liberal order from within has been increasingly recognized. We have travelled a long way from the heady triumphalist days of 1989 and 1991. The current state of affairs has come about because the Western liberal order, suitably reconfigured in the 1980s, succeeded in presiding over a new wave of prosperity and expansion. But the era of globalization and neo-liberalism eventually created the conditions for its own demise. The financial crash of 2008 undermined the foundations of the financial growth model and created significant obstacles to reviving growth and prosperity. At the same time, the perception by the losers from globalization that they had been abandoned by cosmopolitan liberal elites fueled an angry nationalist populism. The growth of inequality, the destruction of traditional livelihoods and communities, and the stagnation of wages all fed this mood. But populist politics crystallized around the issue of immigration and the fears that immigration inspired over the threat to particular forms of cultural identity. The populists have been defeated so far in Europe, at least in the older democracies. But they only need to win once in a major country to pose an existential threat to both the euro and the European Union itself.

Although a new multipolar world is emerging, it remains unclear whether this will be a multilateral world based on agreed rules and institutions or a world of great conflict between antagonistic blocs (Telò 2016). The ability of the EU to survive and continue to provide an example of an open multilateral regionalism, an institutional laboratory for the international order, will be crucial. Brexit is a major blow to the EU but not a terminal one. The UK had always been a semi-detached member of the EU, not part of the Eurozone or Schengen. Some loose associative status for the UK will have to be worked out. Ultimately the EU may emerge stronger for losing its most reluctant member, but in the short run the UK referendum vote was damaging. It emboldened populists everywhere, since—despite the protestations of some Brexiteers—the vote was a vote against multilateralism, against openness, and against the liberal world order, in addition to being an extraordinary act of self-harm. An even greater risk to the prospects of a multilateral world comes from the United States and the erratic policies of the Trump Administration. At the very least, the world must deal with a United States which is much more self-interested and much less willing to play a leadership role. The disengagement of the US, which will be felt in many parts of the world, makes it all the harder to renew the institutions of the liberal international order in ways which make them inclusive for all nations. The United States in some of its current policies validates the populist case not just against globalization and neo-liberalism, but against the liberal cosmopolitan elites who are seeking to build a cooperative, multilateral world that recognizes limits to state sovereignty and seeks agreement on common rules and standards.

## References

Atkinson, A. B. 2015. *Inequality*. Cambridge, MA: Harvard University Press.

Feder, J. L. 2016. "This Is How Steve Bannon Sees the Entire World." Available at www.buzzfeed.com/lesterfeder/this-is-how-steve-bannon-sees-the-entire-world.

Fukuyama, F. 1989. "The End of History." *The Public Interest* 16 (summer): 3–18.

Gamble, A. 2014a. "Ideologies of Governance." In A. Payne & N. Phillips (eds.), *Handbook of the International Political Economy of Governance*. Cheltenham: Edward Elgar, pp. 13–31.

Gamble, A. 2014b. *Crisis without End? The unravelling of western prosperity*. London: Palgrave Macmillan.

Gray, J. 1998. *False Dawn*. London: Granta.

Huntington, S. 1997. *The Clash of Civilizations and the Remaking of World Order*. New York: Simon & Schuster.

Kennedy, P. 1988. *The Rise and Fall of the Great Powers: Economic and military conflict*. London: Unwin-Hyman.

Laderman, C. & B. Simms. 2017. *Donald Trump: The making of a world view*. London: Endeavour Press.

Marsh, D. 2013. *Europe's Deadlock: How the euro crisis could be solved and why it won't happen*. New Haven, CT: Yale University Press.

Milanovic, B. 2016. *Global Inequality: A new approach for the age of globalization*. Cambridge, MA: Belknap Press.

Mudde, C. & C. Kaltwasser. 2017. *Populism: A very short introduction*. New York: Oxford University Press.

Müller, J.-W. 2016. *What is Populism?* Philadelphia, PA: University of Pennsylvania Press.

Piketty, T. 2014. *Capital in the Twenty-first Century*. Cambridge, MA: Harvard University Press.

Rodrik, D. 2011. *The Globalization Paradox*. Oxford: Oxford University Press.

Rostow, W. W. 1960. *The Stages of Economic Growth: A non-communist manifesto*. Cambridge: Cambridge University Press.

Slaughter, A.-M. 2009. *A New World Order*. Princeton, NJ: Princeton University Press.

Telò, M. 2005. *Europe: A civilian power? EU, global governance and world order*. Palgrave Macmillan: Basingstoke.

Telò, M. 2016. *Regionalism in Hard Times: Competitive and post-liberal trends in Europe, Asia, Africa, and the Americas*. London: Routledge.

Wallerstein, I. 1976. *The Modern World System*. London: Academic Press.

Williamson, J. 1989. "What Washington Means by Policy Reform." In J. Williamson (ed.), *Latin American Readjustment: How much has happened*. Washington, DC: Institute for International Economics. Available at www.piie.com/commentary/speeches-papers/what-washington-means-policy-reform.

**PART III**

# Challenges for a common agenda of a new multilateral convergence

# 9

# POPULISM, GLOBALIZATION, AND FUTURE WORLD ORDER

*Qin Yaqing*

Since the end of the Cold War, world order has been an important topic for both academic studies and policy analyses. A liberal international system as advocated by John Ikenberry (2009) and his colleagues, a world of power struggle as John Mearsheimer (2001) envisions, and a recent argument by Amitav Acharya (2014) that sees the end of the US-led liberal world order—all these views have been aired from time to time. In the past few years, populism has begun to make surprising inroads in many parts of the world and anti-globalization is a rising tide in world politics, at least to some degree. What is particularly worrisome is that major powers have taken conspicuous policy measures that seem to cater to extreme nationalism and populism. Where is the world heading? What international order are we going to witness or create? Can resurgent populism and anti-globalization movements reverse the tide of globalization and push us into a Hobbesian jungle?

I argue that the world will not move "back to the future" as Mearsheimer (1990) predicted immediately after the end of the Cold War. Rather it will continue to move progressively ahead. A world order based on multilateralism in its more realistic sense in fact has been the most appropriate way forward, while a rules-based approach to global governance has constituted the best practice for an improved world. I therefore hold that there will be a world order based on what I term a "new multi-lateral institutionalism." It can be defined as a scheme that responds to the changing pattern of power distribution, respects genuine multilateralism, and represents a more democratic decision-making process of global governance: one that is inclusive of multiple interests and embracing a world of multiple cultures.

## The post-Cold War world order

The end of the Cold War ushered in a new world order based on "hegemonic institutionalism." This order was dominated by the United States as the only superpower in international politics, even while offering more room for multi-lateral international institutions to operate. It rested on American domination, took sovereignty as a benchmark, and employed multilateral international regimes as important mechanisms for maintaining stability around the world. Power, sovereignty, and international institutions were the pillars that sustained it.

This order had several prominent features. First, the pattern of "one superpower together with several major powers" replaced bipolarity and became the new way of distributing capabilities in the international system. The Soviet Union, along with its alliance system, collapsed; European states were just moving out of the shadow of the Cold War; and other major players were on the rise, yet still lagging far behind the United States in terms of material capabilities and ideational influence. The United States became the uncontroversial hegemon in the system, staying on top of the systemic power pyramid.

Second, economic globalization and a relatively open world economy were taking shape. The end of the Cold War marked the end of the two economic blocs. The significance of their demise was no less striking than changes in other fields, for it inaugurated an era of genuine economic integration. For the first time in history, major economies became highly interdependent, together creating a world economy marked by a complex "you-in-me and me-in-you" relationship. Particularly worth mentioning is the fact that emerging economies found a more favorable environment for growth, taking advantage of the opening brought about by globalization and integrating themselves fairly rapidly into the world economic system. Their economic strategies and practices have been facilitated by the open global economic system while at the same time pushing this economic system farther along by both broadening and deepening it.

Third, efforts made to deal jointly with global issues were in fact creating a platform for international cooperation. With the rapid development of globalization, global issues and problems have loomed larger and larger. The issues are transnational in nature. Financial crises, terrorism, climate change, epidemics, poverty, refugees, proliferation of nuclear, chemical, and biological weapons, etc.— these problems have become significant threats to human well-being worldwide. They are threats without boundaries that exceed the ability of any single nation-state, no matter how powerful it may be, to resolve them (United Nations 2004). Some analysts believe that we have entered an era of transnational threats, stressing that such perils are even more serious than traditional security threats between states. Due to the transnational nature of global threats, it is wise to establish a basis for cooperation to deal with them effectively.

Fourth, most members of international society now share the view that multi-lateralism is the most important principle of the world order. In the wake of the Cold War's end, naked power politics was seriously questioned and realism as the dominant international relations theory began to lose influence. Since the 1980s, neo-liberal institutionalism has become a highly influential theory, exercising a direct impact on the establishment and maintenance of the world order (Keohane 2012). Robert Keohane (1984) emphasized the feasibility and necessity of an institutional world order, holding that multilateral rules, regimes, and decision-making procedures can function independently of hard, material power. Think-tank reports and strategic proposals identified multilateral institutions as the most distinctive features of an improved post-Cold War order and regarded what I term "institutional power" as one of the most important forms of power in such a world (Ikenberry & Slaughter 2006; Slaughter *et al.* 2008).

These features show that American power did indeed play a key role in the post-Cold War order. As the victor and the most powerful state to emerge from the ashes, the US naturally became the hegemon of the international system, assuming major responsibility for maintaining it. However, it would not be accurate to conflate the post-Cold War order *per se* with the American world order or the US hegemonic world order. No single country, not even the United States, is capable of controlling globalization or overcoming transnational threats. Besides, American liberalism has not been accepted universally (Acharya 2014).

The post-Cold War order, one that has been relatively open and tolerant, was enabled by some important elements of consensus in international circles, of which the most significant is widespread approval of multilateralism. In fact, it is commonly believed that "multilateralism matters" (Ruggie 1993). The Charter of the United Nations is committed to multilateralism, which continues to be the foundation for the institution's ideas and practices. Broadly speaking, the principle got its start after World War I, when many actors realized that naked power and balance of power could not effectively maintain peace and stability and might even result in systemic war. The lesson from the failure of the League of Nations led international society to a firmer belief that multilateralism, with necessary modifications, was the only way toward a better world, and the United Nations itself was the outcome of translating such ideals into reality. Following the end of the Cold War, this belief become even more deeply entrenched, especially when accompanied by the realization that no single state can solve the world's problems on its own.

Another important point of consensus concerns international cooperation. In general, the major players in the international system have tended to prefer cooperation. As globalization has proceeded apace, two major forces have coalesced, one representing established actors including the United States and other Western countries and the other bringing together emerging economies, most notably the BRICS group, whose members have developed rapidly in the process of globalization. On the one hand, the United States realizes that it faces challenges from emerging powers, especially from China, and takes them very seriously (Bernstein & Munro 1997). Nevertheless, it remains quite confident about its ability to direct international institutions, believing that the US-led international regimes were capable of integrating rising powers like China and that no revolutionary change in the international system would occur (Thornton 2008; Ikenberry 2008). In general, it must have seemed to American policymakers that a cooperative approach could serve to integrate new powers even more effectively than a policy of confrontation and exclusion. On the other hand, the newly emerging powers accepted the leading position of the United States; recognized the increasingly high degree of interdependence among various economies; tended to view globalization more as an opportunity for their economic development; and supported the idea that joint efforts were needed to respond to global issues and threats. China, for example, repeatedly stated that it would stick to the path of peaceful development and would not challenge the international order led by the United States (Zheng 2003). Furthermore, it has engaged and integrated with international society in practice (Qin 2016b). As a result, emerging countries also have adopted a more cooperative stance toward the established powers, especially the United States. In reality, the economies of all those countries today are highly interdependent.

A related item of consensus concerns governance by multilateral institutions. Transnational problems that accompany globalization threaten the entire world, all nations included. Furthermore, they are not problems that war can address. It seems that in the history of modern international relations, warfare has created more problems than it has solved. Thus, the most reasonable approach was to create and make use of international institutions. In the process of dealing with transnational threats, policymakers came to understand that the task of reconciling various interests, policies, and priorities required institutions to coordinate and seek compromise among them. In other words, they needed to establish a scheme of global governance based upon multilateral institutions, including effective and legitimate rules and regimes. Such institutions were no longer mere public goods provided by a particular actor, whether a state or an international organization. They also were urgently needed by all members of international society. Governance by multilateral institutions thus became a crucial, highly significant point of consensus among nations in the post–Cold War era, together with the tide of globalization and threats from transnational problems.

Thus, the chief elements of consensus among the members of international society concerning the need for *multilateralism, cooperation,* and *institutionalism* facilitated the formation and maintenance of the world order immediately after the Cold War ended. It was a relatively open and tolerant system, in which stability was largely maintained; an open economic system for development was highly valued; regional integration, such as the European Union and ASEAN forged quickly ahead; and new economies like China and the other BRICS countries developed with remarkable rapidity. Without these areas of consensus, such a world order would have been unthinkable. Moreover, among all the points of consensus enumerated here, multilateralism is perhaps the most significant. It is true that the United States played an important role as the most powerful nation in the world in the post–Cold War system. However, we must not forget it that there is a natural tension between multilateralism and hegemony, for multilateralism itself is a negation of unipolar dominance. The evolution of multilateral institutions and regimes is and will remain the key to world order. Contrary to what proponents of hegemonic stability theory may argue (Gilpin 1981; Organski & Kugler 1980), true multilateralism implies the weakening of hegemonic dominance. Though hegemonic institutionalism is perhaps a reasonable term to describe the post–Cold War order, a world with a much-weakened hegemon or without any hegemony at all is what awaits us in the future.

It is therefore reasonable to argue that the post-Cold War world order is characterized by "hegemonic institutionalism." It recognizes the important role played by the hegemonic power in the international system. This role, however, is possible only given the areas of consensus reached by members of international society at large.

## Problems of globalization

The process of globalization, continuously widening and deepening, has been accompanied by a dramatic spurt of growth in world wealth in general and in high-performing, emerging economies in particular. At the same time, however, problems have come to the fore together with globalization—most notably, the imbalance of power distribution, the unevenness of economic growth, and the deficits of global governance.

### Imbalance of power distribution

The distribution of capabilities among various actors in the international system has undergone rapid and significant change in the past three decades. The most conspicuous of these changes is the simultaneous rise of several major developing economies. The BRICS members have grown far wealthier, with China now having the second largest economy in the world. The United States—still the largest and most powerful country, with substantial global reach and influence—has experienced two Middle East wars, terrorist attacks, and serious financial crises. As a result, its relative power has been on the decline. In its global strategy, there has been a struggle between unilateralism and multilateralism, in which the former sometimes has gained the upper hand. The war in Iraq during the George W. Bush administration and the recent US decision to withdraw from the Paris Climate Accord and other international institutions exemplify unilateralism, which has reduced American soft power and actually weakened multilateralism.

While it remains true that the United States is the world's most powerful state, other players are rising to challenge it. Once again, China provides the best example. Although China was the least powerful major state in the immediate post-Cold War period, its subsequent economic dynamism has led some strategists to argue that the world is witnessing the emergence of a G2 power structure. Regardless, the process of power shifting is a conspicuous reality in the post-Cold War system. The problem is not a change in relative power, which (after all) occurs from time to time. Instead, it is the failure of international society to provide an appropriate and timely approach to deal realistically with that change, leading to a situation marked by imbalances of power, responsibility, and interest. If there is general agreement that multilateral institutionalism provides the most appropriate approach to international governance, then the existing global governing power—that is, the power to frame an issue, set an agenda, and provide rules and solutions—does not reflect power shifts that have occurred in the real world. Developing countries, despite their rapid and remarkable rise, contend with an obvious gap between their increasing capabilities and their relatively static shares of institutional power in global governance. Dissatisfaction follows. This has become a serious problem in the post-Cold War world order.

## Unevenness of economic growth

Despite the overall increase in global wealth since the end of the Cold War, there has been a clear imbalance when it comes to economic growth. By 2015, the national income per capita in the world's richest country was several hundred times more than that in the poorest country. Also, as overall wealth increased in the last decade of the 20th century, the number of people under poverty line rose as well. In many fields—such as the global division of labor, industrial structure, international trade, and the distribution of wealth—uneven development has remained highly visible. It has led to the revival of arguments based on neo-Marxist and/or dependency theory. In many cases, the gap between rich and poor countries has become increasingly evident, and the center/periphery division continues to be a structural fact that may lead to conflict and disorder (Frank 1967; Wallerstein 1974).

In addition to the gap between rich and poor countries, there is another dangerous gap: the one between rich and poor people within a given country. There is a greater risk to global governance and world order when complaints about economic inequality shift from the domestic to the international realm. People in developed countries, for example, complain that their jobs have been taken by workers in developing countries and that international refugees have derailed their lives. Britain's referendum to withdraw from the European Union was fueled very much by the refugee problem, and many other European countries, including major ones like France, also have witnessed a split between those who support globalization and those who oppose it. The 2017 riots that occurred in Charlottesville, Virginia, offer another example of how extreme nationalism can take the form of racism. In developing countries, especially rapidly growing ones such as the BRICS, the gap between rich and poor is also stunning. While the economy as a whole may have burgeoned remarkably, the poor do not feel that their situation is better because they compare it to that of the rich. Their experiences and feelings differ profoundly from those of economic elites.

Unless the world succeeds in reducing the gap between the rich and the poor, it never will achieve stability and peace. Poverty is an important source of instability and resentment about the unfair distribution of wealth, and it often serves as a trigger for revolution. Three decades of globalization, with a conspicuous emphasis on economic growth and market forces, have not successfully solved this problem and in some cases have made it even worse by widening rather than narrowing the economic gap.

## Deficits of global governance

Together with globalization, transnational problems have emerged in an unprecedented manner, and global governance—according to some parties—is necessary for handling them. But despite many serious declarations and much rhetoric, global governance has failed in important respects. Cooperation has not been as effective and reciprocal as predicted by liberal institutionalists, and the tragedy of the commons has arisen in many areas.

The financial crisis that began in 2007 is a telling example. It started in the United States, spread rapidly to other parts of the world, and gravely damaged the global economy. Almost none of the important economies was able to escape its effects. The crisis made people realize that a larger governing institution should be organized to deal with economic and financial problems worldwide better than the G7 had done. The result was the establishment of the G20, which made a crucial contribution to its solution. The G20 is more representative than its predecessor, including major economies as well as some important intergovernmental organizations. By joining the G20, up-and-coming countries like China and India drew closer to the center of world economic governance. However, as the crisis eased following its nadir in 2009, the G20 has not lived up to expectations, nor has it been able to make effective decisions on important economic reforms. Similarly, the Doha Round of world trade negotiations, which began in 2001, ended in failure in December of 2015.

Jones, Pascual, and Stedman (2009) have identified six areas in which transnational and global threats occur, including climate change, nuclear proliferation, the proliferation of biochemical weapons, civil violence, terrorism, and economic and financial crises. More than three decades of globalization have passed and none of the threatening issues in those areas has been dealt with effectively. Governance in the climate change area has met new setbacks by the US decision to withdraw from the Paris Accord, which had been reached after enormously difficult negotiations. Terrorism remains as worrisome as ever, while the menace of nuclear weapons appears to have become acute once again. Problems are accumulating and deficits of governance are daunting, making many people question the effectiveness and competence of the existing international political institutions. Loss of confidence in multilateral institutionalism for global governance constitutes an important condition for returning to unilateralism and power politics, at least in some countries (Qin 2013).

## Populist realism as a reaction against globalization

Voices of anti-globalization have been heard virtually since the trend began; yet now, given the increasing seriousness of global issues, anti-globalization has become something of a popular movement, one that is reflected in policies and strategies of important international players. The Brexit vote and the victory of the Trump campaign are often cited as examples of this tendency. But the situation is more dire than is indicated by those events. European countries have experienced divisive debates over globalization; indeed, the very developed nations that led the globalizing wave are now places where strong opposition to globalization is spreading rapidly. Some argue that anti-globalization constitutes a grassroots movement. No doubt it is, but it is also more than that. A recent manifesto by important conservative intellectuals, entitled "A Europe We Can Believe In" (a.k.a. "The Paris Statement"), has revealed the ideational split among elites (Bénéton *et al.* 2017). In short, as a movement, anti-globalism involves not only the grassroots, but all sectors of society, including intellectuals.

In general, the world is witnessing the rise of what I call "populist realism," a term that is intended to describe the combination of populism and *realpolitik* that has emerged at this historical moment. Populism holds that the identity, the "self," of a nation is the most important and political realism worships material power. The former finds expression in a mass movement, whereas the latter concerns state policy. Populist realism combines the two elements in their extreme forms, stressing the ultimate significance of the self-nation, the ultimate importance of the state interest, and the ultimate utility of coercive power. In recent years, it has been reflected in the resurgence of power politics, state-centrism, and extreme nationalism. It stands in stark contrast to the current of opinion that prevailed in the 1990s and 2000s, when globalization was taken as a positive phenomenon and transnational threats and global issues were high on the political agenda, especially that of important international stakeholders. In the realm of ideas, *realpolitik* was on the defensive, while neo-liberal institutionalism and social constructivism were gaining ground.

## *The revival of power politics*

The revival of power politics in international relations is reflected the worship of material capabilities, especially military might. Power always has been one of the key concepts of international relations and has never completely withdrawn from world affairs (Guzzini 2013). Traditionally, international relations theory defined it mainly in terms of its coercive and conquering aspects—or, to use a more descriptive term, "hard power." It is material in nature and coercive in function. Its core consists of military capabilities that enable conquest. Thus, the classical definition of power is the ability to make others do what they otherwise would not do (Dahl 1957: 2–3).

In the past two decades, however, conceptualization of power, along with the evolution of world politics, has expanded and changed. Scholars now are thinking about the nature of power in new ways. "Soft power," for example, has become an important concept of international politics, while "smart power" is a useful idea for strategists (Nye 2004). The conceptual expansion and reinterpretation of power, no matter whether we are talking about soft or smart power, tend to criticize the notion of naked, coercive power, reflecting a strong resentment against the domineering and violent uses of power emphasized in classical realism. Scholars even have begun to distinguish between "good" and "evil" power: Whereas the former treats others as ends in themselves, the latter regards them only as means. In addition, good power empowers others in a reciprocal manner, while the evil version deprives them of their rights (Haugaard 2012). These ideas about power are not only reinterpretations of the nature of the phenomenon; they also imply a strong criticism of power as coercion and oppression, and a tendency toward transforming power into something at least more persuasive and nonviolent influence. The return of power politics, which seems to be happening now, is regarded by critics as a regressive tendency. The current veneration of material capabilities and of military might suggests that a reversion to past forms of power is indeed underway.

## The return of state-centrism

The return of state-centrism has helped push the state again toward the center of world politics, recovering its status as an exclusive agent of control and coercion. Since 1648, when the Westphalian international system was established, the state has been the dominant actor in world affairs, standing as the highest authority internally and answering externally to no other power. Its identity was often conceived in opposition to an antagonistic "other" or "others," and the international system itself was considered an anarchic Hobbesian jungle characterized by the war of all against all. The struggle between the US and USSR, with its terrifying strategic arms race, provides a telling example: Their respective identities were created and strengthened in contrast to the hostile "other."

Globalization has rendered this conceptualization of the state problematic in three respects. First, the transnational threat allegedly posed by the other does not emanate from any state in particular. Rather, the other seems to encompass the entire world, and the totality of humankind. It is a threat to no single country, but to many or all, or else it is the common enemy of nations and peoples worldwide. Second, no individual country, regardless of how materially powerful it may be, can deal with the threat single-handedly. Although the United States is the world's only superpower, its anti-terrorist activities still need support from other countries and players. Financial crisis and economic sluggishness in today's world are also problems no country can solve on its own because economies worldwide are so closely interrelated. In short, the state, standing alone, is incapable of handling transnational and global challenges in the era of globalization (Nye 2002). Third, social forces have emerged dynamically. Transnational networks and non-governmental organizations have played an important role in various global issue areas, not only making people aware of such problems but also making states participate in the agenda-setting process. Despite the fact that the state continues to be the leading actor in world affairs, social forces have become increasingly influential and have claimed a share in some of the power that used to belong to the state alone. The resurgence of state-centrism attempts to re-establish the state's exclusive, authoritative status. The state is the dominant player in world politics. The most serious threats at the global level are again defined as those coming from other states, and the most effective means to deal with such threats is again defined in terms of hard power, especially military strength.

## *The resurgence of extreme nationalism*

The resurgence of extreme nationalism goes against globalization *per se*. The nation-state as a central concept of international politics reflecting the essence of modernity is itself a product of modernism, indicative of modernist ideas and practices. As such, nationalism was—and remains—a necessary element in the formation of the modernist state, since it evokes and appeals to national sentiment, thus fostering the increased cohesiveness that nation-states require. On the other hand, nationalism also serves to facilitate extremist ideas and forces. Once nationalism reaches truly extreme levels, its dangerous, negative effects become all too obvious. Extreme nationalism assumes the inferiority of every other nation, the citizens of which are seen as hostile aliens whose sole purpose is to serve as means to achieve its own ends. It dismisses the seriousness of transnational threats and refuses to sacrifice any national sovereignty or advantage in order to attain public goods. Once extreme nationalism becomes an influential ideational force and even policy practice, it will derail common efforts to deal with global issues and destroy the consensus in favor of global governance. The global village will be fragmented and nobody will care about the global commons.

Consequently, two camps have formed in world politics: one that continues to support an inclusive international society, an open world economy, progressive regional integration, and effective global governance, and another that promotes populist realism and advocates nationalistic politics regarding economic development, international trade, immigration, and so forth. These forces exist not only at the level of ideas; they are already influencing policymaking and strategic decisions.

## Future world order

Global problems and transnational threats have been left unresolved while the anti-global movement with populist realism at its core has grown stronger and more vociferous. Praise for the virtues of a world without order is now heard almost everywhere. It seems that the international system has come to another crossroads. To move forward to the future or back to the future is the question the world needs to answer (Mearsheimer 1990).

It is almost a certainty that in the foreseeable future, the debate and competition between globalization and global governance, on the one hand, and anti-globalization and populist realism, on the other, will play a crucial role in determining what kind of order will be built. In some countries, including several of the major players on the world stage, policies and strategies will lean more toward the second alternative. However, most of the world will move forward. In other words, the world will have an order based primarily on multilateralism and will rely on multilateral institutions as its main governing mechanisms. Along with the evolution of world politics, international society needs an order that more faithfully reflects a balance among various forces and that rests more firmly on genuine multilateral institutions and rules. The United States as the most powerful country in the world will continue to play an important role, but multilateral consultation and coordination will become more common in global governance. It will be increasingly a consultative, ruled-based multilateralism, or what I would like to term "the new multilateral institutionalism". In this process, hegemonic domination will decline, multilateral consultation will increase, and multiple cultures and values will find more representation. A world order based on multilateral institutionalism will continue to improve and consolidate.

The world order cannot simply move back to a Hobbesian future, as Mearsheimer has predicted, for globalization has become a part of our new reality and cannot be undone, as some would wish. Just as Columbus discovered two new continents and thereby expanded both the world and human consciousness of the planet's geography, the end of the Cold War expanded human connectivity across the board, starting in the economic realm and spreading quickly to almost all other arenas. It is practically impossible for human and national activities to shrink back to their original corners. Globalization, together with the transnational forces and technological innovations that have helped to push it forward, has connected the world into a multiple and complex whole, whose parts are closely related and interdependent. Acharya (2014) quite rightly believes that it is something like a multiplex cinema, with different films being shown in different theaters, giving moviegoers an opportunity to choose which they prefer to see. Moreover, the theaters should not be treated as isolated from one another; indeed, the themes of the films they present should be thought of as cross-influencing. Different films interpenetrate and intermingle. In other words, the world is more like a web with everything related to everything else; that is—again metaphorically—the themes of the different films interpenetrate and intermingle. The globalized world is more like a place where movement in one part will affect other parts and indeed the whole system (Qin 2016a). In such a situation, no country is able to stand alone, move alone, and withdraw alone. The cost of withdrawal from globalization is enormous.

Furthermore, globalization has changed people's mindsets to a large extent. While it is true that the world today retains many important aspects of the past, at the same time we need to recognize that great ideational changes have occurred in terms of power and responsibility, global commons and governance, communication and connectivity, and even the meaning of life itself. In the foreseeable future, we undoubtedly will see an intensive struggle between the forces for and against globalization and multilateral institutionalism. We may face a world that sometimes will seem quite strange to us and certainly different from what we have experienced over the last few decades. But globalization is largely irreversible, and the ideational change it has brought about will not move back to the future. For example, despite policies designed to slow or halt globalization and multilateralism, the United States will not be able to withdraw to the isolationism of the past. It is also impossible for China to re-close its door to the rest of the world as it had done before the reform and opening policy was adopted.

Moreover, the world will not move back to the future for another reason: A world order based on multilateral institutionalism is the most appropriate form so far discovered in the history of international relations. Globalization will press forward and global governance will continue to be indispensably necessary. Accordingly, how to govern, and why, will continue to be a major issue, both in theory and in practice. Despite the inadequacy of existing international institutions, the use of multilateral institutions to deal with global issues and transnational threats continues to be the most reasonable approach. An imperial system long since has been consigned to the dust bin of history. Hegemonic world order resembles autocracy in domestic affairs. We may wish to have a benign hegemon, but no one can guarantee such an outcome. An order resting on balance of power never was suited for the job of resolving global issues, and has proven unable to maintain peace. To some extent, the multilaterally institutional order, as embodied by the principles and practices of the UN system, was a response to the inability of the balance of power regime to prevent war. It will continue to be the most reasonable and democratic world order ever seen in international relations, especially when compared with imperialism, hegemony, and balance-of-power politics.

To a large extent, the long peace that had prevailed since the end of World War II owes to the multilaterally institutional order associated with the United Nations. It has changed the belief and international practice according to which war is the final solution to conflict in foreign relations and in human affairs in general. Its purposes and principles—namely, resolving conflict through multi-lateral institutions and saving the nations of the world from the scourge of war—laid the foundation for the contemporary order and have made positive contributions to peace and prosperity. Despite its various shortcomings and inadequacies, and despite inevitable interference by powerful countries, the United Nations has been the optimal, paradigmatic venue for governance based on multilateral institutionalism. From time to time, its working mechanisms have obliged important players to resist the impulse to use force at critical moments and enabled the world economic system to keep moving toward more open and inclusive arrangements. Its norms have introduced new and progressive ideas in world affairs, such as cross-civilization dialogue and an emphasis on human security. The most important thing, however, is that from the very outset of globalization its firm belief in multilateral institutionalism has set the stage for global governance through multilateral institutions. The United Nations has shown that multilateralism, as embodied in its own principles and practices, is what international society wants and needs. What is more, a UN-style system of multilateral governance corresponds to the interests of the majority of nations in the world; thus, it should count as the most reasonable world order in the history of international relations. It is more democratic than the imperial order; it is more peace-oriented than power politics and balance of power; and it is more open and inclusive than hegemony.

Of course, this does not mean that rules and institutions are all perfect and effective. The fact that global problems and transnational threats have not been effectively dealt with, let alone solved, demonstrates the failure of existing institutions to meet the needs of globalization. The current institutional system does not reflect a balanced distribution of institutional power, nor does it contain an effective mechanism for balanced socio-economic development and fairer distribution of wealth. Likewise, it does not display a genuine inclusivity of multiple cultures and practices in today's world. In addition, serious deficits in the supply of institutions, both qualitatively and quantitatively, have begun to appear. In terms of quality, the existing international institutions were designed for managing inter-state relations, and therefore by design they are not meant to govern the global commons or to coordinate the efforts of various actors to attain shared goals. In performance they have already shown this critical weakness. In terms of quantity, they are also far from adequate. Together with globalization and technological innovation, new fields and frontier areas have emerged rapidly, for some of which almost no agreed-upon rules and institutions exist. Rules designed to manage conflict between two states, for example, are unable to respond effectively to climate change or international refugees. Rules and regimes governing such new areas as the space or the internet are yet to become acceptable, let alone institutionalized, even though there has been an increasing awareness that these areas should be governed. To some extent, anti-globalization voices and policies demonstrate just how important it is to update and upgrade existing international institutions along with the changing global scenario to meet current needs. The reform, supplementation, and perfection of existing international institutions are practical actions we need to take to build an order better designed for the era of globalization and of transnational threats.

New multilateral institutionalism provides a reasonable approach to insuring more effective global governance and a more sustainable world order. What I mean by "new multilateral institutionalism" is a kind of multilateral institutionalism that takes institutions as the primary mechanism for global governance and that embraces *pluralism,* values *partnership*, and encourages *participation* on an equal footing. Resting firmly on the belief in and practice of multilateralism and institutional governance and facing an era of declining hegemony, new multilateral institutionalism is, by definition, no longer the hegemonic institutionalism which, though recognizing the importance of institutional governance, tends to lecture the members of international society, especially the lesser ones, on what they should do and even who they should be (Finnemore 1996). In other words, it is not the kind of institutionalism that hegemonizes and homogenizes. Rather, it recognizes diversity and respect heterogeneity. It is more democratic, more inclusive, and therefore more legitimate. For the new multilateral institutionalism, pluralism, partnership, and participation are the key words that apply throughout the process of globalization and global governance.

## Conclusion

International society continuously evolves. Despite the anxiety, crisis, and even regressive tendencies that may endure for a period of time, that evolution is generally progressive over the long run. Mearsheimer's prophecy that the world would move "back to the future" (Mearsheimer 1990) has not and will not become true. Nor, despite its messy look now, will the world regress toward a Hobbesian jungle. A multilateral institutional order reflects the evolution of international society, and is a principle better than any other form in international relations history: i.e., it is more representative, democratic, and legitimate. It may not be as "effective" as hegemony or rule by power, but it is headed in the right direction, and it facilitates global governance as a legitimate process of consultation, coordination, and cooperation. Compared with other forms of world order, it is in line with interests of the majority of nations and acceptable to sovereign states and other international actors as well.

At the same time, reform is very much needed. The rise of the anti-globalization movement and populist realism accent both the need for and the urgency of change. Reform, however, is not intended to overthrow existing international institutions and replace them with something completely different. Moreover, it is by no means supposed to negate the principle of multilateral institutionalism as the key to global governance. Rather, it is meant to reinforce multilateral institutionalism through a more balanced distribution of institutional power and a more adequate institutional framework to deal with global issues in various areas. Reforms should enable us to sidestep the logic of collective action and the tragedy of the commons. To complement such reforms, it is absolutely necessary that members of international society, especially its important stakeholders, to rebuild their consensus for a more resolute support of multilateral institutionalism as the foundation for the world order and to make joint participation, consultative cooperation, and inclusivity its essential elements and practices.

## References

Acharya, A. 2014. *The End of American Order*. Cambridge: Polity Press.
Bénéton, P. *et al.* 2017. "A Europe We Can Believe In." Available at www.the trueeurope.eu.
Bernstein, R. & R. H. Munro. 1997. *The Coming Conflict with China*. New York: Alfred A. Knopf.
Dahl, R. 1957. "The Concept of Power." *Behavioral Science* 2(3): 201–215.
Finnemore, M. 1996. *National Interests in International Society*. Ithaca, NY: Cornell University Press.
Frank, A. G. 1967. *Capitalism and Underdevelopment in Latin America*. New York: Monthly Review Press.
Gilpin, R. 1981. *War and Change in World Politics*. Cambridge: Cambridge University Press.
Guzzini, S. 2013. *Power, Realism and Constructivism*. New York: Routledge.
Hauguaad, M. 2012. "Rethinking the Four Dimensions of Power: Domination and empowerment." *Journal of Political Power* 5(1): 33–54.

Ikenberry, J. 2008. "The Rise of China and the Future of the West." *Foreign Affairs* 87(1): 23–37.

Ikenberry, J. 2009. "Liberal Internationalism 3.0: America and the dilemma of liberal world order." *Perspectives on Politics* 7(1): 71–87.

Ikenberry, J. & A.-M. Slaughter. 2006. *Forging the World of Liberty under Law: U.S. strategic security in the 21st century—Final report of the Princeton Project on National Security*. Available at www.princeton.edu/~ppns/report/FinalReport.pdf.

Jones, B., C. Pascual, & S. Stedman. 2009. *Power and Responsibility: Building international order in an era of transnational threats*. Washington, DC: Brookings Institution Press.

Keohane, R. 1984. *After Hegemony: Cooperation and discord in world political economy*. Princeton, NJ: Princeton University Press.

Keohane, R. 2012. "Twenty Years of Institutional Liberalism." *International Relations* 26(2): 125–138.

Mearsheimer, J. 1990. "Back to the Future: Instability in Europe after the Cold War." *International Security* 15(1): 5–56.

Mearsheimer, J. 2001. *The Tragedy of Great Power Politics*. New York: W. W. Norton.

Nye, J. 2002. *The Paradox of American Power: Why the world's only superpower can't go it alone*. New York: Oxford University Press.

Nye, J. 2004. *Soft Power: The means to success in world politics*. New York: Public Affairs.

Organski, A. F. K. & J. Kugler. 1980. *The War Ledger*. Chicago, IL: The University of Chicago Press.

Qin, Y. 2013. "Quanqiu Zhili Shiling yu Shijie Zhixu Linian de Chongjian" ["Global Governance Failure and Ideational Reconstruction of the World Order"]. *Shijie Jingji yu Zhengzhi* [*World Economics and Politics*] 4: 4–18.

Qin, Y. 2016a. "A Relational Theory of World Politics." *International Studies Review* 18: 33–47.

Qin, Y. 2016b. *Shijian yu Biange: Zhongguo Canyu Guoji Tixi Jincheng Yanjiu* [*Practice and Co-evolution: China's engagement with the international system*]. Beijing: World Affairs Press, 2016.

Ruggie, J. (ed.). 1993. *Multilateralism Matters: The theory and praxis of an institutional form*. New York: Columbia University Press.

Slaughter, A.-M. *et al*. 2008. *Strategic Leadership: Framework for a 21st century national security strategy*. Available at http://fsi.stanford.edu/sites/default/StrategicLeadership.pdf.

Thornton, J. 2008. "Long Time Coming." *Foreign Affairs* 87(1): 2–22.

United Nations. 2004. *A More Secure World: Our shared responsibility*. Report of the High-level Panel on Threats, Challenges and Change. New York: United Nations.

Wallerstein, I. 1974. *The Modern World-System, vol. I*. New York: Academic Press.

Zheng, B. 2003. "Zhongguo Heping Jueqi de Xin Daolu yu Yazhou de Weilai" ["The New Path of China's Peaceful Rise and the Future of Asia"]. Speech at the Bo'ao Forum. Available at www.sina.com.cn.

# 10

# THE TRIUMPH OF EXTERNAL FREEDOM

## Conflicting liberties and modernities in comparative perspective

*C. K. Martin Chung*

Because the Chinese have had too much freedom, that's why China needs revolution. The aims of the Chinese Revolution are different from the aims of foreign revolutions.

*Sun Yat-sen, 1924*

Freedom, politically understood, is primarily a moral, domestic-political concept. … The German concept of freedom was always directed to the international context … [It was] a concept of protest, of self-centered defense against anything curbing nationalistic-racial egotism.

*Thomas Mann, 1945*

As World War I (1914–1918) approached its centennial anniversary, the world remembered its horrors and commemorated its victims. With major monographs from Christopher Clark's *The Sleepwalkers* to Margaret MacMillan's *The War That Ended Peace*, both published in 2014, popular and scholarly debates on the causes and legacies of the Great War have been going on ever since. The concurrent dramatic turn of the Ukraine crisis in late 2013, culminating in the Russian take-over of Crimea in March of the following year, only further heightened public sensibilities towards the possible and perhaps even imminent repetition of the mistakes of the 20th century. After all, when Russian President Vladimir Putin addressed the State Duma on March 18, 2014 on the occasion of the official annexation of Crimea, he spoke of restoring the unity of "historical Russia" (kremlin.ru 2014). One can only gasp at the prospect of others emulating Putin's Russia to restore "historical Mongolia" or "historical Germany."

This reflective impulse linking past and present, however, did not stop at the theatre of the original conflict. Not a few students of history have asked whether Europe then could be a useful "mirror" for present-day antagonists elsewhere. Mac-Millan notes, for instance, that it is "tempting—and sobering—to compare today's relationship between China and the US with that between Germany and England a century ago" (MacMillan 2013: n.p.). The Oxford historian was hardly the only one tempted to compare the European past and the Asian or Pacific present. Those who study German history and foreign policy speak of the "striking parallels between the prewar situation of the Kaiserreich and China's current condition," especially in terms of their international status ambitions and the problems these entail (Wolf 2014: 186). And, in terms of the relationship between economic and political freedom, both cases suggest that "economic modernization and trade integration do not by themselves lead to political openness" (Grimmer-Solem 2015: 117). Some commentators also point to the sense of humiliation shared by Germany after the Treaty of Versailles and China ever since the Opium Wars, while others question squarely the increasingly assertive Chinese foreign policy under the present Communist Party of China chief Xi Jinping (Ferdinand 2016; Cabestan 2017) and whether this recent shift resembles that of the German empire under Wilhelm II (Gwyn 2013). The common undertone of these comparative reflections is that the "sleepwalking" Europe—especially Germany—of the past century can offer an invaluable object lesson for "rising" Asia or "dreaming" China (Wang 2014) of the so-called Pacific Century: a reflective angle also explored by some within contemporary China itself (Yu 2010).[1]

While conscious of the Sinophobic potentials and deterministic tendencies of such Sino-German comparisons across time, such as the kind of Eurocentric-trajectory thinking identified by Goody (2006: 25), this essay aims to further this comparative endeavor by way of humanistic and political philosophical reflection. It borrows from Thomas Mann's post-1945 self-critique of previous German political thought and political culture, especially what he called the German misconception of freedom (*Freiheit*). The basic assumption is that what Mann diagnosed as the tragic German preoccupation with "external freedom" (*äußere Freiheit*) at the expense of "internal freedom" (*innere Freiheit*) in the European age of nationalism,[2] which is linked, according to him, to the "failed German revolutions,"[3] may not be a characteristic unique to pre-1945 Germany. After all, there is much to be said about Asian nationalisms that, despite significant differences, share profound similarities with their European predecessors or counterparts (Zhao 2004). It will be argued here, in fact, that the tension between internal and external freedom as identified by Mann also exists in Chinese revolutionary thinking: namely, to borrow an early observer's terms, the tension between "national liberty" and "individual liberty" (Linebarger 1937: 98–99). Evidence is sought in the key writings of Sun Yat-sen (1866–1925), *the* quintessential Chinese revolutionary revered across the Taiwan Strait. In a nutshell, it can be argued that for Sun, the "father of the nation" and first president of Republican China, external freedom trumped internal freedom, which he saw rather as a root cause of imperial China's lack of external freedom. In other words, it appears that there are not only values in conflict, such as freedom and equality, two of the key values of modernity since the Enlightenment shared by both liberals and socialists (Gamble 2000: 36), but that there is also a conflict within the value of freedom itself.[4] Furthermore, manifestations of such a conflict are not only confined to the revolutionary era in the past. A case in point is the contemporary example of the Chinese

Communist state arrogating to itself the concept of *weiquan* (維權) or "rights protection/defense"—an internal-liberal concept—for the alleged protection of China's territorial and maritime rights. A brief examination of this "new" manifestation of the "old" conflict between internal and external freedoms will be conducted in the third section of the essay.

We begin by explicating Mann's two concepts of freedom as put forward in a 1945 speech at the Library of Congress in Washington, D.C., entitled "Germany and the Germans."[5] Equipped with these conceptual tools, we proceed to analyze key passages from Sun Yat-sen's *Three Principles of the People* (三民主義 *sanmin zhuyi*), in which Sun problematized the concept of freedom (自由 *ziyou*) in relation to the revolutionary vision he had for post-dynastic China. This analysis provides support for the aforementioned argument that the tension between external and internal freedom, as observed by Mann in pre-1945 German history, with the fateful recurring triumph of external freedom as the overarching political obsession legitimizing internal oppression, is also present in Chinese history, even during revolutionary times, when internal freedom—to follow Mann—should have taken center stage. To interpret these difficult passages of Sun's from a liberal viewpoint, some hermeneutical maneuvers will be proposed at the end of the essay.

## Thomas Mann's two concepts of freedom

In his 1945 speech marking his 70th birthday (Mayer 1992: 41, 45), the Nobel laureate delivered to his audience what must have sounded like a confession-cum-indictment of his fellow Germans. "I am to speak to you today on Germany and the Germans—a risky undertaking, not only because the topic is so complex ... To deal with it purely psychologically, *sine ira et sine studio*, would appear almost immoral in view of the unspeakable that this unfortunate people has done to the world. Should a German avoid this subject today?" (Mann 1947: 9–10). Forewarning his audience that their speaker was part and parcel of *that* Germany being criticized, who "does have something to do with German fate and German guilt," Mann began his at first personal and then collective self-revelation of what he was suggesting as the "secret union of the German spirit with the demonic" (Mann 1947: 14). It was in this context that he brought up the person of Martin Luther, a "gigantic incarnation of the German spirit," whose politics and legacy were partly to blame for the German problem (Mann 1947: 17).

Among other misgivings the writer had about the theologian was the latter's much-criticized position during the Peasants' Revolt of 1524–1525.

> [Luther] was a freedom hero—but in the German style, for he knew nothing of liberty. I am not speaking now of the freedom of the Christian person (*Christenmensch*),[6] but of political freedom, the freedom of the citizen (*Staatsbürger*)—this freedom not only left him cold, but its stirrings and demands were deeply repugnant to him.
>
> *(Mann 1947: 19)*

Luther's "anti-political servility" was to blame for having shaped the "centuries-old, obsequious attitude of the Germans towards their princes and all state authorities," their "political immaturity" (Mann 1947: 22).

Mann, however, did not go on to distinguish Christian or theological freedom from civic or political freedom. Instead, he expounded the differences between what he called external and internal freedom:

> Freedom, politically understood, is primarily a moral, domestic-political concept. A people who is not internally free and answerable for their own actions does not deserve external freedom ... The German concept of freedom was always directed to the international; it meant the right to be German, only German and nothing else and nothing beyond that. It was a concept of protest, of self-centered defense against anything curbing nationalistic-racial (*völkisch*) egotism.
>
> *(Mann 1947: 22–23)*

In other words, external freedom (*äußere Freiheit*) is understood in the context of a people's relations to the outside world. It demands the right to be oneself and to act according to the will of the people in defense against anything that attempts to limit that collective individualism. Internal freedom (*innere Freiheit*), on the other hand, is to be understood in the context of the relationship between the citizens and the state: that is, to what extent state power is put under sufficient and effective control so that the rights of the citizens are not at its mercy. Mann lamented that in German history, the concept of external freedom had always triumphed over the concept of internal freedom. "[It is] an externally oriented defiant individualism in relation to the world, to Europe, to civilization. Internally, it comes with a disturbing measure of illiberality, immaturity, and insipid subservience" (Mann 1947: 22–23).

Mann was hardly the lone voice along this line of postwar German reflection. Fritz Bauer (1903–68), the state attorney general of Hesse who was instrumental in the (West) German transitional justice processes,[7] also sought to pinpoint an aspect of the fateful internal-external tension in German culture and history. Commenting on the pedagogical aims of the first Frankfurt Auschwitz trial[8] in 1963, the German-Jewish jurist said,

> Although heroic valor has been celebrated in Germany—there was bravery and courage in every direction against the external enemy—there has been a complete neglect [of the fact] that civil courage, i.e. the courage before the enemy [of justice] in one's own people, is just as great if not greater, and is in no way less required. One has fully overlooked that it is both honorable and a duty to work for justice also in his own state.
>
> *(Perels & Wojak 1998: 114)*

In a wider perspective, Mann's expressions of "internal" and "external" freedom call further to mind the twin security as *raison d'être* of Hobbes's *Leviathan*: (internal) protection/peace/conservation and (external) defense of the people. For "if there be no Power erected, … they can expect hereby no defense, nor protection, neither against a Common enemy, nor against the injuries of one another" (Hobbes 1904: chapter 14). At first glance, the two dualisms appear as mere reformulations of each other. However, beneath the surface lies significant divergence. To begin with, Mann's internal freedom is not about being free from the whims and violence of one another as common citizens; rather, it is about freedom from that "militant slave mentality" (*militanter Knechtssinn*) that characterized the German citizen-state relationship (Mann 1947: 23). And when it comes to external freedom, the difference is more complicated. On the one hand, Mann minced no words when criticizing the *German* version of the idea. "The German idea of freedom is nationalistic-racial (*völkisch*), anti-European, bordering on the barbaric," he said, and "against civilization" (Mann 1947: 24–25). Such a "freedom" is "narrowing and depressing" (Mann 1947: 24). On the other hand, however, against this dark version of external freedom, Mann also outlined a benign and self-opening vision of such freedom: the French "nation" is a "revolutionary and liberal (*freitheitlich*) concept that includes what belongs to humanity (*das Menschheitliche*) and means freedom in the domestic-political sphere and Europe in the international context" (Mann 1947: 23–24). According to Mann, Goethe, in contrast to his German contemporaries, "approved everything of a broad and generous nature: the supranational (*das Übernationale*), the Germanism of the literature of the world" (Mann 1947: 25). This stands in sharp contrast to the self-enclosing "German monoculture": "separatist, anti-Roman, anti-European" (Mann 1947: 17).

It is clear from the context that Nazi Germany was for Mann the tragic example of a people having absolute external, "ultranational" freedom while being internally unfree in the extreme. But how did Germany arrive at that horrid state of affairs? And how did the confusion of the two freedoms come about in German history in the first place? On this point Mann was largely in agreement with a version of the German *Sonderweg* thesis, according to which the fact that Germany had never had a "successful" revolution was paramount (Kontje 2011: 154–56):

Why does the German yearning for freedom always have to end up in inner unfreedom? Why did it finally have to culminate in the assassination attempt on the freedom of all others and on freedom itself? The reason is that Germany has never had a revolution and learned to unite the concept of the nation with the concept of freedom.

*(Mann 1947: 23–24)*

In other words, the so-called "liberal nationalism" (Kontje 2011: 154; Auer 2004) found, or purportedly found, in other European countries was absent in pre-1945 German history due to the lack of a *successful* revolution in which success would be indicated by the express goal and the actual achievement of internal, domestic-political freedom for the citizens vis-à-vis state power. Hence Mann would even object to calling Germany a "nation," given the term's "historical connectedness with freedom" (Mann 1947: 24). The failure of "great men," including Goethe, to undo the "Lutheran dualism of spiritual and political freedom" was also to blame for the lack of integration of the political element into the concept of education (Mann 1947: 25–26).

To conclude, before we move on to the next section to identify similar struggles in Chinese revolutionary thought, let us summarize Mann's argument. He claims that the tension between external and internal freedom, or even the perennial domination of the former over the latter, has burdened German history up until 1945, with tragic consequences—and not only for victims of German aggression. In this sense, it can be deduced that the reversal of such domination, that is, the restoration of the primacy of internal freedom over the obsession with external freedom (in the ultra-national rather than the supra-national sense),[9] necessarily accompanies successful social transformations, whether through reform or revolution. While one might rightfully consider this to be but a belated classical-liberal conviction in postwar Germany, Mann's self-criticism still deserves credit for its forceful emphasis on the ideas of external freedom and collective individualism as having a potent hold on the political imagination of particular nationalities with distinctive cultural and historical trajectories. In the following, it shall be demonstrated that these powerful ideas have also left their mark on the Chinese Revolution of 1911, and possibly beyond.

## Sun Yat-sen's "nationalism" and "rights of the people"

Between January and August of 1924, about twelve years after the end of the Qing Dynasty (1644–1912) and one year before his own death, the 58-year-old Sun Yat-sen delivered a series of speeches at the Kwangtung Higher Normal School, which are collectively known as *Sanmin Zhuyi*, or the *Three Principles of the People* (Wilbur 1976: 197–198). It wasn't the mature revolutionary who had first published his three principles in a Tokyo newspaper in 1905, after having reached the age of 39 and suffered a couple of failed revolts. It was a much older Sun, who had been made "president" twice (provisional and extraordinary) and grand marshal against usurpers and who had seen and experienced a number of intrigues, betrayals, and even attempts to restore the imperial system (in 1915 and 1917). The apparently perennial fragmentation and warlordization of the newborn republic wearied him.[10] Sun's resentment can be palpably felt in the sixteen *sanmin* lectures, which contain complaints not only against "Tatar barbarians" (i.e., the Qing Manchus as a foreign minority ruling over the Han majority) and Western aggressors, but also against internal factiousness, or what he called the "sand-like looseness"[11] of the Chinese nation. In the very first of the six lectures on "Nationalism" (民族主義 *minzu zhuyi*). he lamented that

> [I]n spite of four hundred million people gathered together in one China, we
> are in fact but a sheet of loose sand. We are the poorest and weakest state in

the world, occupying the lowest position in international affairs; the rest of mankind is the carving knife and the serving dish, while we are the fish and the meat. Our position now is extremely perilous; if we do not earnestly promote nationalism and weld together our four hundred millions into a strong nation, we [will] face a tragedy—the loss of our country and the destruction of our race. To ward off this danger, we must espouse nationalism and employ the national spirit to save the country.

*(Sun 1929: Nationalism Lecture 1, pp. 7–8)*[12]

As Sun explained in plain language, his *Sanmin-ism* is but save-the-country-ism [救國主義 *jiuguo zhuyi*] (Sun 1929: Nat. Lect. 1, p. 1). The survival of the (Han-) Chinese nation[13] was threatened by foreign powers externally, and by the incompetence and recalcitrance of the ruling Manchus internally (Sun 1929: Nat. Lect. 1, pp. 19–20). Given this overarching preoccupation with (Han-)national survival from the depredations of "foreign" enemies both inside and outside China, it comes as little surprise that the first mentions of freedom (自由 *ziyou*) in *Three Principles* are externally contextualized: It is about China's "freedom" to set customs duties for foreign imports, and small nations' "freedom" from European imperialism (Sun 1929: Nat. Lect. 2 and 4).

The most substantial elaboration on freedom, however, took place in the second of Sun's six lectures on "the rights of the people" (民權主義 *minquan zhuyi*), or the principle of democracy. It is also here that one can see clearly the tension between what Mann called external and internal freedom. In short, the mostly negative connotations of internal freedom—i.e., in the context of citizen-state relations—that are found in this particular lecture leave little interpretive room for a positive evaluation of the concept within *Sanmin-ism*. In fact, Sun blamed "too much" internal freedom outright for China's lack of external freedom:

Because we have had too much liberty without any unity and resisting power, because we have become a sheet of loose sand and so have been invaded by foreign imperialism and oppressed by the economic control and trade wars of the Powers, without being able to resist. [In order to be able to resist foreign oppression in the future, we] must break down individual liberty and become pressed together into an unyielding body like the firm rock which is formed by the addition of cement to sand.

*(Sun 1929: Democracy Lecture 2, p. 42)*

That "cement," Sun argued, is "our revolution-ism" or revolutionary principles (革命主義 *geming zhuyi*), which is *Sanmin-ism* and the five-power constitution (Sun 1929: Dem. Lect. 2, p. 45).[14] The cementation process, aside from overthrowing the Qing yoke and establishing the republic, also should involve the sacrifice of individual nationals' freedom for the freedom of the national—that is, collective—individual in the international context:

The individual should not have too much freedom, but the nation should have complete freedom. When the nation can act freely, then China may be called strong. To make the nation free, we must each sacrifice his personal freedom.

(Sun 1929: Dem. Lect. 2, p. 44)[15]

Sun's illiberal definition of internal and external freedom does not seem to be a mere passing remark. Rather, the founder of the Kuomintang, one of Taiwan's two major parties at present, was at pains to outline the major differences between European and Chinese political/historical trajectories. He argued that premodern Europe was far more despotic, or internally unfree,[16] than dynastic China, hence the European need to arrive at internal freedom through revolution. But, he continued, this was not the case for China:

We today cannot imagine what the people of Europe suffered under their feudal rule; it was far worse than anything the Chinese have ever suffered under their autocracies. ... [T]he dynasties and governments which followed the Qin adopted a much more liberal policy towards the people; apart from paying the regular grain taxes the people had almost no relation with the officials. The European tyranny in one way or another pressed directly down upon the shoulders of the common people. As this lasted very long and despotism developed more and more systematically, conditions became worse than anything we have ever experienced in China. ... We can see from this that the Chinese people have not been directly subjected to the oppression of autocracy. ... The Chinese people, therefore, felt very little resentment against their emperors.

(Sun 1929: Dem. Lect. 2, pp. 32–34)

For this reason, China did not need to have a revolution for the sake of internal freedom, which, according to him, "the Chinese had already aplenty" (Sun 1929: "The People's Rights," Lecture 2, p. 38). Rather, revolution was needed in China for its "cementing" effect on national strength and, ultimately, external freedom. "Because the Chinese have had too much freedom, that's why China needs revolution. The aims of the Chinese Revolution are different from the aims in foreign revolutions. ... [T]he aims of our revolution are just the opposite of the aims of the revolutions of Europe" (Sun 1929: Dem. Lect. 2, p. 42). In other words, the ruling Manchus or the Chinese dynastic system as a whole had to be replaced not primarily because they were illiberal, but due to their inability to attain China's external freedom, as a result of which ordinary Chinese suffered "indirect tyranny":

Their sufferings have come indirectly. Because our state has been weak, we have come under the political and economic domination of foreign countries and have not been able to resist. Now our wealth is exhausted and our people are destitute, suffering poverty. This kind of suffering is indirect, not direct [from the tyranny of one's own state].

(*Sun 1929: Dem. Lect. 2, p. 33*)

Because of this unjust suffering, Sun would even go further, reprimanding those Chinese youths who were "seduced" by the anti-nationalistic cosmopolitanism (世界主義 *shijie zhuyi*) of some Western thinkers, which—although conducive to the attainment of internal freedom in different compositions of majority-minority power relations within a state—was deemed by the ailing revolutionary as counterproductive to the more urgent goal of external freedom and to the "mission" of the Chinese, the "victimized nation" (受屈民族 *shouqu minzu*).

Now we want to revive China's lost nationalism and use the strength of our four hundred million to fight for mankind against injustice; this is our divine mission. The Powers are afraid that we will have such thoughts and are setting forth a specious doctrine. They are now advocating cosmopolitanism to inflame us. … [L]ed astray by this doctrine, some of China's youths … have been opposing nationalism. But it is not a doctrine that victimized nations should talk about. We, the victimized nation, must first recover our position of national freedom and equality before we are fit to discuss cosmopolitanism.

(*Sun 1929: Dem. Lect. 4, p. 67*)

Sun's supposition that Western powers harbor ulterior motives in their preaching of cosmopolitanism should sound eerily analogous to present-day Chinese critiques (both official and popular) against the so-called "Western universal values." A *People's Daily* editorial in 2017 read: "Being superstitious and blindly following Western values will [lead one to] fall into the trap of Western 'universal values,' bow down before others, and even upset the foundation of our nation" (People's Daily 2017). A century or so after the overthrow of China's last dynasty, the editorial writer could have drawn a quotation or two directly from the "Father of the Nation" himself to strengthen the Communist regime's claim to be his true heir.

## From internal to external *weiquan:* The perennial triumph of external freedom?

What is worrisome, from the present point of view, is not only that Sun *can* be used by supporters of an illiberal political order, a problem to be dealt with below,[17] but the seemingly perennial triumph of external over internal freedom from past to present. A case in point is the gradual and subtle transformation of the concept of *weiquan* (維權) or "rights protection/defense" in China from a specifically internal-liberal claim (the citizens vis-à-vis their state) to an increasingly externally oriented one (the People's Republic of China vis-à-vis other states).

Though a section of an essay is hardly ideal for a thoroughgoing conceptual history of the term, a few anecdotes nonetheless may suffice here to describe the core of the transformation under examination. According to the online library catalogue of Tsinghua University, *weiquan* as an acronym for *weihu quanyi* (維護權益) or protection of rights and interests appeared first in Chinese academic and semi-official writings in the early 1990s, applying mostly in the contexts of defending the rights of youth and women. In this early "social" phase, the term was not yet "politicized" in the sense of highlighting the one-party state as the originator of rights infringement; rather, what needed "overcoming" were certain pre-existing social structures and barriers—often with the help of the Party or party-controlled organizations (cf. Zhang 1991; Wang 1993).

A decisive turn in the concept's connotation seems to have taken place in the late 1990s, when it was used in the context of consumer rights protection and more specifically denoted the protection of lawyers' rights against possible encroachment (e.g., by the state). In 1998, the Committee for the Protection of Lawyers' Lawful Rights and Interests was established within the All-China Lawyers' Association with the specific task of, inter alia, "providing assistance to lawyers who, in the legal process of fulfilling their duties as lawyers, suffer infringement of their professional, physical, and property rights and interests by certain agencies [i.e. state/party organs], organizations, and individuals" (Zhu 2004: 62; People's Daily 1998).

It wasn't long before the eventual metamorphosis of lawyers' *weiquan* (律師維權), or lawyers' protection of their own rights, into *weiquan* lawyers (維權律師), or lawyers protecting the rights of others. With the advent of the "*weiquan* movement" at the turn of the century, the political-legal connotation of the term began to dominate. Writing in 2007–2008, Fu Hualing and Richard Cullen observe that "*weiquan* is the term now typically used in China to identify the type of legal activities commonly referred to in the West as 'cause lawyering' or public interest legal work" (Fu & Cullen 2008: 111).[18] Teng Biao, one of the prominent *weiquan* laywers, points to 2003 as the "generally regarded … symbolic year for the rights defense movement (維權運動 *weiquan yundong*)" (Teng 2012: 29). He names a number of incidents around the time from Dr. Jiang Yanyong's 2003 exposure of the SARS epidemic to the *Yazhou Zhoukan* making 14 Chinese rights-defense lawyers the collective persons of the year in 2005.

In the ensuing decade or so, the concept of *weiquan* has witnessed considerable dissemination and dissimilation on the Mainland. Aside from the continual application of the concept in the contexts of consumer rights, expanding into the area of intellectual property, there have also been clear attempts to apply it in *external* contexts, such as the maritime territorial disputes in the South China Sea. *Haishang weiquan* (海上維權), or maritime rights protection, has now become an established "subject term" in both academic and semi-official publications in the People's Republic of China.[19] Increasingly, *weiquan* is being reinterpreted to mean primarily *weihu zhuquan* (維護主權), or the protection of (state) sovereignty. Specifically, externalized *weiquan* calls for the need to "unite as one body" from Party to government to army, police, and citizenry in concerted self-defense (e.g. Zhang 2017; Xue & Zheng 2015). With the renewed persecution of lawyers standing up for citizens' rights against undue state infringement at present (Gan 2017), coupled with the media's—including those in both Hong Kong and Taiwan—sometimes unsuspecting adoption of the term *weiquan* in non-liberal contexts (i.e., those having nothing to do with internal freedom), it is difficult to be optimistic about the outcome of this "new" fight between internal and external freedoms, or the conceptual struggle over what constitutes fundamental *weiquan*, and which consequently should enjoy precedence over the other.

## Conclusion: Towards a hermeneutical solution

Returning to the "old" struggle: The previous analysis and juxtaposition of Thomas Mann's two freedoms and Sun Yat-sen's "nationalism" and "people's rights" has shown a comparable tension between the internal and external struggles for freedom in both pre-1945 Germany according to Mann[20] and revolutionary China as reflected in the writings of Sun.[21] In the latter case, as shown above, not only was internal freedom, or people's rights against their state's undue interference, sidelined by the primal endeavor for external freedom, or China's international status among the "Powers," but even the very source of the internal liberal conflict—internal despotism and lack or insufficiency of freedom—was *externalized*. According to Sun, there had been ample, even perhaps excessive, internal freedom in dynastic China, but external enemies took advantage of this "weakness" and brought "indirect suffering" to the Chinese people, who now needed a revolution to unify themselves to fight for external freedom. In other words, to risk pushing the argument to its logical conclusion, if dynastic China had been able to fend off foreign economic and political oppression, there would not have been a need for Chinese revolution. External freedom was the sole "liberal" revolutionary purpose. As David Lorenzo puts it: "Sun displaces liberty by favoring unity" (Lorenzo 2013: 76).

The purpose of the foregoing is not to vilify Sun or his democratic constitutional legacy in China. Rather, as is the case with any revered tradition, coming to terms with the "difficult" or less-than-convenient aspects of the person and his thought is an essential procedure of the cultural process to keep the tradition alive. For present-day Chinese liberals to deal with what is illiberal in the Chinese liberal tradition is akin to Christians struggling with biblical texts ostensibly teaching violence, or Confucians preaching *ren* or compassion but also dealing squarely with—instead of shying away from—the problem of revenge in Confucian classics (Pfister 2017). In the same spirit, it will be attempted here to offer some hermeneutical pathways to address the problem of freedom in Sun's passages cited above.

To begin with, Sun's conception of freedom (自由 *ziyou*) is problematic, for he equates it with *fangdang buji* (放蕩不羈), which literally means "dissolute" (*fangdang*) and "unbridled" (*buji*) (Sun 1929: Dem. Lect. 2). Since the basic meaning of freedom is assigned such a negative connotation, it should come as no surprise that internal freedom is viewed negatively as contributing to the "loose sand-like" quality of the Chinese people, which only has "sacrificial" value for a higher good. To rework Sun's bias against internal freedom, one can then proceed in two ways: either begin by reconceptualizing freedom positively, or at least in such a way that does not rule out self-restraint and cooperation—à la Locke's reworking of Hobbes's "condition of nature"[22]—or by extending the same negative connotations to external freedom: i.e., arguing with Sun (using his own conceptions) that adding one more "free" egoistic nation to the community of egoistic nations poses no solution to the problem of international conflict. The abasement of freedom to the status of the dissolute cannot be a first step toward any higher moral status, whether Chinese or Western, either. If one chooses the first strategy, historicizing Sun's concept of freedom can be an effective initial move (cf. Zhang 2010). If the second option is preferred, one probably can develop and connect such a critique of external freedom in the Chinese context to the discontent with nationalism and the nation-state system in postwar Europe (e.g., Liu 2006). No doubt this course will require addressing Sun's supposition of Western "ulterior motives." However, that can be dealt with by a more nuanced approach to differentiate official double standards and hypocrisy from intellectual endeavors to rise above the narrow confines of nationalistic thinking.

Another hermeneutical option is to go back to the earlier, younger Sun, who first pronounced the Three Great Principles in 1905.[23] In this earlier source, it can be deduced that "democracy" or the principle of people's rights is not to be subsumed under "nationalism," but rather is intended to solve the very problem created by it. In his own historiography of Europe, Sun wrote that

> the rise of nationalism came after the end of Rome, and European nations became independent. Since then came imperialism in these various states, in which tyranny reigned supreme, hence the rise of democracy.
>
> *(Sun 1965: 281)*

In other words, national independence, from a systemic point of view, does not come without its own problems. The resultant absolute power brings about tyranny, to which democracy is the antidote. Such a hermeneutic maneuver can essentially lend support to the interpretation that Sun's three principles are not necessarily hierarchical, with nationalism enjoying precedence over people's rights and livelihood; instead, they may be held in tandem, possibly balancing and solving one another's problems.[24] As has been noted by Marie-Claire Bergère as well (Bergère 1998: 360), nationalism was not always present as a guiding principle in Sun's revolutionary program in the years between 1905 and 1924, thus demonstrating its dispensability rather than centrality. In this interpretive framework, internal freedom does not occupy an inferior position to external freedom, but can and should co-exist with it.

By the end of World War II, however, Thomas Mann would not accept even this apparently "balanced" approach to internal and external freedom. "A people who is not internally free and answerable for their own actions does not deserve external freedom," he argued. "They are not able to contribute meaningfully to the discussion on freedom, and when they make use of the reputable term, they distort it" (Mann 1947: 23). It seems as though the writer was convinced that internal illiberality is not conducive to learning how to be free responsibly, and hence external freedom in the hands of such an illiberal state would only result in irresponsible state actions on the international stage. That is to say, internal freedom is the precondition for (responsible) external freedom. In view of the size, economic power, and military budget of the People's Republic of China, one can only hope that this conviction of Mann's does not always correspond to reality.

Finally, it would probably be mistaken to place the blame entirely on "international status obsession" or the prioritization of external freedom. To ignore altogether the fear of external aggression based on past experiences of victimization (doubtless also partly exaggerated by certain historical narratives that enlarge one's own victimhood and minimize or even hide altogether one's own role as a perpetrator)[25] would strike many as an affront to historical justice. Therefore, to overcome such preoccupations would likely also require positively addressing the sense of insecurity in the national historical self-understanding. In the words of the late Nobel laureate, Liu Xiaobo (1955–2017), this process involves "squeezing out the 'wolf's milk' (狼奶 *langnai*) that had seeped into human nature" (Liu 2009). Such a process will be complete and external freedom will have ceased to be the dominant political preoccupation when, to paraphrase his "final statement," a people can muster enough confidence to say "we have no enemies" in an environment where partners and forces "curbing national egotism" elsewhere are ready to be found.

## Notes

1  Unless otherwise stated, all quotations from non-English sources are the author's own translations. Following Chinese conventions, family names are generally placed before given names.
2  Mann would object to the use of the term "nationalism" in the context of pre-1945 Germany with his distinctive understanding of French nationalism; see subsequent section.
3  On the appropriate and inappropriate uses of the term see Langewiesche (1998).
4  The value of equality is in no way less contentious, especially surrounding the relative emphases on equality before the law, equality of opportunities, and equality of outcomes. For a concise update on relevant debates in connection with the different conceptions of freedom, see Meyer (2016).
5  While originally delivered in English, the quotations from this speech in this essay are modified by the author based on the German version published in Stockholm in 1947. Search results from the Higuchi Goethe-Mann Corpus (www.flc.kyushu-u.ac.jp/~hgmc) show that the terms *"innere Freiheit"* and *"äußere Freiheit"* only appear in this speech of Mann's.
6  Referring to Luther's *Von der Freiheit eines Christenmenschen* (1520).
7  On Fritz Bauer's life and achievements, see Wojak (2009). On his intellectual contributions to transitional justice in postwar Germany, see Chung (2018).
8  The Frankfurt Auschwitz trials in the 1960s gave new impulse to the German process of self-purification through trial proceedings that continue up to the present. See, among others, Wittmann (2012) and Douglas (2016).

9  It is unclear from Mann's text, however, what the intrinsic connection between the obsession with external freedom in the ultranational sense and the realization of internal unfreedom is. There are only a couple of hints pointing to his thinking in this regard: Employing the Goethean either-or dichotomy of civilization (*Kultur*) and barbarism, Mann argued that to be anti-European is to be anti-civilization, hence barbarous—with both external *and* internal manifestations (Mann 1947: 25). It seems there is the assumption that by opening up to the outside world ("Europe"), civilization can be attained; but by walling itself off, Germany achieves nothing but barbarity. Such an assumption appears also in the passage where Mann quoted Goethe's "wish" for the German diaspora, which would purportedly bring out the good in the German character (Mann 1947: 37–38).

10  On the multiple sources of Sun's frustration, especially with Western governments, and the purported Russian exploitation of this fact to fan Sun's growing anti-Western sentiments as expressed in the *sanmin* lectures, see Wilbur (1976: 204–12).

11  Cf. Yu Ying-shih's characterization of Chinese culture as "loose sand" and "personalism" (Yu 2007).

12  English translation modified from Sun (1981) based on the Chinese original (1929).

13  Sun basically equated the "400 million Chinese (中國人 *zhongguoren*)" as one "Han people" (漢人 *hanren*): "四萬萬中國人,可以說完全是漢人。同一血統, 同一言語文字, 同一宗教, 同一習慣, 完全是一個民族" (Sun 1929: Nation 1, p. 7).

14  "余之革命主義內容, 賅括言之, 三民主義、五權憲法是已" (Sun 1989: 356). The five-power structure proposed by Sun consists of the executive (行政), the legislature (立法), the judiciary (司法), examination (考試), and control (監察).

15  Going beyond the internal-external dichotomy, state interference in individual freedom can also be justified on other grounds in the Chinese tradition. For instance, in differentiating Confucian and liberal theories of individual freedom, Joseph Chan (2014: 156) argues that Confucianism, even in its "reconstructed" and "modernized" form, "would not categorically reject moralistic or paternalistic state interference in people's lives," though favoring incentives over coercion.

16  Sun cited the relative lack of liberty of thought, liberty of speech, liberty of movement, and liberty of belief in Europe (Sun 1929: Dem. Lect. 2, p. 34).

17  See but one of the latest episodes in the decades-long public and academic dispute over Sun's liberal and illiberal qualities in Law (2017) and Li (2017).

18  See also their work on the "radicalization" of *weiquan* lawyers (Fu & Cullen 2011).

19  According to the online library catalogue of Tsinghua University, one of the earliest entries of the equivalent term *haiyang weiquan* (海洋維權) can be found in Yu (2003). The actual popularization of the term, however, came later. According to Factiva search results of archived simplified Chinese news and official sources, there were but a handful articles with either term (i.e., *haishang* or *haiyang weiquan*) before 2006. Between 2006 and 2010, the terms became increasingly salient, being applied mostly in relation to the ongoing Sino-Japanese disputes over the Senkaku/Diaoyu Islands, but also beginning to appear in the contexts of emerging maritime disputes with Southeast Asian neighbors. From 2011 onwards, the term's popularity has undergone exponential growth, with emphasis now increasingly shifted to the South China Sea, coinciding with former president Hu Jintao's 2012 call for China to enhance its maritime capabilities to become a "maritime power" (Manicom 2014: 177) and with the publication of the multi-volume *Code for Safeguarding the Rights and Interests of China on the Sea* (Wu 2012).

20  It would be interesting to explore, in a subsequent investigation, whether and in which actual forms such a tension manifested itself in German history as claimed by Mann. For instance, can one simply lump together the different dimensions of *Freiheit* longed and fought for in the *Befreiungskriege* of 1813–1815 and in the *Märzrevolution* of 1848? See Nipperdey (1983), Winkler (2002) and Mommsen (1989).

21  According to Wilbur (1976: 7), when it comes to intellectual innovation, Sun "absorbed and popularized [ideas fashionable in his time] more than he innovated." Or, as Chang and

Gordon (1991: 93) refer to his *Sanmin-ism* as a whole, it incorporated "new principles for old traditions," signifying synthesis and continuity.
22 Instead of presuming the natural condition of humankind as a state of war, of "every man against every man" (Hobbes 1904: chapter 13), Locke posits the state of nature as "a state of liberty … not a state of license" (Locke 1821: chapter 2, section 6).
23 See similar comparative efforts in Wells (2001: 68–70), who echoes the assertion of Wilbur (1976: 204) that the anti-Western and anti-imperialist sentiments in the later Sun's nationalism were partly a result of Russian influence.
24 Interestingly, the principle of livelihood (民生主義 *minsheng zhuyi*), or probably better translated as "welfarism" in this earlier text, is considered to be overtaking democracy as the overarching political movement of the 20th century (Sun 1965: 281).
25 In the German context, see for example Nolan (2005) and Thielicke and Diem (1948). In the Chinese context, see Wang (2012) and Chung (2015).

# References

Auer, S. 2004. *Liberal Nationalism in Central Europe*. London: Routledge.

Bergère, M.-C. 1998. *Sun Yat-sen*. Stanford, CA: Stanford University Press.

Cabestan, J.-P. 2017. "China's Institutional Changes in the Foreign and Security Policy Realm Under Xi Jinping: Power concentration vs. fragmentation without institutionalization." *East Asia* 34(2): 113–131.

Chan, J. 2014. *Confucian Perfectionism: A political philosophy for modern times*. Princeton, NJ: Princeton University Press.

Chang, S. & L. Gordon. 1991. *All Under Heaven: Sun Yat-sen and his revolutionary thought*. Stanford, CA: Hoover Institution Press.

Chung, C. K. M. 2015. "Chinesische Vergangenheitsbewältigung: Hindernisse und Ressourcen in vergleichender Perspektive." *Jahrbuch für Politik und Geschichte* 6: 115–133.

Chung, C. K. M. 2018. "Against Loveless Judging: Fritz Bauer and transitional justice in postwar Germany." *International Journal of Transitional Justice* 12(1): 9–25.

Douglas, L. 2016. *The Right Wrong Man: John Demjanjuk and the last great Nazi war crimes trial*. Princeton, NJ: Princeton University Press.

Ferdinand, P. 2016. "Westward Ho—The China Dream and 'One Belt, One Road': Chinese foreign policy under Xi Jinping." *International Affairs* 92(4): 941–957.

Fu, H. & R. Cullen. 2008. "Weiquan [Rights Protection] Lawyering in an Authoritarian State: Building a Culture of Public-Interest Lawyering." *China Journal* 59: 111–127.

Fu, H. & R. Cullen. 2011. "Climbing the Weiquan Ladder: A radicalizing process for rights-protection lawyers." *China Quarterly* 205: 40–59.

Gamble, A. 2000. *Politics and Fate*. Cambridge: Polity.

Gan, N. 2017. "Human Rights Lawyer Swept Up in '709 Crackdown' to Face Court in Tianjin for Subversion." *South China Morning Post*, February 16.

Goody, J. 2006. *The Theft of History*. Cambridge: Cambridge University Press.

Grimmer-Solem, E. 2015. "The Mature Limited Access Order at the Doorstep: Imperial Germany and contemporary China in transition." *Constitutional Political Economy* 26(1): 103–120.

Gwyn, R. 2013. "Is China Making the Same Mistakes as Kaiser Wilhelm's Germany?" *The Star*, December 9.

Hobbes, T. 1904. *Leviathan*. Cambridge: Cambridge University Press.

Kontje, T. 2011. *Thomas Mann's World: Empire, race, and the Jewish question*. Ann Arbor, MI: The University of Michigan Press.

kremlin.ru. 2014. "Address by President of the Russian Federation, March 18, 2014." Available at http://eng.kremlin.ru/transcripts/6889 (accessed March 20, 2014).

Langewiesche, D. 1998. *1848 und 1918—Zwei deutsche Revolutionen.* Bonn: Friedrich-Ebert-Stiftung.

Law, W-s. 2017. "誰害怕「逆權」韓流?" ["Who is Afraid of the Korean Culture of Resistance?"]. *Ming Pao,* October 13.

Li, W. 2017. "孫中山是獨裁者嗎? 與羅永生教授商榷" ["Was Sun Yat-sen a dictator? A rebuttal to Law Wing-sang"]. *Ming Pao,* October 19.

Linebarger, P. 1937. *The Political Doctrines of Sun Yat-sen: An exposition of the San Min Chu I.* Baltimore, MD: Johns Hopkins University Press.

Liu, X. 2006. 單刀毒劍,中國民族主義批判. [*A Critique of Chinese Nationalism.*] Taipei: Broad Press.

Liu, X. 2009. "I Have No Enemies: My final statement." Available at http://www.nobelprize.org/nobel_prizes/peace/laureates/2010/xiaobo-lecture_en.pdf (accessed February 12, 2015).

Locke, J. 1821. *Two Treatises of Government.* London: Whitmore & Fenn, & C. Brown.

Lorenzo, D. J. 2013. *Conceptions of Chinese Democracy: Reading Sun Yat-sen, Chiang Kaishek, and Chiang Ching-kuo.* Baltimore, MD: Johns Hopkins University Press.

MacMillan, M. 2013. *The Rhyme of History: Lessons of the Great War,* Kindle edition. Washington, DC: Brookings Institution Press.

Manicom, J. 2014. *Bridging Troubled Waters: China, Japan, and maritime order in the East China Sea.* Washington, DC: Georgetown University Press.

Mann, T. 1947. *Deutschland und die Deutschen.* Stockholm: Bermann-Fischer Verlag.

Mayer, H. 1992. "Abermals: Deutschland und die Deutschen 1991." In T. Mann, *Deutschland und die Deutschen 1945.* Hamburg: Europäische Verlagsanstalt, pp. 41–62.

Meyer, T. 2016. "Gleichheit—warum, von was und wie viel?" *Neue Gesellschaft/Frankfurter Hefte* (11): 42–46.

Mommsen, H. 1989. *Die verspielte Freiheit: Der Weg der Republik von Weimar in den Untergang. 1918 bis 1933.* Berlin: Propyläen.

Nipperdey, T. 1983. *Deutsche Geschichte 1800–1866: Bürgerwelt und starker Staat.* Munich: C. H. Beck.

Nolan, M. 2005. "Air Wars, Memory Wars: Germans as victims during the Second World War." *Central European History* 38(1): 7–40.

People's Daily. 1998. "全國律師維權委員會成立." ["Establishment of the Committee for the Protection of Lawyers' Lawful Rights and Interests"]. *People's Daily,* July 21.

People's Daily. 2017. "讓核心價值觀融入社會生活." ["Let Core Values Seep into Social Life"]. *People's Daily,* June 16.

Perels, J. & I. Wojak (eds.). 1998. "Zu den Naziverbrecher-Prozessen: Gespräch im NDR." In J. Perels & I. Wojak (eds.), *Die Humanität der Rechtsordnung: Ausgewählte Schriften.* Frankfurt: Campus, pp. 101–118.

Pfister, L. 2017. "Ruist Traditions of Revenge and Alternative Resources for Ruist-Inspired Reconciliation." In A. Frieberg, A. & C. K. M. Chung (eds.), *Reconciling with the Past: Resources and obstacles in a global perspective.* Abingdon: Routledge, pp. 69–82.

Sun, Y-s. 1929. 三民主義 建國大綱. [*The Three Principles of the People and Fundamentals of National Reconstruction*]. Shanghai: Commercial Press.

Sun, Y-s. 1965. "民報發刊詞." ["Foreword" to the Inaugural Issue of Min Bao]. *Guofu Nianpu,* vol. 1. Taipei: Zhonghua minguo gejie jinian guofu bainian danchen choubei weiyuanhui xueshu lunzhu bianzuan weiyuanhui, pp. 280–283.

Sun, Y-s. 1981. *San Min Chu I: The Three Principles of the People.* Taipei: China Publishing Co.

Sun, Y-s. 1989. "中國革命史." ["History of the Chinese Revolution."] In X. Qin (ed.), *Guofu Quanji*. Vol. 2. Taipei: Jindai Zhongguo Chubanshe, pp. 354–364.

Teng, B. 2012. "Rights Defence [weiquan], Microblogs [weibo], and the Surrounding Gaze [weiguan]." *China Perspectives* 3: 29–41.

Thielicke, H. & H. Diem. 1948. *Die Schuld der Anderen: Ein Briefwechsel*. Göttingen: Vandenhoeck & Ruprecht.

Wang, S. 1993. "深化改革中的婦聯維權工作." ["The Rights-Protection Work of the All-China Women's Federation during the Deepening of Reform"]. *Collection of Women's Studies* 3: 25–26.

Wang, Z. 2012. *Never Forget National Humiliation: Historical memory in Chinese politics and foreign relations*. New York: Columbia University Press.

Wang, Z. 2014. "The Chinese Dream: Concept and Context." *Journal of Chinese Political Science* 19(1): 1–13.

Wells, A. 2001. *The Political Thought of Sun Yat-sen: Development and impact*. Basingstoke: Palgrave.

Wilbur, C. 1976. *Sun Yat-sen: Frustrated patriot*. New York: Columbia University Press.

Winkler, H. A. 2002. *Der lange Weg nach Westen: Deutsche Geschichte vom Ende des Alten Reiches bis zum Untergang der Weimarer Republik, vol. 1*. Munich: C. H. Beck.

Wittmann, R. 2012. *Beyond Justice: The Auschwitz trial*. Cambridge, MA: Harvard University Press.

Wojak, I. 2009. *Fritz Bauer 1903–1968: Eine Biographie*. Munich: C. H. Beck.

Wolf, R. 2014. "Rising Powers, Status Ambitions, and the Need to Reassure: What China could learn from imperial Germany's failures." *The Chinese Journal of International Politics* 7(2): 185–219.

Wu, Z. (ed.). 2012. 中國海上維權法典. [*Code for Safeguard Rights and Interests of China on the Sea*]. Dalian: Dalian Maritime University Press.

Xue, G. & J. Zheng. 2015. "Safeguarding Rights and Interests in the South China Sea: Legal support of military operations other than war of the PLA navy." *Humanities and Social Sciences Journal of Hainan University* 33(6): 1–7.

Yu, H. 2003. "Preliminary Analysis of Current Laws and Regulations on Maintaining Marine Rights and China's Situation in Maintaining Marine Rights." *Marine Information* 3: 25–26.

Yu, J. 2010. 從柏林圍牆到天安門—從德國看中國的現代化之路. [*From the Berlin Wall to Tiananmen.*] Taipei: Yunchen Wenhua.

Yu, Y-s. 2007. 知識人與中國文化的價值. [*Intellectuals and the Values of Chinese Culture.*] Taipei: China Times Publishing.

Zhang, B. 1991. "共青團維權工作的回顧與展望." ["The Rights-Protection Work of the Communist Youth League of China: Review and prospect"]. *China Youth Study* 3: 3–4.

Zhang, B. 2010. "孫中山自由觀的多變性與一貫性." ["Continuity and Change in Sun Yat-sen's View on Liberty"]. *Guangdong Social Sciences* 5: 89–95.

Zhang, L. 2017. "構建海上作戰與急時維權一體化國防動員體制." ["Establishing Consolidated Mobilization for Maritime Warfare and Rights Protection"]. *National Defense* 3: 4–7.

Zhao, S. 2004. *A Nation-State by Construction: Dynamics of modern Chinese nationalism*. Stanford, CA: Stanford University Press.

Zhu, S. 2004. "Reforming State Institutions: Privatizing the lawyers' system." In J. Howell (ed.), *Governance in China*. Lanham, MD: Rowman & Littlefield, pp. 58–76.

# CONCLUSION

*Mario Telò*

The chapters of this volume point to one overarching conclusion. The excessive focus on identity politics as well as the redefinition of cultural differences as conflicts over national interests make it far harder to find points of convergence, continue projects of multilateral cooperation, and preserve peace in the world.

New political actors have challenged the culture of modernity—at least as it is understood in the Western world—and offered wide-ranging alternatives to it. As we try to sort out those challenges, we must distinguish carefully among four phenomena.

First, within the globalized world, there are alternative cognitive priors or alternative cultural backgrounds that the West did not respect sufficiently in the past. The authors seek to discover convergences among those alternatives that would dispense with traditional eurocentrism and eschew any self-glorifying, imperial vision of Western primacy. The latter certainly helped justify not only the worst excesses of colonial domination but also recent neo-colonial relations and, in new forms, even some interregional approaches developed during the 1990s.

Second, however, the authors also agree in distinguishing two related but very different phenomena. They tend to share a radical criticism of traditional arrogant ideas of Western supremacy and its legacies (see the chapters by Meyer, Qin, and Flôres). Yet at the same time, they differentiate between the understandable wish of national and regional cultures to assert their value and distinctiveness and resist the diffusion of Western norms, on one hand, and the recent revival of political authoritarianism in its various forms, on the other. The latter emphasize, and sometimes manipulate, the unique features of national or regional cultural traditions as though they were shields to block any and all initiatives toward multilateral cooperation.

Third, we must clearly differentiate between countries in which elites claim the right to a non-Western, alternative path to modernization and plain anti-modernism in its various forms of exclusive identity politics. Multiple modernities *qua* tradition-based forms of inclusive government seem to be proliferating (Russia, Turkey, China, Iran). The latter phenomenon differs essentially from the conspicuous process of rebalancing the relative cultural and political weight of modern versus anti-modern socio-political milieus in most Western democracies, whether in Europe or North America (cf. the chapter by Meyer). We should pay greater attention to the worrisome challenge posed by several variants of the extremist religious and political fundamentalism that pursue the politics of identity and advocate new forms of highly exclusionary theocracy (cf. the chapter by Latif).

Fourth, most recently, neo-populist political actors and parties and neo-nationalist and xenophobic movements have gained political power even in Western electoral democracies, including the United States, Britain, Poland, Italy, and Hungary. Many have deployed ethnic or religious identity politics not just against the harmful aspects of globalization but even against immigration, openness, and multilateral cooperation at the regional and global levels. This fragmentation is particularly strong within the EU, as the chapters by Gamble and Cerutti (among others) demonstrate.

Not only has the model of Western modernity as such been challenged; in addition, fundamentalists and extreme nationalists from within all of the cultural traditions retard the peaceful convergence of cultures and nations upon a revised scheme of multilateral cooperation—one that would transcend the hegemonic system of the past.

This book should contribute to a clearer understanding of the diverse types of challenge to the culture of the West and to reviving the dialogue between partners such as the EU and China, the EU and Brazil, and the EU and the Arab world within the post-bipolar global context. In contrast to more narrowly focused research strategies that examine only economic and trade relations and conflicts, this volume also explores the political/cultural dimension of what often are called "hybrid interregional multipurpose and multidimensional relations." That is, many of the authors wish to include not only full-fledged states, but also regional entities such as the EU, ASEAN, and MERCOSUR.

New entities such as these, well-suited to function in a multipolar world, have emerged fairly recently as significant international actors, usually following crucial historical turning-points, notably 1945 and, more recently, 1989–1991. The latter, of course, marked the collapse of the Soviet Union and the rise and eventual decline of the US as the dominant hegemonic power. These emergent regional and global actors realize that they must strike a balance between two goals. They want to preserve and defend their cultural identities (whether incipient or fully formed) and the diverse paths towards modernity that incorporate those identities. Yet, at the same time, they recognize that they need international cooperation toward a better, more culturally pluralist, more participatory, and even multilateral system of governance for the global commons.

The present volume brings to bear fresh research approaches upon the intersection of these two related sets of theoretical problems. Congruent with our earlier book, *Multiple Modernities and Good Governance* (Routledge, 2018), several chapters—including those by Meyer, Qin, Hinchman, and Latif—define the philosophical and cultural framework of the discussion. They emphasize the "diversity" aspect of multiple modernities, groping their way toward a more deeply post-hegemonic conceptualization while distancing themselves from evolutionist, deterministic, and American- or Western-centric models. Yet where respective concepts of good governance, along with its guiding values and principles, is concerned, they seek to avoid any new version of fatalistic relativism.

What challenges lie ahead? First, populist nationalists tout identities and history, and claim that they want to take back full control over national or sub-national borders. They harbor the illusion that they can halt or reverse globalization while breaking the power of cosmopolitan elites. Indeed, their more extreme factions claim to act in the name of exclusiveness, cultural intolerance, and the protection of "Made in _____" labels. Their political assertiveness may put at risk the very idea of peace between previous enemies and socio-economic integration among neighboring countries. Were they to prevail, regional and global peace would be threatened.

If we assume that multilateral, multilevel cooperation is teetering on the brink between collapse and renewal, then those who defend such cooperation ought to search for ways to make a new beginning. Here we should not overlook the advantages of cultural dialogue, nor should we underestimate the potential for confrontations on values. In the context of the emergence of China, India, Brazil, Indonesia, and other post-colonial and developing countries, one theoretical issue has emerged that often—and wrongly—has been oversimplified. The present volume's chapter by Martin Chung (drawing on the political thought of Sun Yat-sen) introduces an original interpretation of the unresolved dispute over values by opposing internal and external forms of freedom. As developing countries assign absolute priority to independence from imperialism and emphasize "sovereignism" in international relations, they may generate problematic side-effects, such as limiting the domestic development of human rights and personal freedom and/or retarding secularization by strengthening fundamentalism. Efforts to rally the "unity of people against the external influences" may bring to the fore new combinations of populism, nationalism, and authoritarianism in some parts of the world.

How deep are the challenges ahead? The chapters by Qin, Song, Telò, Cerutti, Flôres, and Gamble explore the diverse cultures of modernity, distinctive paths to modernization (diverging from the American model), and the variety of secularization processes and regionalist policies, especially those in their respective neighborhoods: the Mediterranean basin, Eastern Europe, South America, the Asia-Pacific region, and central Asia. Meanwhile, Gamble focuses on the consequences that the long recession beginning in 2009 had in influencing the crisis of democratic regimes. What we are witnessing is the convergence between the populist revolt and what Qin defines as populist realism.

Many of the authors also deliver messages of concern. For example, both Qin and Telò point out the surprisingly high degree of consensus in the elite discourses of Europe and China about the shape of a post-hegemonic, diverse, plural, and multilayered scheme of multilateralism. But they also raise the question (still unanswered) about whether the West is experiencing a clash between neo-nationalist ideas of sovereignty and democracy and multilateralism. At the same time, the authors note that populist authoritarianism and nationalism are making a comeback in developing countries as well, mainly as rhetorical tools for simplifying the management of internal troubles. Both authoritarian and democratic regimes are channeling fear, intolerance, and people's demands for protection into a variety of defensive measures from hard borders to physical barriers like walls. We can see the practical outcome of such isolationism in the triumph of populist leaders or movements in both Western democratic regimes and those in the developing world: Trump, Brexit, Salvini, Orbán, and Kaczynski, but also Bolsonaro, Maduro, and Duterte in Brazil, Venezuela, and the Philippines, respectively. The populist wave has put the world on notice. The authors of this book have attempted to analyze the reasons for its success and the harmful, even disastrous, consequences if it is not checked and reversed.

# INDEX